K–8 Classroom Methods
From Teacher Reflection to Student Responsibility

Randi N. Stanulis
Michigan State University

Brenda H. Manning
The University of Georgia

Merrill
Prentice Hall

Upper Saddle River, New Jersey
Columbus, Ohio

Library of Congress Cataloging in Publication Data

Stanulis, Randi N.
   K–8 classroom methods : from teacher reflection to student responsibility / Randi N.
Stanulis, Brenda H. Manning.
      p. cm.
   Includes bibliographical references and index.
   ISBN 0-13-022522-3 (pbk.)
   1. Elementary school teaching. 2. Effective teaching. 3. Motivation in education. I.
Manning, Brenda H., II. Title.

LB 1555 .S79 2003
371.102--dc21   2002074820

Vice President and Publisher: Jeffery W. Johnston
Executive Editor: Debra A. Stollenwerk
Editorial Assistant: Mary Morrill
Production Editor: JoEllen Gohr
Production Coordination: Carlisle Publishers Services
Photo Coordinator: Cynthia Cassidy
Design Coordinator: Diane C. Lorenzo
Cover Designer: Rod Harris
Cover art: Superstock
Production Manager: Pamela Bennett
Director of Marketing: Ann Castel Davis
Marketing Manager: Krista Groshong
Marketing Coordinator: Tyra Cooper

This book was set in Times by Carlisle Communications, Ltd. It was printed and bound by Banta Book Group.
The cover was printed by Phoenix Color Corp.

Photo Credits: Scott Cunningham/Merrill, pp. 3, 123, 207; KS Studios/Merrill, p. 1; Anthony Magnacca/Merrill,
pp. 121, 235; Barbara Schwartz/Merrill, pp. 31, 89; Anne Vega/Merrill, pp. 55, 149, 171.

Pearson Education Ltd.
Pearson Education Australia Pty. Limited
Pearson Education Singapore Pte. Ltd.
Pearson Education North Asia Ltd.
Pearson Education Canada, Ltd.
Pearson Educación de Mexico, S.A. de C.V.
Pearson Education–Japan
Pearson Education Malaysia Pte. Ltd.
Pearson Education, *Upper Saddle River, New Jersey*

10 9 8 7 6 5 4 3 2 1
ISBN: 0-13-022522-3

Dedication

Dedicated with love to my three boys:
  Tom, Scott, and Alex

Dedicated with love to my girls:
  Jill, Ginger, and Megan

Preface

K–8 Classroom Methods: From Teacher Reflection to Student Responsibility presents K–8 methods with the aim of developing teacher reflection and student responsibility. Anyone who aspires to teach will find this book beneficial, especially those preparing to teach for the first time.

The book is centered around two main themes. We begin with the teacher's role as a reflective practitioner (chapter 1) to become more mindful of

(a) creating a classroom community with special attention to the often forgotten verbal environment (chapter 2);

(b) promoting students' social responsibility (e.g., cooperation with others) and productive school work habits (e.g., concentrating, focusing attention, finishing school assignments promptly and accurately) (chapter 3); and

(c) using multiple models of classroom guidance for the diverse classrooms of today (e.g., Gordon's Teacher Effectiveness Approach, Dreikurs' Logical Consequences Approach, Manning's Cognitive Self-Instruction) (chapter 4).

The first theme, "From Teacher as Person to Teacher as Guide," stresses the importance of the purposeful thinking of the excellent teacher who plans a healthy environment that is conducive to optimal learning.

The second theme, "From Teacher as Planner to Teacher as Strategist," is comprised of five chapters. These chapters present a new twist to planning (chapter 5), communicating (chapter 6), developing and using best practices (chapters 7 and 8), and assessing student learning (chapter 9). Our perspective is driven by learner responsibility; therefore, each of the teaching/learning processes aims for student autonomy. In addition to this perspective, we address timely topics that every prospective and practicing teacher should know, such as home-school connections and service learning (chapter 5); using computers as tools to foster student learning (chapters 5 and 6); classroom-tested teacher suggestions for fostering students' attention skills, organizational skills, and research skills (chapter 7); current cognitive/metacognitive learning strategies such as the powerful reciprocal teaching and metamemory strategies (chapter 8); and authentic assessment, digital portfolios, and student-led parent-teacher conferences (chapter 9).

Many examples, activities, cases, and suggestions for classroom practice are included in this book. Each is derived from our work with teachers. These are not made-up, imaginary suggestions—they were either field-tested by teachers in everyday K–8 classrooms and deemed successful via classroom teacher research, or field-tested in actual classrooms as a component of the university research in collaboration with teachers and also deemed successful. Thus, the text is reality-based, not only on university research, but authors' more importantly on K–8 classroom research. This is a major strength of this text, especially when we consider that many classroom methods texts do not include classroom strategies that actually have been applied by K–8 classroom teachers. If hypothetically based methods are published before teachers have tested them in the classroom, subsequent follow-up by teachers can be disappointing and discouraging. Thus, we have attempted to address this limitation by including methods that teachers have documented as being beneficial for them and their students.

Other features of the book include self-questions, Learning Out Loud exercises, the teacher's role in setting up the classroom environment, current practicing teachers' application of methods, and summaries.

Self-Questions—At the beginning of each chapter, Bloom's Taxonomy is used to frame questions readers can ask themselves. These self-questions orient readers to the content and scope of each chapter. Readers can answer the self-questions as they begin the chapter or return to them after reading to check their comprehension of the chapter's content. In the literature, self-questioning is documented as an effective technique for improving comprehension. Specifically, self-questioning serves to focus attention, frame a perspective for reading, and assess one's own learning. Instructors using the book might also use the self-questions to focus their students' attention or assess their understanding of the chapters' conceptual breadth and depth. Because Bloom's six levels (knowledge, comprehension, application, analysis, synthesis, and evaluation) are included in every chapter as a precursor to reading, instructors can be assured that they have considered multiple levels of understanding and performance for their students' learning.

Learning Out Loud exercises—Learning Out Loud exercises represent the outward expression of self-talk that guides thinking, planning, reflection, and action. As teachers and students become more aware of and learn to guide their reflections and actions through problem defining, self-guiding, self-coping, self-correcting, and self-reinforcing, they move from *intra*psychological processes (within self) to *inter*psychological processes (among people). This shift is the point at which we "learn out loud," or make the inner world public. Once a learner has reflected on a particular idea and has turned it over in his or her mind and internalized the implications of an idea, he or she is then ready to articulate this idea. The ability to learn and teach "out loud" involves both awareness and experience—only by practicing and monitoring ways to regulate their own thinking, and experiencing success with the effects of such regulation, can teachers help others become more independent learners. As teachers learn "out loud," they can understand the motivation that comes from inside in order to set their own goals and work toward goal completion. Such a framework encompasses the joy involved in being your own best teacher—where you can learn out loud as you bring your inner awareness to a conscious level.

In each chapter, the Learning Out Loud exercises serve to ensure a greater understanding of the knowledge and skills within the text. Without them, readers may miss the richness of understanding that will increase their use of these skills in their own classrooms with their own students. Bear in mind that the Learning Out Loud exercises are only suggestions for increasing reader participation and retention. Instructors using the text may want to modify, add, or delete certain exercises to meet their particular needs.

The Teacher's Role in Setting Up the Classroom Environment—A primary purpose of this text is to foster the development of motivation, metacognition, and optimal learning, constructed within a socially supported environment. The goal of such an approach is independent self-guidance, including goal setting, monitoring, coping, and reinforcing. We believe that the teacher plays a critical role in setting up an effective learning environment where the aforementioned goals can be achieved. Teachers need to provide direct, explicit instruction to help students move to levels of higher learning. Thus, our approach blends constructivism and direct instruction, as we promote ways for students to develop personal and social responsibility within the classroom community through structured teacher support. To provide effective learning environments that promote deep learning and socially responsible pupils, teachers need to be metacognitive and need to be aware of and practice many different instructional strategies.

Considering our major focus on teachers' responsibility to scaffold, model, ensure student practice, and prompt students to employ self-regulated learning strategies, this text centralizes the teacher as a model of cognition and metacognition.

Current Practicing Teachers' Application of Methods—We provide many concrete examples of how teachers have successfully applied the philosophies, approaches, methods, strategies, and suggestions presented. In almost all cases, the methods we advocate for classroom use have been field-tested by our students who currently teach in typical classrooms. Readers can rest assured that in many cases and examples these methods are not unrealistic and, indeed, can be trusted. We have made a serious attempt to highlight the best approaches supported by teacher action research of our students, who are now teachers.

Summaries—Each chapter ends with a summary section that brings together the chapter's major points. Like self-questioning, the summaries serve to improve comprehension by consolidating thinking and synthesizing the important topics of each chapter.

The central belief undergirding this text is that teachers play the major role in setting up and maintaining an effective environment where students can become active and responsible learners. All nine chapters address the various ways that teachers unfold these responsibilities (e.g., planning, guiding, and assessing the learning of school children) and illustrate specifically and concretely how this might be accomplished.

Acknowledgments

Acknowledgments for Randi N. Stanulis

The idea for this book was conceived during the summer of 1999, when Brenda Manning and I co-taught a graduate course based on her extensive research and development of cognitive self-instruction. The two of us blended our strengths and passions to develop a tool teachers could use to reach their potential and help to unlock the potential within their students. Though the process of writing this book has been very eventful, through moves across country and through the College of Education, I am ever grateful for my close association to an inspirational teacher and scholar, Brenda Manning. The book would not have been written, however, were it not for my best friend and husband, Tom Stanulis, who cooked many dinners, changed many diapers, and drove to many tennis and swimming lessons with our two children in order to support my writing time. I hope that this book in some small way can contribute to a better education for tomorrow's teachers. In that wonderful way, I feel like we are making a difference for my children, Scott and Alex.

Acknowledgments for Brenda H. Manning

Writing books is usually an introspective task that takes one away from the routine of one's life and family. Therefore, my first thoughts of gratitude go to my wonderful family. I wish to thank my soul-mate husband, W. Stewart Manning, without whom life would be much less complete, exciting, warm, tender, and enjoyable. Thank you, Stewart. My adult children and grandchild—Jill, Tim, Megan, Ginger, Aimee, and Doug—without a doubt remain the finest supporters and best cheerleaders a mom could ever imagine. You are the best and I love each of you deeply.

I also wish to express my sincere appreciation to my colleague and friend, Randi N. Stanulis, for sharing this experience with me—it has been frustrating and fulfilling simultaneously. In the midst of "the book," Randi gave birth to her second son, I became a grandmother for the first time, Randi and her family moved from UGA to MSU, and I moved offices twice. Understandably, there were times when we could not even find the book manuscript. The birth of this book has been an exercise in patience and a learning experience of shared emotions for the two of us. However, we believe the end result is an important book that will be helpful in our field. If so, this will be the greatest reward of all. Thank you, Randi.

From Both of Us

Many, many thanks are generously sent to Stephanie Bales from the University of Georgia for her expert assistance in typing the manuscript, and to Jennifer Rosenberger from Michigan State who helped with manuscript preparation in the eleventh hour. A deep thank you goes to Dr. Carol Pearson, who helped gather the latest research for Chapter 5; and to Dr. Stacey Neuharth-Pritchett and Dr. Gert Nesin, who wrote Chapter 9 based on their expertise in different forms of assessment. In addition, a wholehearted thank you goes to our students, as preservice and inservice teachers, whose projects, work, and ideas add the classroom reality often missing in a text like this one. Without a sprinkling of teacher seasoning across this book, the disconnection between theory/research to classroom practice would have been perpetuated once again. Thanks for stabilizing us in the real world of teachers. Finally, we would like to thank those who reviewed this manuscript and gave us their thoughtful comments: Sue R. Abegglen, Culver-Stockton College; Devon Brenner, Mississippi State University; Margaret M. Ferrara, Central Connecticut State University; Joyce W. Frazier, University of North Carolina, Charlotte; Mary Lynn Hamilton, University of Kansas; Dwight Hare, Mississippi State University; Stephen Lafer, University of Nevada, Reno; Frank Miller, Pittsburg State University; and Donna Strand, Baruch College at City University of New York.

Randi N. Stanulis and Brenda H. Manning

Brief Contents

Contents

From Teacher as Person to Teacher as Guide

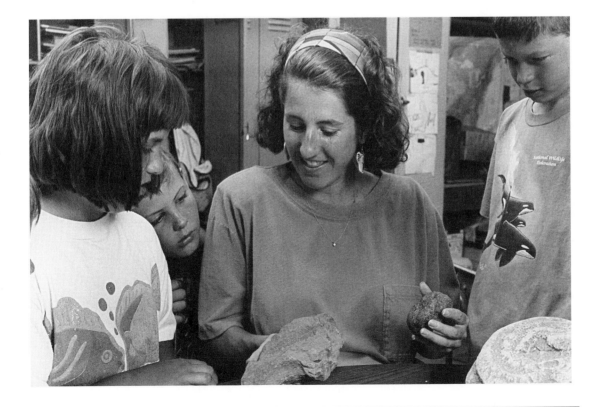

Developing as Reflective Practitioners

Self-Questions

Knowledge: Identify one way to analyze self-guiding talk.

Comprehension: Define *self-monitoring* in a classroom setting.

Application: Describe your preferred way to analyze your own self-guiding talk.

Analysis: Explain the main differences between novice versus experienced teacher's self-guiding speech during teaching dilemmas.

Synthesis: Considering the ways to foster language of teacher self-support, write a plan to improve a specific habit that has hindered your accomplishment of a goal.

Evaluation: Debate the advantages and disadvantages of developing as a self-monitoring teacher.

Introduction

Teachers play a critical role in setting up and maintaining an effective classroom environment where students can become active and responsible learners. To set up and monitor a productive learning environment, teachers must continuously reflect, question, plan, and assess. Students often hear the word *reflection* during their teacher preparation. Indeed, many teachers lament, "Don't ask me to reflect anymore! Just let me *do* my teaching." However, "doing teaching" effectively requires conscious and concrete reflection.

The concept of *reflective practitioner* will become concrete when you understand the meaning of three terms that are central in this text: metacognition, self-regulated learning, and self-guiding speech (commonly referred to as self-talk). *Metacognition*, the centerpiece of reflection, involves both awareness and regulation of teacher thinking. In plain terms, metacognition includes thinking about one's own thinking and guiding a response based on that deliberation. *Self-regulated learning* builds directly on metacognition—learners who are self-regulated are "metacognitively, motivationally, and behaviorally" active participants in their own learning and teaching process (Zimmerman & Schunk, 1989, p. 4). Reflection involves deliberate mental monitoring and adjusting prior to, during, and after instruction. The skills of self-regulation that promote reflection include self-questioning, self-directing, self-coping, self-correcting, and self-reinforcing. *Self-guiding speech*, hereafter referred to as *self-talk*, provides a more concrete way to analyze your own reflection.

Within this chapter, we provide many examples to help you understand and regulate your own thinking by becoming aware of, classifying, and analyzing your own self-talk. The primary goal of this text is to develop reflective practitioners who then can help students develop similar habits and skills that will lead to responsible and active learning.

Analyzing Self-Talk

Individuals make about 55,000 self-talk utterances per day (Helmstettler, 1986). The way we talk to ourselves impacts our feelings, health, self-esteem, stress levels, and interpersonal relationships. Clinical studies (Butler, 1992) revealed that 75% of our daily self-talk works against us—it is largely counterproductive. We say things to ourselves that we would never dream of saying to someone else. If we were as careful about how we talk to ourselves as we are about how we talk to others, we would improve the quality of our personal and professional lives. But this is not an easy task. However, when we realize that productive and healthy self-talk can improve our feelings, our health, our self-esteem, our stress levels, and our interpersonal relationships, what can be more important? If teachers improve in these five areas, students in our classrooms will have better teachers. The "Teacher As Person" theme maintains this premise: The teacher in the classroom is only as good as the person inside the teacher. But how can we change the way we have been talking to ourselves for at least 20 years, maybe more?

The first step is *awareness*. To monitor our thoughts as teachers, we must first become aware of what we are saying to ourselves. This teacher reflection, or self-talk, is as critical to the quality of our schooling today as is our diet to our overall health. We would not expect to be very healthy if we ate chocolate candy bars at every meal for 3 months. Why is it that we can say mean, scary, discouraging, critical things to ourselves routinely and consistently and never consider the harm we are reaping? If not for ourselves, at least for the sake of our K–8 students, let's take steps to become aware and then change what we say to ourselves. Teachers who have taken this kind of action repeatedly report better lives: They stop smoking; they lose weight; they reduce or even eliminate panic attacks; they are calmer and more in control; and they like their teaching, their students, and even their principals better.

Before we venture into how you (and we) can develop as self-monitoring teachers who have improved our own self-talk, let's take a quick look at Manning's (1990) study of over 500 K–8 students' self-talk during independent school tasks over the last 15 years. From these longitudinal data, we have examples of what more productive K–8 students and less productive K–8 students say to themselves to focus their attention on tasks, follow through, and finish their independent school work. This student self-talk is divided among the categories of problem defining, self-starting, self-guiding, self-coping, and self-reinforcing. These categories are known as the *skills of self-regulation* (Brown & DeLoache, 1978). Figure 1–1 shows the verbatim self-talk examples taken from each group of K–8 students' usual self-talk profiles while they worked on independent school tasks. The labels of *most productive* and *least productive* were provided by each student's classroom teacher. The teachers were asked to name their most productive workers and their least productive workers. *Productivity* was measured by how promptly students started their work, if they continued working without unnecessary delays, and if they finished their schoolwork promptly and accurately. The most productive workers were also most frequently the students with the highest grades. Although there is an undeniable correlation between productive school work habits and high achievement, there are some K–8 students who are high achievers with poor school work habits and some K–8 students with excellent school work habits who are low achievers. These are the exceptions to the rule, however.

LEARNING OUT LOUD 1–1

Divide yourselves into two groups. One group will read the most productive students' voices and the other group will read the least productive students' voices. It seems to be most powerful to hear the least productive voice first, followed by the most productive voice for each square on the chart. Read these aloud and with expression. Do all of the focus column, then the follow-through column, and finally the finish column. The first person in group one reads, "I don't know what to do. I can't do any of this anyway!" The first person in group two answers with, "What did the teacher say to do first? Where do I start?" Then the second person in group one reads, "This is really stupid stuff. I'm not going to waste my time." The second person in group two responds with, "Get started on spelling. Better get going."

As you can see from the research findings described in Figure 1–1, student self-talk can either facilitate or constrain learning. Unfortunately, most of us are unaware that we are even talking to ourselves. Further, we have little idea that much of our self-talk is so critical! To help students become aware of the ways they talk to themselves, and to intervene to improve the nature of self-talk, classroom teacher and masters student of Manning's, Traci Rojo designed a helpful classroom application. Her project is one example of many that you will read about in this text to help you learn about the concept of reflection, including metacognition, self-regulation, and self-talk.

	Focus	Follow-Through	Finish
Problem Defining			
Most Productive Students	What did the teacher say to do first? Where do I start?	How much time do I have to complete spelling? After spelling I'll work on the math page.	Make sure I finished all the assignments. Check it off from the board.
Least Productive Students	I don't know what to do. I can't do any of this anyway.	I finished one. Time for a break. I hate working and working all morning.	Finish—that's a joke. I'm supposed to finish five assignments. Be real.
Self-Starting			
Most Productive Students	Get started on spelling. Better get going.	I need to get back to spelling right now if I want to finish. Stop staring.	Just one more problem. Look up this word first. Then I'll be finished.
Least Productive Students	This is really stupid stuff. I'm not going to waste my time.	I'm not going to continue this silly stuff. Keep working, she says. Who cares about me?	Try to finish. No! No! I got more than half. That's good for me. I'm slow.
Self-Guiding			
Most Productive Students	Now put the periods in this time. Watch out. This looks tricky.	Now slow down and read this one more time—carefully. Did I skip a sentence just now?	Count the pages—1,2,3. Name on every paper?
Least Productive Students	What is this stuff? Mark has finished five already.	Not another definition. I give up! Where is number three? Forget it.	Andrea will laugh because I didn't finish. Just stop.
Self-Coping			
Most Productive Students	I'm kind of tired today, but I'll get started anyway. These look long and too hard, but I can figure it out.	I may not be getting every one of these right, but I'm trying.	It's hard to get it all done today, but I'll make it. Hang in there—just two more.
Least Productive Students	I'm tired. This is going to be too hard. This is too much work.	I'll miss all these anyway. Why work on them? I've had it. I quit.	This is too much work. I won't finish again.
Self-Reinforcing			
Most Productive Students	I'll get started right away without wasting time. I'm a good worker.	I can stick with this stuff. Even the intercom didn't bother me.	Awesome! I finished! Looks good.
Least Productive Students	I'm far behind everyone else. I'll get another F.	I'm the slowest one in class. I hate all this school junk.	Stupid—that's me. I can't ever finish.

Figure 1–1 The Self-Talk Statements and Questions of Most Productive and Least Productive Students. *Source: From "Self-Talk and Learning," by B. H. Manning, 1990, April,* Teaching K–8, *pp. 56–58. Reprinted with permission of the publisher, Early Years, Inc., Norwalk, CT 06854.*

TEACHER PROJECT: TRACI ROJO

My project consists of a PowerPoint presentation called *The Superhero of Self-Talk*. *The Superhero of Self-Talk* is an introduction to self-talk and how it can help students. It starts with a class that is failing despite their teacher's efforts. Then, one day, the Superhero of Self-Talk flies in and shows the students how they can help themselves by using helpful self-talk.

I am fortunate to be able to loop with my class to second grade next year. When thinking about my project, I considered many ideas. I tried several CSI/SRL related strategies with my class this spring (Concentration Zapper, modeling of helpful self-talk songs, and a few checklists) and was pleased with the results. I felt, however, that I was just applying random strategies and had not given my class a way to connect everything. That's when I came up with the idea of creating a project that would serve as an introduction and springboard for further CSI/SRL related strategies.

First, immediately following the presentation, I plan to brainstorm with the students the various scenarios/activities in which they feel they might use self-talk. (I think they will be very open to share due to the supportive relationships we've established this year.) Then we will brainstorm unhelpful self-talk we might say in each situation and change each unhelpful statement to a helpful one. We would probably work on one situation a day, depending on how the students are understanding the concepts.

Eventually, I would like to categorize the situations and helpful self-talk to aid the students in seeing *all* the times when we might use self-talk (happy times, non-school situations, etc.) I would challenge them to think of new situations we haven't thought of yet to add to our list.

I also plan to implement a self-talk journal (for myself *and* the students). I will start by stopping periodically throughout the day to have students share any self-talk they remember saying up until that point of the day (and whether they feel it was helpful or unhelpful). I know this may interrupt instruction for awhile, but I think the benefits to their awareness of their own self-talk will outweigh the effects of instruction. After doing this for a few weeks, I will move into the students writing down the self-talk statements in their journals and categorizing it as helpful or unhelpful.

Also, during the time I am facilitating these activities, I will be implementing other CSI/SRL strategies. For instance, I want to implement several of the "racing" organization strategies shared last week, as well as collaborative strategic reading, homework strategies, and several checklists.

Once my students have become fairly proficient at using helpful self-talk (hopefully by Christmas), I plan to have them work on a skit, play, puppet show, centers, etc. (whatever they come up with) to use as a follow up to the presentation. I'm very excited about sharing the presentation and subsequent activities with my current student teacher, Ms. Zadarosni. She was very impressed with the activities I implemented this spring and how they impacted the students. She will be teaching kindergarten at our school next year and is motivated to learn more about CSI/SRL and how her kindergartners may benefit. I also hope to show the presentation and related activities to other interested teachers and their classes next year. (I've had several express an interest.)

I haven't completely decided on other strategies I want to use or other ways to use this presentation. I feel I have an exciting opportunity, though, to really jump into using CSI to benefit my students since I've spent a year learning what they need to succeed. I can't wait to get started!

(continued)

LEARNING OUT LOUD 1–2

The following section (in italics) shows a teacher's self-guiding classroom talk. As you read what Oppong is saying to himself, ask yourself if you consider his inner speech helpful or unhelpful. Keep in mind that negative or unhelpful self-talk can impede the learning process for both teacher and student. Self-talk that does not generate positive or helpful outcomes may indeed hinder the desired results, and may prevent you from teaching effectively and prevent your students from learning.

Building on Traci's project, we next provide an example of a fourth-grade teacher, Oppong, who has made his thinking visible so that he can learn more about how he naturally uses self-talk within a typical teaching lesson. During a science lesson, this second-year teacher described his natural self-talk as he recalled it while watching a video of himself teaching the lesson.

"Oh no! She's already tuned me out. No, no, why aren't they understanding this? Why isn't he listening? She needs this more than anybody in here. I'm not just talking to the wall. I wish they'd all look at me and listen when I'm talking. How irritating."

Now compare this to the same lesson in which he deliberately focused on constructing positive or helpful self-talk. He uses his helpful self-talk to guide his thinking in order to implement an effective lesson.

"I hope this lesson works this time! It is important for them to understand this. I need to review where fossils are found. They seem to be confusing this with our earlier discussion. I should have them work firsthand with some fossils. Maybe that will help. 'All eyes up here.' [Students are invited to go to the various stations where different types of fossils are displayed.] All right. Maybe I should start over. Obviously they need reteaching. I need to remember, it's not unusual for them to have trouble with this. Hmmmm . . . my brightest students seem to understand this, but the slower kids are lost. Maybe this is over their heads. I'm really going to praise them for trying.

I need to use more firsthand experiences with them. It's too distracting to just travel from one station to another without more direction. They can't seem to discriminate the different types of fossils. Hey—more of them understand this than I thought! I am making progress. We are going to need to reinforce this in small groups. I know this is hard for them. I shouldn't expect mastery so soon. Keep those perfectionist thoughts to yourself, Oppong.

I need to wrap up with a short review and closure. That was a pretty good lesson. At least we are working on this in depth. That makes me feel pretty good."

As you can see, the kinds of learning opportunities created depended largely on how Oppong guided his mental deliberation. When he was positive and open to change, he could see many possibilities for ways to reorganize the lesson and focus on student learning.

LEARNING OUT LOUD 1–3

Make a column labeled *helpful* and a column labeled *unhelpful*. In pairs or small groups, generate a teaching scenario and then write five helpful and five unhelpful self-guiding statements or questions for each column.

The Importance of Context and Individuality for Analyses of Teacher Reflection (Self-Guiding Speech)

Self-talk units are defined as words, phrases, or sentences that the teacher determines comprise a complete thought. Standing alone, a self-guiding speech unit is not inherently positive/ helpful or negative/unhelpful. The context and individuality of the *teaching situation* and the *specific teacher* must be considered. Teacher self-talk occurs before a specific teaching episode, during teaching, and after teaching. Depending on the specific context, a particular self-talk comment usually considered a *positive/helpful* self-guiding statement might, in reality, be *negative/unhelpful*. For example, if you are teaching some very bright children and one of them just had a terrific idea that you, as the teacher, have never even imagined, you might say to yourself in delight, "He can teach this lesson better than I can!" Unless one knows the specific context, this same statement could be coded as *negative/unhelpful*.

One reason why you continue to read *positive* with *helpful* and *negative* with *unhelpful* is because teachers have told us that *helpful* and *unhelpful* communicate more clearly what they mean when they are analyzing these self-talk reflections. *Positive* and *negative* are too inherently value-laden; whereas *helpful* and *unhelpful* are more context- and teacher-specific. You might be asking yourself about now, "Well, who determines if self-talk is *helpful* or *unhelpful*, and based on what?" Good question!

Helpful self-talk for teaching means that the self-talk creates or maintains a positive classroom climate/environment and/or moves you, the teacher, toward a professional goal you have for yourself or your students. On the other hand, *unhelpful self-talk* creates or perpetuates a negative classroom climate/environment and/or moves you away from the intended professional goal you have set for yourself or your students.

The other part of the previous question, "Who determines if a self-talk statement is helpful or unhelpful?", is also an important part of the equation: The speaker (teacher) must analyze his or her own self-guiding speech/reflection. In any specific context before, during, or after teaching that you have experienced or envisioned, the accompanying self-talk is unique to you and can only be fully understood, explained, and analyzed by you. If you say a particular self-talk statement is *helpful*, then it is *helpful*—same for your self-determined *unhelpful* self-talk. This is your own analysis—it is not second-guessed by others. Nevertheless, others may want to understand better why you coded a particular self-talk as you did, especially those self-talk comments that appear counterintuitive (i.e., positive-coded negative and negative-coded positive).

LEARNING OUT LOUD 1–4

Collect 25 self-talk statements or questions while you are teaching. If you are not teaching, collect 25 self-talk statements or questions while you are working on a teaching-related task (e.g., developing a lesson plan or a professional portfolio, preparing to teach a mini-lesson to your peers). Bring these 25 examples to class. Using the *Coding Self-Talk* forms shown in Figures 1–2 and 1–3, code your self-talk as either *Helpful* or *Unhelpful*. You will see in Figures 1–2 and 1–3 that *Helpful* coding is broken down further into the categories of self-correcting, self-guiding, self-coping, and self-reinforcing. Therefore, if you decide your example (self-talk) is helpful, you must look at it more closely and determine if it is correcting, guiding, coping, or reinforcing. If it does not fit into any of these four categories, you can code it simply as *Helpful/Other* or name another category, such as *Helpful/Questioning*. The same decision-making process is used for *Unhelpful Self-Talk*. After you have finished coding your 25 self-talk statements or questions, discuss your decisions with a peer or in a small group during class time.

Helpful	Unhelpful
Correcting	*Criticizing*
Example: This is not the right road! I should have turned left.	Example: How stupid I am!
Guiding	*Complaining*
Example: Put the car in reverse.	Example: I didn't want to drive all the way to North Carolina anyway!
Coping	*Discouraging*
Example: I just need to take a deep breath, stay calm, keep it all in perspective. This, too, shall pass!	Example: I'm exhausted. I'll never make it through all this hassle. I just want to resign—today!
Reinforcing	*Panicking*
Example: I handled that situation very well. Good for me!	Example: Oh no, oh no! I'm lost—which way? Oh my word, which way now? I don't remember! What if . . . ? (Rehearsal of all the potentially negative things that might happen.)
Other	Other
(Utterances that you can't classify may suggest another category.)	(Utterances that you can't classify may suggest another category.)

Figure 1–2   Coding Self-Talk (Self-Talk Statements or Questions).
Source: From "Self-Talk and Learning," by B. H. Manning, 1990, April, Teaching K-8, *pp. 56–58. Reprinted with permission of the publisher, Early Years, Inc., Norwalk, CT 06854.*

Figure 1–2 shows examples of coded self-talk utterances. These utterances are more personal than the professional teacher statements discussed in Learning Out Loud 1–4. However, if you find the professional utterances are not relevant enough for you to understand well, switch to a collection of 25 personal utterances to do this coding exercise. Our teachers really enjoy this exercise and report that, for the first time, they are more aware of what they are saying to themselves and how it affects both their personal and professional lives. We hope you will find this coding a concrete way to analyze teacher reflection or verbal self-guiding statements and questions.

Awareness of Self-Guiding Talk

As mentioned earlier, Butler (1992) offers the idea that the first step to improve self-talk is awareness. Once we realize the power of our self-talk to affect the quality of our lives, we are much more apt to change what we say to ourselves. All of us talk to ourselves. How much we talk to ourselves is not the important issue, although too much self-talk can become distracting to the task at hand. In fact, the research on children with learning disabilities (e.g., Manning, Glasner, & Smith, 1996) evidences that one discriminating factor between children with learning disabilities and their non-disabled peers is that the former talk to themselves significantly more. This continuous mind chatter serves to distract children

Helpful Self-Talk	I'm a very good speller. *(Provide example of your own.)*
Neutral Self-Talk	Slow down on number 6. *(Provide example of your own.)*
Unhelpful Self-Talk	Who needs stupid mathematics? *(Provide example of your own.)*

Figure 1–3   Categories and Examples of Self-Talk.

with learning disabilities. Thus, more is not always better. In the quantity/quality discussion, the quality of your self-talk is the focus, not the quantity. Therefore, as teachers, you will focus on the quality of self-talk as a way to make your reflection more concrete.

In this regard, Matthews (1978) found that neutral self-guiding speech is much more task-facilitative than either positive or negative self-talk. Can you speculate as to why this is so? Take a few minutes and make several predictions. According to Matthews, either positive or negative self-guiding speech takes the mind off the task at hand and usually misdirects our thinking toward more personal characteristics (e.g., positive self-talk: "I'm really good at this!" or negative self-talk: "I hate learning this."). While "positive" self-talk is more beneficial to attitude, task persistence, task completion, and so forth, "neutral" self-talk is even more helpful because we are referring to ongoing task performance (e.g., neutral self-talk: "Underline the subject once and the predicate twice") and "negative self-talk" is the most detrimental to accomplishing our goals via activities/tasks. Figure 1–3 summarizes these three types of self-talk and provides an example for each.

Next, we include five short teaching dilemmas and accompanying self-talk written by student teacher Todd Nickelsen, a student of Manning's, so that he could become more aware of his context-specific self-talk. Todd was placed in a sixth-grade classroom in a large, rural school for his teaching internship.

TEACHER PROJECT: TODD NICKELSEN

TEACHING DILEMMA #1

On Monday morning, there was a sixth-grade team meeting. One of the issues discussed was how many tallies the teachers should assign the students for not returning a packet of forms that needed to be completed, signed by parents, and returned by Thursday. Although there was initial disagreement, the five teachers eventually agreed on assigning two tallies. However, when my mentor told her fourth-period class that she would be assigning two tallies to students who did not return their forms, one student informed her that another teacher already told the class that the offense warranted three tallies. Due to the length of the pause between the student's comment and her response, it was obvious that my mentor teacher was not sure what exactly to say. In the end, she stuck with her original comment by saying, "Well, I don't know about that. We agreed on two tallies."

(continued)

TEACHER PROJECT: TODD NICKELSEN (CONTINUED)

My Self-Guiding Speech
- Students are incredibly perceptive. They pay attention to details and consistency, especially when it affects their social life or free time.
- Students will call attention to inconsistencies. I've seen this many times while observing and have experienced it as a substitute teacher. Students are more than ready to point out to an adult that he or she is not performing the task the same way other teachers perform the task.
- Based on today's observation and my past experiences, I believe that consistency is a crucial element of structure, and students in middle school definitely need a certain level of structure.
- How will the teachers deal with this situation? I already listened to them discuss the matter and reach consensus. However, the teacher who originally suggested three tallies maintained her original opinion even after she agreed to assign two tallies. How will they rectify the situation?
- Will the issue of inconsistency arise again? If so, how will the teachers deal with it? How will it affect the students?

TEACHING DILEMMA #2

Prior to the beginning of the first lab of the year, my mentor teacher discussed the lab rules in great detail with the class. One of the rules is that students must not touch the lab materials until directed to do so by the teacher. My mentor teacher also explained that students who broke the rules would not participate in the lab and would take a zero. Immediately after discussing the rules and passing out the materials, a group of four boys began to distribute the supplies among themselves. My mentor teacher addressed the situation by mildly scolding the four boys. She did not, however, restrict them from participating, nor did she assign them a zero.

My Self-Guiding Speech
- Were the boys consciously disobeying their teacher or did they not listen to her?
- If they did listen, how is it possible that they didn't "hear" her? In other words, how is it possible that students sit in the same room with a teacher, respond to her by saying "Yes, ma'am," but still don't "hear" what she is saying?
- How can we teach students to listen and follow instructions better? Is this something that can be taught?
- The teacher warned the students about the consequences of not following directions. However, she did not punish the boys like she said she would. What sort of message does this send to her students?
- What would I have done? Would I have restricted the boys from participating in their first lab?
- If you aren't going to follow through with a consequence, shouldn't you make it clear that students will always get one warning?

TEACHING DILEMMA #3

During a lab on Wednesday, my mentor teacher realized that part of the procedure had been omitted. Instead of telling the students what to do, she asked them what they thought should be done.

My Self-Guiding Speech

- I wonder why she didn't just tell the students what to do. Did she have her own idea or was her mind blank? Did she really need their input?
- I like that she included students in the decision-making process. Inclusion empowers them and makes them feel important.
- To what extent should you include students in making decisions, especially decisions about curriculum, content, methodology, and discipline?
- When including students in the decision-making process, how do you decide which student's suggestion/idea is best? Do you strive for consensus or settle for compromise?
- How do students perceive teachers when the teachers aren't fully prepared for the day? Do they see the teacher as incompetent or do they think some teachers intentionally do not prepare for all aspects of a lesson so that they can include student input?

TEACHING DILEMMA #4

At the end of each class, my mentor teacher reminds the students to put their papers in the correct section of their toolkits. One day she noticed that, instead of placing his papers in the correct locations, one student simply stuffed his papers into the pockets of his toolkit. She used his toolkit as an example of what not to do.

My Self-Guiding Speech

- How did this student feel when she used him as a negative example? Will his feelings cause him to change his "filing" system, or will his possible embarrassment lead to an increase in his current approach to filing?
- When referring to negative examples, should teachers call attention to specific students or should they speak in hypothetical terms?
- Why do some students lack organizational skills?
- How can we convince students of the need to be organized if they are not organized? Is it right to force students to be organized? Is it not the case that some people simply don't need to be organized? Don't some people work better when their desk is scattered with books and papers?
- Assuming it is true that an individual is in need of being organized, how do you teach him/her to become organized?

TEACHING DILEMMA #5

After 2 weeks of school, one particular student (I'll refer to him as Jonathan) finally made it out of the special education room and into his appropriate science classroom, which is my mentor teacher's fourth-period science class. For Jonathan, the fact that he even made it to school is a major event. He suffers from severe separation anxiety and his mother refuses to medicate him. Unfortunately, he is a major distraction. For the first 10 minutes of class, he cried and whined about going home. My mentor teacher addressed this distraction by asking him to pay attention and stop crying. Unfortunately, Jonathan did not respond. He had to be removed from the class until he calmed down again. When he was removed, my mentor teacher spoke to the class about Jonathan and his special needs.

My Self-Guiding Speech

- How will the students react to Jonathan? Will they accept him like my mentor teacher requested or will they tease him?

(continued)

TEACHER PROJECT: TODD NICKELSEN (CONTINUED)

- How fair is it that this student "gets away with" unacceptable behavior while other students are expected to act in a more mature manner?
- What sort of lesson will the students learn from Jonathan? Will it be a positive lesson or will they learn that all they have to do is cry to get their way?
- Why does Jonathan's mother let her son get away with such unacceptable behavior? Why does she not medicate him?
- Where do you draw the line with the inclusion of special education students into regular education classrooms?

Source: Created by Todd Nickelsen. Used with permission.

LEARNING OUT LOUD 1–5

Choose one of the five teaching dilemmas you just read and rewrite the self-guiding speech (SGS) in a way you would have responded. Analyze your SGS by coding each of your utterances as *Helpful* or *Unhelpful* and also as *Other-Directed* or *Self-Directed*. After completion of your coding, pair with a classmate and discuss each of your analyses. Bring your most interesting codings to a large group discussion when all pairs in the class have completed their conversations and selections.

Impacting Personal Lives via Self-Guiding Speech

Burns (1980) and other cognitive theorists such as Ellis (1977) and Meichenbaum (1977) convince us that changing our thinking can change our behavior. Building on such work, Pamela Butler (1992) discusses the kinds of self-talk we use that impact our personal lives. She mentions that we often use overbearing *judges* rather than realistic *guides*. She has developed a procedure for changing these judges into a language of support. One of the first steps involves learning to recognize our unhealthy self-talk. We mentioned this first step as awareness of your unhelpful or negative self-talk.

Butler's work has implications for teachers' self-talk. She analyzes self-talk as three judges that drive us beyond realistic expectations, that stop us from doing the things we want to do, and that confuse our thinking. Manning, in Manning and Payne (1996a), adapted Butler's more general work to the world of teaching. Butler terms our unhelpful self-talk as drivers, stoppers, and confusers. She follows the unhelpful with the helpful permitter voices that cause us to be a better friend to ourselves. Although there are a number of these, we hope you will take the time to do some dramatic reading or even skits to act out the detrimental effects of these mental drivers, stoppers, and confusers on our lives as teachers.

LEARNING OUT LOUD 1–6

Pair up with a classmate. One of you will read aloud the example self-talk for the five drivers: be perfect, hurry up, be strong, please others, and try hard. As the reader says each driver self-talk, the other person will answer with the permitter self-talk. For example, you read with a dramatic voice: Be perfect: "If I can't teach this lesson perfectly, I won't try at all." Then your classmate answers with the be perfect permitter self-talk: "There are no perfect human beings. Why do I keep trying to be a perfect teacher? Doing my best and accepting mistakes is a healthier way to teach." Continue this dramatic reading for the other four drivers (see Figure 1–4).

Driver Teacher Self-Talk: The unrealistic, relentless internal push to "get busy," "do it right," etc. Not to be confused with motivation or drive, which can be healthy.

1. **BE PERFECT VOICE**: Pushes us constantly to perform at unreasonable levels. Limits us to 100% or nothing, with nothing in between; all-or-nothing attitude.

    BE PERFECT/DRIVER SELF-TALK: "If I can't teach this lesson perfectly, I won't try at all."

    BE PERFECT/PERMITTER SELF-TALK: "There are no perfect human beings. Why do I keep trying to be a perfect teacher? Doing my best and accepting mistakes is a healthier way to teach."

2. **HURRY UP VOICE**: Pushes us to do everything quickly. One of the major contributors to Type A behavior, associated with heart disease.

    HURRY UP/DRIVER SELF-TALK: "I better hurry because all the other teachers are ahead of me in this book."

    HURRY UP/PERMITTER SELF-TALK: "It's okay to take the time these students and I need. We will learn well what we are learning instead of trying to finish the book first."

3. **BE STRONG VOICE**: Regards any need as a weakness to be overcome. Feelings of loneliness, sadness, or hurt are intolerable. Prevents us from asking for needed help.

    BE STRONG/DRIVER SELF-TALK: "I'm a new teacher. If I ask too many questions, they'll think I'm dumb."

    BE STRONG/PERMITTER SELF-TALK: "It's okay to have feelings and okay to express them. It is okay if I feel sad about where some of my students have to sleep at night."

4. **PLEASE OTHERS VOICE**: Involves an intense fear of rejection, even when the disapproving person is unimportant to us. We lose sight of our own feelings.

    PLEASE OTHERS/DRIVER SELF-TALK: "These students may not like me if I am too demanding. They have to like me or it will be awful."

    PLEASE OTHERS/PERMITTER SELF-TALK: "Pleasing others is rewarding, but it becomes maladaptive when we lose sight of our own feelings in exchange. It's okay to please myself, too. I will lose who I am if I do not acknowledge my needs."

5. **TRY HARD VOICE**: Involves feeling impervious to the setting of appropriate limits for ourselves. Taking on more and more responsibility without considering our own limitations. The inability to say no.

    TRY HARD/DRIVER SELF-TALK: "Why do I keep saying I'll be on another committee? I don't have a single free night during the week. I'm exhausted."

    TRY HARD/PERMITTER SELF-TALK: "It's okay to recognize my own limits; it's okay to give my responsibilities enough time, backing, and energy to succeed."

Figure 1–4   Driver Self-Talk.
Source: Adapted from Talking to Yourself: Learning the Language of Self-Affirmation *(pp. 26–31), by Pamela Butler, 1992, San Francisco, CA: Harper Collins. Adapted with permission of the author.*

Teachers like yourselves, who have begun to talk back to their "drivers," report mostly success and, at least, self-satisfaction that carries over into a more relaxed classroom. These results are worth wading through Butler's mental *stoppers* (Figure 1–5). These are set up just like the drivers in Figure 1–4 and can be used for information only, or you can continue with your dramatic reading or even act out these with scenarios you develop.

The final group of Butler's judges is called *confusers*. These ways of talking to ourselves should be made visible to you, as a future teacher. The only way we can stop confusing ourselves is to first become aware of these distorted ways to verbally guide our teacher behavior and then to combat confusers with the permitter self-talk shown in Figure 1–6.

Learning a language of support for teachers and students in classrooms necessitates self-directing, self-coping, self-questioning, self-correcting, and self-reinforcing. These skills of self-regulation foster healthy, facilitative self-talk speech. Once accomplished, talking to ourselves in more healthy, appropriate ways leads naturally to talking to others in more productive, facilitative ways, thus improving the verbal environment in the classroom (discussed in chapter 2).

Stopper Teacher Self-Talk: Interferes with our spontaneous self-expression and therefore limits us. These are the internal messages that tell us "no," "don't," "only if," etc. Stoppers keep us from asserting ourselves.

1. **CATASTROPHIZING VOICE:** Verbally rehearsing horrible events that might occur if we were to engage in certain behaviors. We exaggerate the risk of engaging in that behavior so much that we decide to do nothing.

    CATASTROPHIZING/STOPPER SELF-TALK: "If we go on field trips, the bus may break down, or the students may be more unruly, or we may get too far behind in our other work."

    CATASTROPHIZING/PERMITTER SELF-TALK: "So what if? So what if the bus breaks down? They'll just send another one to carry us. It might not be so pleasant, but it won't be catastrophic, or even awful."

2. **NEGATIVE SELF-LABELING VOICE:** Attaching arbitrary judgments to natural, healthy impulses.

    NEGATIVE SELF-LABELING/STOPPER SELF-TALK: "I'd really like to tell my principal how much I appreciate all that she does, but she might think I'm trying to get a raise or something extra, so I won't."

    NEGATIVE SELF-LABELING/PERMITTER SELF-TALK: "Many good acts of mine are squelched because I call myself or my behavior bad names. When I start this again, I'll just ignore it!"

3. **RIGID REQUIREMENTS VOICE:** Imposing a set of conditions that must occur before an action can take place. Usually begins with the word *if.*

    RIGID REQUIREMENTS/STOPPER SELF-TALK: "If everyone will approve of my suggestion, then I'll speak out at our next faculty meeting."

    RIGID REQUIREMENTS/PERMITTER SELF-TALK: "These 'ifs' keep limiting my alternatives and block my feelings and behaviors. Next time I hear a rigid 'if,' I'll just go beyond it!"

4. **WITCH MESSAGES VOICE:** Restraining ourselves with the word *don't.* Some examples are "don't change," "don't be yourself," "don't grow up," "don't be different."

    WITCH MESSAGES/STOPPER SELF-TALK: "Don't be so strict about this. Just because we aren't told ahead of time about afternoon faculty meetings—don't be fussy about this."

    WITCH MESSAGES/PERMITTER SELF-TALK: "Assert my right to listen and honor all aspects of myself."

Figure 1–5   Stopper Self-Talk.
Source: Adapted from Talking to Yourself: Learning the Language of Self-Affirmation *pp. 26–31, by Pamela Butler, 1992, San Fransisco, CA: Harper Collins. Adapted with permission of the author.*

Confuser Teacher Self-Talk: Using confuser self-talk distorts our own reality. This kind of self-talk, like the other two, is a maladaptive way of talking to ourselves. Some people have referred to the confuser self-talk as defective, or irrational, thinking.

1. **ARBITRARY INFLUENCE VOICE**: Conclusion that is drawn without careful consideration of all the facts involved.

   ARBITRARY INFLUENCE/CONFUSER SELF-TALK: "The students are not looking at me so they must not be listening to me. They aren't learning this! I'm such a failure as a teacher."

   ARBITRARY INFLUENCE/PERMITTER SELF-TALK: "Be specific here. When I say 'I'm a failure as a teacher,' what I really mean and should say is half of my class is not paying attention to this lesson."

2. **MISATTRIBUTION VOICE**: The direction of blame or responsibility is moved away from the real causative agent onto something or someone else.

   MISATTRIBUTION/CONFUSER SELF-TALK: "That student makes me furious."

   MISATTRIBUTION/PERMITTER SELF-TALK: "Students don't really make me furious. I choose to react in a negative way to their classroom behavior. What steps can I take to react in a more positive way? I am in control of my emotions; my students are not."

3. **COGNITIVE DEFICIENCY VOICE**: The failure to be aware of the complete picture; tunnel vision.

   COGNITIVE DEFICIENCY/CONFUSER SELF-TALK: "The reason Stewart is failing is because he does not concentrate."

   COGNITIVE DEFICIENCY/PERMITTER SELF-TALK: "What's the whole picture? A school problem is rarely so simple that it can be explained by one factor. What are other contributing factors to Stewart's problem?"

4. **OVERGENERALIZATION VOICE**: To recognize only the similarities between people or events and to ignore differences. Racial, cultural, and gender prejudices are based on this confuser.

   OVERGENERALIZATION/CONFUSER SELF-TALK: "I'll carry to class some of my *Sports Illustrated* magazines for my boys to read."

   OVERGENERALIZATION/PERMITTER SELF-TALK: "Oops, watch it! Ginger is the best basketball player in my class. Why did I assume that only the boys would want to read *Sports Illustrated*? Come to think of it, Sam would rather read poetry than play sports at recess."

5. **EITHER-OR THINKING VOICE**: Seeing everything as black or white, agree or disagree; no consideration is given for degrees, continuum, or in-between ground. *Dichotomous thinking* is a synonym.

   EITHER-OR THINKING/CONFUSER SELF-TALK: "Because I am a teacher, I keep being asked if I am authoritarian or permissive. I'm really not either, but I feel forced to choose one."

   EITHER-OR THINKING/PERMITTER SELF-TALK: "I can think in degrees, and in between ends of continua. I will stop allowing others to categorize me so easily as either this or that. It often is not that simple and depends a great deal on the specific situation."

6. **VAGUE LANGUAGE VOICE**: The use of words that have not been defined clearly by ourselves (e.g., success, happiness, wealth).

   VAGUE LANGUAGE/CONFUSER SELF-TALK: "I just want to be a success in my teaching."

   VAGUE LANGUAGE/PERMITTER SELF-TALK: "Success is in the eye of the beholder, just as beauty is. I must be sure I know how someone is defining her success, her happiness. What does success in teaching mean to me?"

7. **MAGNIFICATION VOICE**: Overestimation of the importance of an event or a situation; blowing something out of reasonable proportions.

   MAGNIFICATION/CONFUSER SELF-TALK: "I am a terrible teacher."

   MAGNIFICATION/PERMITTER SELF-TALK: "Bring it down to size by dating and indexing. *Dating* means to tell precisely at what particular time something occurred (e.g., I was a terrible teacher last Friday when I was having a headache). *Indexing* means being specific about the uniqueness of each person or event (e.g., Ms. X is a stricter teacher during academic learning time and Ms. Y is a stricter teacher during free time)."

Figure 1–6 Confuser Self-Talk.
Source: Adapted from Talking to Yourself: Learning the Language of Self-Affirmation *pp. 26–31, by Pamela Butler, 1992, San Fransisco, CA: Harper Collins. Adapted with permission of the author.*

The Origins of Self-Talk

Have you asked yet, "Where does my self-talk come from?" Eventually, someone asks this very important question. Thinking about its origins often helps us to become more aware of our self-talk. Beyond awareness, identifying the origins of self-talk helps us to change the negative voices in our head to more positive, helpful ones. Awareness sets us free to rescript our lives if we don't like the way others have "put words in our heads." It is quite reassuring and encouraging to know that we don't have to live with lots of verbal, negative baggage from our parents, past teachers, and the significant others in our lives. On the other hand, we can pay attention to and emphasize the positive, helpful messages from our past.

By completing Learning Out Loud 1–7, you can identify the voices from your past and the verbal messages you are still replaying in your mind. These messages are the origins of your current self-talk. These origins directly affect the quality of your self-talk and, thus, also affect your current and future professional life as a classroom teacher. Because your self-talk affects your teaching and, therefore, your future students' education, the activity is an important one. Take it seriously because, indirectly, it can improve your teaching and your students' learning.

LEARNING OUT LOUD 1–7

Draw a circle in the middle of a page about the size of a silver dollar. Write *ME* in the middle of the circle. Draw spokes from the edge of the circle with arrows at both ends of the spokes (refer to Figure 1–7). On each spoke write the name of one significant person, institution, book, etc. that has had an impact on your life. This might be a family member, coach, teacher, friend, book title, church, school, etc. Under or beside each name write a verbal message that represents a central and consistent message sent to you by this influence on your life. Figure 1–7 shows two examples from teachers enrolled in a middle school teacher preparation program. As you see, you may have more than one spoke for any one influence. For example, you might have three spokes for *MOM* with three different verbal messages she has sent you.

After constructing your Origins of Self-Talk Mind Map, clarify the single word or single sentence messages as part of a discussion about the mind map exercise. How do you think these messages will affect your teaching? Be specific. For examples, read the two mind maps and Connections to Teaching sections shown in Figure 1–7.

Teacher Reflection of Self-Talk Before, During, and After Teaching

Teacher self-talk affects all aspects of classroom functioning before, during, and after teaching. All too often, teacher reflection is considered something we engage in after teaching acts have occurred. We retrospectively think back on them—reflecting on how we could have done this or that better. This is important. However, self-talk is not only used after teaching; it is also used before and during teaching. We are always talking to ourselves and this speech-to-self or self-talk is always influencing our teaching behaviors and decisions. Exemplary teachers constantly and consciously monitor their teaching: before, during, and after. To emphasize this on-going, continual mental awareness and regulation, complete Learning Out Loud 1–8.

LEARNING OUT LOUD 1–8

Before working with your classmates on self-talk, spend solitary time thinking about your mental deliberations *before* you begin teaching a lesson to your target age group. Envision yourself getting ready to teach. On paper, put your classmates in the context you envision as you prepare to teach. Describe where you are and what you are planning to teach. This can be based on a real situation you have encountered or one you completely make up.

    A.   Describe the situation prior to teaching.

_____

_____

        What do you say to yourself *before* you teach?

_____

_____

        Now you are standing or sitting with your target students and you are teaching something to these students. What are you teaching? What materials are you using?

    B.   Describe the in-flight teaching situation.

_____

_____

        What do you say to yourself *during* the teaching act?

_____

_____

        Now the lesson is over. The students are no longer in the class. They have been dismissed. The room is suddenly quiet.

_____

_____

    C.   Describe the empty classroom after the lesson is over.

_____

_____

        What are you saying to yourself *after* the class as you reflect back over the lesson you just taught?

_____

_____

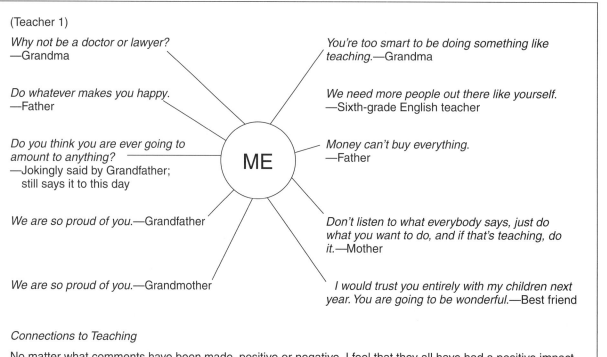

(Teacher 1)

Why not be a doctor or lawyer?
—Grandma

Do whatever makes you happy.
—Father

Do you think you are ever going to amount to anything?
—Jokingly said by Grandfather;
   still says it to this day

We are so proud of you.—Grandfather

We are so proud of you.—Grandmother

ME

You're too smart to be doing something like teaching.—Grandma

We need more people out there like yourself.
—Sixth-grade English teacher

Money can't buy everything.
—Father

Don't listen to what everybody says, just do what you want to do, and if that's teaching, do it.—Mother

I would trust you entirely with my children next year. You are going to be wonderful.—Best friend

Connections to Teaching

No matter what comments have been made, positive or negative, I feel that they all have had a positive impact on me. Despite my father's parents encouraging me to pursue a different career, I decided to take my father's advice and choose a career that would make me happy. I am saddened to this day nearly each time I talk to my father, for I know he despises his job. The only reason he sticks with it is to support his three daughters. I can remember when our family was most happy, and that was when my father had a job that he loved and took pride in, which was working for a private business. Since then, my parents have split and my father is stuck in a job he hates. I know he does not want this to happen to me, so I continue to pursue the career of my dreams that will fulfill my life and make me feel needed. As for my best friend, she alleviated the fear I felt as a first-year teacher. I was telling her how frightening it was for me to picture myself molding the lives of such young, vulnerable children in less than a year. I mean, I'm still so young and have no clue where my life is going other than my profession. I know she meant it when she said she would trust me with her children (if she had any!) and that I would make an excellent teacher! So watch out, teachers of America, I'm coming!

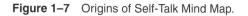

Figure 1–7   Origins of Self-Talk Mind Map.

Connecting Self-Regulation Theory to Classroom Teaching

Vygotsky (1978) posited that language originates in our social exchanges and requires two separate functions: communication and self-guidance. Vygotsky's work was not aimed at education or even at adult learners. Instead, it was aimed toward children's learning behaviors during novel, complex, and challenging task performance. However, learning to teach and teaching itself are also characterized as novel, complex, and challenging (Gallimore, Dalton, & Tharpe, 1986; Manning & Payne, 1996a). Thus, when the focus shifts from age-dependent to task-dependent considerations, Vygotsky's theoretical perspective

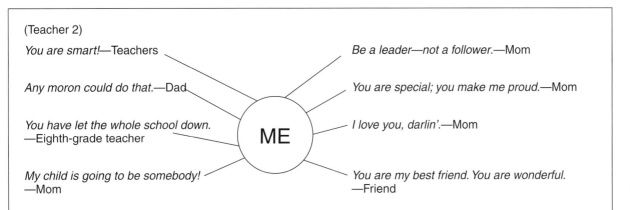

(Teacher 2)

You are smart!—Teachers

Any moron could do that.—Dad

You have let the whole school down.
—Eighth-grade teacher

My child is going to be somebody!
—Mom

ME

Be a leader—not a follower.—Mom

You are special; you make me proud.—Mom

I love you, darlin'.—Mom

You are my best friend. You are wonderful.
—Friend

Connections to Teaching

This exercise has helped me to recall some positive and negative voices from the past. Two of the most influential voices have come from my parents. It really amazes me how different their voices sound to me. On one hand, my mom was and still is my biggest influence. Sometimes I refer to her as my "cheerleader." She has always been at my side with positive messages. One of her favorite quotes is "Be a leader—not a follower." I have heard my mom say this to me a million times. These words have inspired me to be an original, voice my opinions, stand tall, and be proud of myself. On the other hand, my dad was usually very negative. He was always downplaying my achievements and successes by saying, "Any moron could do that." I do not think that he will ever realize how those words belittled me and hurt my self-esteem and self-image.

Another voice from the past comes from one of my eighth-grade teachers and cheerleading sponsor. At least once a week, she took me aside in her classroom to let me know that I had shamed my classmates and humiliated my peers. My teacher said these words to me over 8 years ago, but I still feel horrible whenever I remember those comments. I wonder if she knows how destructive those words are to a 13-year-old girl.

As a middle-school teacher, I have the responsibility of shaping young minds. In addition, I also have an influential voice in my classrooms. I realize that it would be impossible to be 100% positive every day to all my students, but this exercise has helped me to understand that my words can shape a life. I am very fortunate to have a mom who was so positive and wonderful in her verbal comments. However, I will have students in my classroom who do not hear positive reinforcement at all. If I could be that one positive voice to my students, what a difference I could make!

Figure 1–7   *(continued)*

of planned, self-directed speech aimed toward goal accomplishment is as useful for psychological applications in schools as it is for understanding children. To extend the notion of self-regulated teaching, using Vygotsky's notions of verbal self-guidance as the cornerstone, an example of translation into classroom practice follows.

Self-Regulated Teaching*

Rohrkemper and Corno (1988) discuss the need for teachers to refrain from protecting students from frustration and boredom. Instead, they recommend that teachers "deliberately promote the development of students' adaptive learning within a supportive classroom environment" (p. 297). They define frustration as the "stress of difficulty" and boredom as the

*The section "Self-Regulated Teaching" originally appeared in Manning & Payne, 1996a, pp. 58–61.

"stress of tedium" (p. 298). The adaptive learning techniques recommended for students appear well-matched to the complexities of teaching. Adaptive learning strategies can serve as a useful tool for classroom teachers, themselves, as well as for their students. When classroom teachers are excellent verbal role models for dealing effectively with their own difficulty and tedium, students are more likely to exhibit similar coping strategies. Students of all ages are always learning from the significant adults in charge of providing their learning experiences. Effective and ineffective verbal coping skills are modeled by teachers whether or not they deliberately plan to model these skills. Therefore, an important goal for you is to learn self-regulated teaching skills for dealing with your own classroom frustration because you will then be able to serve as an excellent language model for your students.

Self-regulated teaching is dependent upon teachers having realistic expectations for classroom reality. You know ahead of time not to expect the expected and are not undone when confronted by the complexity and unpredictability inherent in teaching. For example, self-regulated teachers realize that one of the stable characteristics of teaching is flexibility. Plans are more often revised during a lesson than implemented precisely as the teacher envisioned. Teachers who are adaptive and prepared expect the complexity, multidimensionality, spontaneity, immediacy, simultaneity, and unpredictability associated with classroom functioning. You realize, for example, that lesson plans rarely are implemented exactly as they are written.

Complexity, or *multidimensionality*, relates to the many facets of teaching. For example, a teacher is required to diagnose, revise, and develop plans, implement lessons, provide meaningful experiences, communicate with parents, and involve all the learners. Teachers have, on average, 1,000 face-to-face interactions per day (Jackson, 1968), make critical decisions approximately every 2 minutes (Clark & Peterson, 1986), and lose 55% of their instructional time to disruption (Gottfredson, 1989, May, personal communication). These statistics illustrate the complexity inherent in teaching.

Spontaneity and *immediacy* in the classroom are related to classroom demands that require teachers to think "quickly on their feet." Spur-of-the-moment, can't-wait answers are frequent occurrences in the classrooms. For example, a frantic parent calls wanting to know why his or her child is having too much homework. The teacher is called upon to give an immediate answer. Or, perhaps a student has been hurt on the playground—the teacher must react quickly.

Simultaneity is reflected in the variety of teacher tasks that must be dealt with all at the same time. Teachers who successfully manage more than one task at a time, and perform both or all tasks reasonably well, exhibit simultaneity. Teachers are familiar with this requirement of teaching—they are often exhausted because of it. Some teachers are very skilled at dealing with the simultaneous demands of the classroom. For example, the teacher who can read a story with expression while comforting an upset child in her lap and touching another child to calm him epitomizes a self-regulated teacher (during this particular teaching episode). This same teacher may or may not exhibit self-regulation during a different lesson or at a different time of the school day. Self-regulated teaching as a concept is fluid and dynamic, not a fixed, permanent label.

Unpredictability in a classroom means that the events are not guaranteed to occur as expected. It is easy to be lulled into thinking that a certain occurrence will happen in an expected manner. And just when we are comfortable with that order, the unexpected happens. For example, as a third-grade teacher, Manning was reading aloud one of her favorite books, that, for the past 5 years, students had really enjoyed. However, the responses of this particular group of children seemed to indicate boredom: sighs and squirms. One child in the group walked forward toward the book in Manning's hand. Manning believed that this child was coming closer to see the pictures better. But just as the child reached Manning's knee, he grabbed his belt and asked, "Do you know how much this belt costs?" This example typifies the unpredictability of a teacher's job.

Instead of complaining, moaning, and groaning about the complexity, spontaneity, and other characteristics of teaching, self-regulated teachers (who exhibit self-regulation most of the time) would be surprised if their school day were simple and predictable. Teachers searching for and expecting calm, predictable, and tranquil working conditions will stand on the verge of hysteria in most typical classroom scenarios. Jacob Kounin's work (1970) is an excellent resource for fostering knowledge of teaching reality. He found that certain teacher practices were highly related to effective classroom management. He also identified requirements for teacher coping—qualities necessary for dealing with the complexity, spontaneity, simultaneity, and unpredictability in classroom teaching. Teachers can minimize their frustration and boredom with "withitness," overlapping, smoothness, momentum, and group alerting (Kounin, 1970).

Teachers who are aware of what is going on in their classrooms—dealing with student behavior and academic tasks—and who demonstrate this awareness to their students have more impressive student involvement with tasks and less student misbehavior. Kounin terms this awareness "withitness." *Overlapping* practices—attending to two events or situations at the same time and performing both of these tasks reasonably well—are also associated with successful classroom functioning. For example, a teacher may present a concept in mathematics at the board while pointing toward the note she needs the paraprofessional to take to the principal. *Smoothness* is exhibited when teachers stay with the logical organization of instruction. Examples are when teachers continue with a learning activity without mentioning unrelated topics, being distracted easily, interrupting students when they are trying to work, leaving a lesson in midstream, or reversing directions. Smoothness means that teachers organize their time in such a way that their behavior does not interfere with the goal of the lesson. *Momentum* relates to the pacing of a learning activity. An example of lack of momentum is when teachers spend too much time on a point that students already understand. The first teacher practice that Kounin found to be highly related to effective classroom management is *group alerting*. These are teachers' behaviors that keep students alert and "on their toes," not knowing when or if they will be called upon to demonstrate their skills and/or knowledge. An example is calling on students at random. *Nonalerting* practices are those that overprotect students from being held accountable, such as round-robin reading.

If we complement Kounin's work with helpful self-talk, we can greatly increase our ability to cope with negative emotional reactions such as frustration. Figure 1–8 explains Kounin's concepts and provides examples of accompanying self-guidance.

Self-regulated teaching is a skill that all teachers should be able to demonstrate and use with confidence. Teaching requires planning; making quick, important decisions; goal-setting; coping; evaluating; organizing; and managing students' behavior. Such processes will require you to monitor and regulate your own thinking to improve planning, interactive instruction, and classroom organization and management. Therefore, one primary reason for promoting helpful self-talk is because teaching, by its very nature, requires metacognitive skills and self-regulated teaching. All of us who are familiar with a typical teaching day know what happens when teachers act impulsively, rushing through the day without thought and prior mental planning. You will not want this to happen to you and we don't either.

Educational researchers Good and Brophy (1984) state that teachers who self-monitor during teaching are more aware of the complexities of teaching. Implicit in this statement is ongoing self-monitoring that guides and directs teacher behavior. The emphasis is on proactive, deliberate teacher monitoring (self-talk) prior to teaching acts, not simply reactive reflection on a teaching act that has already occurred. We refer to these processes as self-regulated teaching to develop self-monitoring teachers. We believe the skills of self-regulated teaching and SGS are teachable and learnable.

Good and Brophy (1984) believe teachers are too often unaware of many classroom events because they have not learned to monitor their own thinking and to study their own

Kounin's Idea	Helpful Self-Talk—Sample Comments That Effective Teachers Make to Themselves
"Withitness" • Keep alert to sights and sounds in the class. • Arrange students for easy visibility. • Scan the entire classroom when working with an individual or small group of students. • At the first detection of misbehavior, use a brief acknowledgment to let the class know that you are aware of the misbehavior.	• "I can tell they are all on task." • "Gerry keeps hiding behind the taller person in front of him. Better move him." • "Glance across the room at everyone. See what the back table of students is up to." • "I see Jill looking over at Susan. She is writing a note to Susan and trying to distract her. I need to ask Jill to get back to work."
Overlapping • Attend to two events at the same time whenever necessary to keep the classroom functioning moving optimally. • When instructing one group, acknowledge difficulties that students outside of the group may be having, but keep group instruction moving. • Correct misbehavior, but keep instruction moving.	• "Listen to the message on the intercom and write Jonathan's mother a quick note about his behavior." • "I need to get David to keep explaining that math problem out loud to us, while I check Ginger's problem. David. . ." • "I can't even hear Stewart read. I need to remind the class quickly to quiet down so I can hear Stewart."
Smoothness • Preplan the lesson so that extraneous matters are taken care of beforehand. • Once students are absorbed in their work, do not distract them. Leave them alone to work and assist them individually.	• "Don't forget to get the overhead for this next lesson and make sure it is working correctly." • "I certainly would like to interrupt them to tell them about the lunch menu, but that can wait until they aren't so absorbed in their projects."
Momentum • Keep the lesson moving briskly. • Do not dwell on a minor or already understood part of the lesson. • Correct students quickly without nagging and return to the lesson promptly. • Have students move from one activity to the next without having to wait for each other on each subpart of the transition.	• "Don't explain this three times. Once is enough." • "I know they understand this part—move on to the next level." • "It would be better if Brenda put away her toys for right now. Brenda, all eyes on the chalkboard for the next problem." • "I believe everyone should be on page 216. I need to go on with the discussion even if one or two are still looking for the right page."
Group Alerting • Call on students at random. • Raise group interest by interspersing suspense between questions by such statements as, "This is a very important question. Can you work this one out? You have not worked on this before." • Have the entire group or class respond in unison using signaled responses such as agree/disagree cards, thumbs up/thumbs down, Is it a? • Physically move around the room and ask students to show what they have done. • While asking one student to respond, look at other students.	• "I keep calling on the same students over and over. Call on some nonvolunteers." • "I want them to get more interested in this lesson. Remember to tell them motivating clues such as, 'This is a new idea.' " • "While Stephanie was answering, this whole side of the room was off task. I will use some agree/disagree cards to involve them in their peers' thinking." • "I need to move over to that back group of girls and take a look at their poster." • "Beverly is responding, but I need to scan the entire room and then come back to Beverly to reassure her that I am listening to her answer."

Figure 1–8 Helpful Self-Talk Applied to Kounin's Characteristics of Effective Teachers.

Source: From Manning, B. H., & Payne, B. D., Self-Talk for Teachers and Students. *©1996 by Allyn & Bacon. Adapted by permission of the publisher.*

behavior. We define self-regulated teaching as the use of helpful self-talk to apply and control higher-order teacher thinking. For example, when teachers are confronted with complex classroom problems, they deliberately select and apply certain teaching practices they have reviewed mentally and deemed successful. By doing this, you will come to realize your self-talk serves as the guide for your teacher activity. Two central issues are related to teacher self-regulation: (1) the quantity of self-talk and (2) the quality of self-talk.

Quantity of Self-Talk

The goal of self-regulated teaching is not to increase the amount or quantity of self-guiding speech. In fact, merely increasing the amount without paying attention to the high quality of self-guidance is often counterproductive. Simply talking to oneself can be distracting, especially if the talk does not involve task-related, neutral comments. As stated earlier, Matthews (1978) found that very positive or very negative affective comments spoken to oneself divert attention from the task at hand. Therefore, the critical issue in self-talk for teachers is not how much you talk to yourselves but, instead, the nature of what you say. Thus, teacher self-talk should be characterized by task-specific, neutral utterances that inform and direct effective decisions and behaviors that are beneficial to you, as a teacher, and/or your students.

Quality of Self-Guidance

What teachers say to themselves as they ponder teaching decisions affects the quality of those decisions. It is important to note that self-regulated teaching, using self-talk as the core mechanism, is not an all-or-nothing designation. The quality of self-guiding teacher talk will vary among teachers by time of day, classroom context, specific interactions, and with specific individuals. No one is self-regulated all the time. The goal is, therefore, to diminish unhelpful self-talk, increase helpful self-talk, and become more purposefully self-regulated during challenging and frustrating teacher tasks and activities. The ultimate purpose of self-regulated teaching is to use high-quality self-talk so frequently during specific tasks in specific contexts that it becomes automatic, routinized, and is no longer needed at a conscious, deliberate level.

Obviously, the use of self-regulated teaching is contextually bound. To illustrate this, an example of self-regulated teaching during instructing is provided on the next page.

Self-Regulated Teaching During Instruction

A teacher's interactive cognition, resulting in high levels of on-task behavior and higher achievement scores, is typified by rapid judgment and a willingness to change the flow of classroom interaction in midstream when necessary (Clark & Lampert, 1986). Becoming adept at monitoring thinking while in the midst of teaching is a complex skill that requires awareness, practice, and reminders. However, its result appears to be increased on-task behaviors and higher achievement scores.

One of the most powerful and potent ways to teach is via modeling (Bandura, 1986). Therefore, it is highly probable that children will not learn to be adaptive, responsible learners in the classroom until the teacher-model is first responsible and adaptive. Therefore, beginning with teacher modeling of self-regulated teaching may be more productive than explicit lessons directed at teaching children to be self-regulated learners. This teacher modeling may be operationalized as the teacher "thinks aloud" his or her own coping statements while teaching (e.g., "This lesson is not going so well. I believe I just need to start over again."). This kind of naturalistic modeling is not simply modeling aloud a suggestion for an adaptive student response. While this is also very important as a later stage of teaching self-regulated learning strategies,

---

EXAMPLE OF AN INTERACTIVE SITUATION

I am attempting to teach my second graders to alphabetize by the second or third letter of a word. Even though I am confident that they will grasp the concept eventually, I realize they are frustrated right now. I can tell by their faces and their posture. When they get this frustrated, they often become disruptive. As the lesson moves along, I say to myself:

Unhelpful Self-Guidance	Helpful Self-Guidance
Good Grief! They aren't even listening. I've had it!	This lesson is hard to teach, but I can do it. It's important for them to understand this. (self-coping)
No! No! Why aren't they getting this—are they just stupid?	I need to review alphabetizing by the first letter. This seems too hard for several of them. I'll pull them together in a small group later. (self-guiding)
Why isn't she listening? She needs this more than anybody in here. I'm not talking to the wall, or maybe I am.	I need to remember it's not unusual for them to have trouble when I first introduce something. (self-coping)
I hate teaching! This job stinks.	
	Oops, I'm calling on the same children over and over again. I should call on the nonvolunteers also. (self-guiding)
I wish they'd all look at me when I'm talking! How irritating!	Hmm, three or four seem to have it now—Dimetrious, Ted, and Felicia have it! (self-reinforcing)
	I need a visual. This is too abstract for them to just listen. They can't seem to deal with this. I'll change the assignment for some of them. (self-guiding)
	Hey! More of them understand this than I thought earlier. Good. (self-reinforcing)
	I'm going to need to reinforce this in a small group for Maria, Rudolfo, Antonio, and Marcus. (self-guiding)
	What time is it? Oh, 10 more minutes until P.E. Not bad! (self-questioning)

Source: From Manning, B. H., & Payne, B. D., Self-Talk for Teachers and Students. ©1996 by Allyn & Bacon. Adapted by permission of the publisher.

---

it may be insufficient for most youngsters if the teacher fails to model these strategies in the classroom. In addition, a natural and spontaneous display of teachers' "think aloud" to cope with the challenging demands of teaching and the sometimes tedious, boring tasks of teaching may be a prerequisite to students' adaptive responses, associated with the frustration and boredom that is sometimes a part of learning. Teachers need to model aloud their everyday teaching situations, as well as model planned instructional "think aloud" to help students use more adaptive responses to school blocks (see Rohrkemper & Corno, 1988). It certainly seems logical that self-regulated teaching would enhance the teaching profession. What do you think?

Many populations have experienced benefits when their self-guiding speech was modified, including many classroom teachers and future teachers like you.

LEARNING OUT LOUD 1–9

Read an article about teacher thinking, especially teacher reflection or cognitive self-direction. Using poster sessions, depict as creatively as possible your reading about teacher thinking. Include the following steps:

1. Find a chapter or article related to teacher thinking.
2. Put the most interesting points on a poster, using colorful markers and neat, legible printing.
3. Fill out the Recent Related Reading (RRR) Summary Form (page 118 in chapter 4) and make a copy for each person in your class and one for your professor/teacher.
4. Put up the posters around your college/university classroom, usually about five or six at a time. The other members of your class will divide themselves as evenly as possible as the small-group audience for each poster. You can put four or five chairs around your poster for your listeners to use while at your session.
5. Spend 8 to 12 minutes describing what you learned about teacher thinking from your reading to your group of four or five classmates. Simultaneously, four or five of your peers should present their poster information to their small groups.
6. After the first poster presentation session, the instructor flicks the light and groups move clockwise to the next poster session. Then you present your information to the next group. You present four to five times as groups rotate through your session.
7. After all groups have heard all four to five poster sessions, the posters are taken down and four or five more posters are put up. Steps 4–7 are repeated until all students have had a chance to present their teacher thinking reading.

Summary

There is a variety of ways to help you, as a teacher, develop an awareness of the three concepts central to our definition of reflection. *Metacognition*, which includes awareness and regulation of teacher thinking, is the centerpiece of reflection. *Self-regulated learning and teaching* includes the skills of self-questioning, self-directing, self-coping, self-correcting, and self-reinforcing, and relies heavily on metacognition to monitor our thinking. *Self-guiding speech*, or *self-talk*, involves the helpful and unhelpful ways in which we talk to ourselves and guide our daily actions.

Throughout this chapter, we provide ways for you to analyze the quality of your own self-talk and to see how self-talk affects classroom teaching and learning. We offer self-talk as a concrete way to reflect, to heighten personal awareness, and to monitor the impact of self-talk on our personal and professional lives.

Self-regulation theory has a direct connection to classroom teaching. The classic work of Jacob Kounin is used as a basis for linking helpful self-talk to effective teacher characteristics, such as "withitness" and momentum. Such discussion highlights the importance of constant reflection to monitor teacher behavior in the classroom.

Creating a Classroom Community—
The Verbal Environment*

Self-Questions

Knowledge: Describe characteristics of positive and negative verbal environments. Give three reasons for being aware of the verbal and nonverbal environment that we create.

Comprehension: Explain the impact of nonverbal behavior on the classroom environment.

Application: Write a well-remembered event about a teacher-student relationship that you have observed.

---

*An adapted version of a portion of this chapter appeared in Randi Stanulis and Brenda Manning (2002). "The Teacher's Role in Creating a Positive Verbal and Nonverbal Environment in the Early Childhood Classroom," *Early Childhood Education, 30*(1), 3–8.

Analysis: Describe the reasons to use self-instructions to manage classroom anger. What is the significance of following such a process?

Synthesis: Referring to the examples of classroom situations wherein teachers and students use self-guiding speech to work through incidents of provocation, develop your own scenario that integrates the theories discussed within this chapter.

Evaluation: Explain the benefits and drawbacks of practicing steps for managing classroom anger effectively.

Introduction

Elements of the classroom environment can affect students' affective and cognitive growth. The way in which a classroom environment is set up affects students' sense of worth and motivation for achievement. As classroom teachers, it is important that you understand how the discourse that you set up affects students' important developing sense of self. This chapter discusses (1) the verbal and nonverbal environment of the classroom, (2) teacher-student relationships, and (3) verbal mediation to promote healthy classroom interactions.

Understanding How Teacher Talk Influences the Verbal Environment

He sat at his desk—last seat, last row—and looked at the chart on the wall next to him. Of course there was no gold star next to his name... As long as his name was Bradley Chalkers, he'd never get a gold star. They don't give gold stars to monsters.

— From *There's a boy in the girls' bathroom*, L. Sachar, 1987

Bradley's quest for a gold star and his perception of himself as a "monster" illustrate the significant influence of the verbal and nonverbal environment created by teachers and students.

The verbal environment structured by the teacher plays a powerful role in establishing acceptable norms in the classroom. Students take cues from their teacher and peers in developing and reflecting appraisals of others. Building on a Vygotskian framework, we agree that all social interactions provide opportunities for children to learn more about their environment (Goodman & Whitmore, 1995). As teachers, you will provide modeling that is very influential, even though you may not always realize it. When you act a certain way toward a student over time, other pupils often observe and imitate your behavior. Gradually, this treatment is reinforced as a cultural norm in the classroom. If students observe their teachers reacting to a student in a way that is potentially damaging, students might be reinforced to believe that these behaviors and actions are appropriate. Consider the following excerpt from Sachar's (1987) book as the teacher sets the tone for interactions in her classroom. A new student, Jeff, has joined Mrs. Ebbel's classroom and she is finding a place for him to sit:

"Well, I guess we'd better find you a place to sit." She looked around the room. "Hmm, I don't see anyplace except, I suppose you can sit there, at the back."

"No, not next to Bradley!" a girl in the front row exclaimed.

"At least it's better than in front of Bradley," said the boy next to her.

Mrs. Ebbel frowned. She turned to Jeff. "I'm sorry, but there are no other empty desks."

"I don't mind where I sit," Jeff mumbled.

"Well, nobody likes sitting... there," said Mrs. Ebbel. (p. 4)

Within this excerpt, Mrs. Ebbel is sending the message to the new student, Jeff, that nobody wants to be near Bradley. She allows other students to speak in disparaging ways about Bradley, and even apologizes because Jeff will have to sit next to Bradley. Although the author is clearly dramatizing the event, it is possible that this kind of interaction can occur, either implicitly or explicitly.

Many scholars have written about the "informal literacy club" (see, for example: Henkins, 1998; Smith, 1988) that accepts some students and excludes others in everyday classroom interactions. Obviously, Bradley has been denied membership in this classroom club. Despite this consistent rebuffing, it is obvious that Bradley wants Mrs. Ebbel's approval. For example, later in the book, Bradley meets his new friend, Jeff, to complete homework together. As he anticipates this time with a friend, Bradley thinks to himself, "*after he did his homework, Mrs. Ebbel might give him a gold star*" (p. 54).

In contrast, the teacher in the book *The Flunking of Joshua T. Bates* (Shreve, 1984) creates a positive learning environment for Joshua as he repeats the third grade. Although Joshua entered the classroom hostile and bitter, Mrs. Goodwin responded by creating an environment where Joshua could experience success. On the first day of school, Joshua understandably did not feel like he belonged. His previous negative experiences in third grade colored his image of Mrs. Goodwin. As Joshua feigned illness, Mrs. Goodwin said, "*We'll see how you feel after reading. I need you to help me in reading class*" (p. 24). During reading, Joshua helped a child with phonics, and during social studies Mrs. Goodwin asked Joshua to share what he knew about Native Americans' lives on reservations. "*She didn't mention the fact that Joshua already knew about Indians because he had already studied them in third grade once. She simply acted as if Joshua T. Bates... was the smartest boy she had met in several months*" (pp. 24–25). Mrs. Goodwin provided Joshua with numerous opportunities to prove *to himself* that he really was bright and could achieve. As a result of these positive experiences reinforced within Mrs. Goodwin's verbal and nonverbal environment, Joshua began to believe that he was smart, and others believed it as well.

Many teachers serve as mental models of positive and accepting self-regulating behavior. As described in chapter 1, self-regulated learners are metacognitively, motivationally, and behaviorally active participants in their academic achievement (Zimmerman & Schunk, 1989). Based on Bandura's (1986) triadic theory of social cognition, Zimmerman (2000) suggests that students' efforts to regulate their behavior and learning involve three dimensions: personal processes, their environment, and their behavior. In order for students to exhibit self-regulative behavior, they must be provided with a positive environment in which to learn.

Clearly, the model promoted by this text is the image of teacher as mental model of positive and acceptable self-regulating behavior. The adult in this setting should be keenly aware that she, the teacher, provides the standard by which appropriate verbal and nonverbal behavior within the classroom environment is measured. Kostelnik, Stein, and Whiren (1988) believe that teachers create either positive or negative verbal environments. These components include both verbal and nonverbal messages, including words and silence (see Figure 2–1). "How much adults say, what they say, how they speak, to whom they talk and how well they listen" (p. 29) all influence a student's estimation of self-worth and the impressions students have about each other.

Negative Verbal Environments	Positive Verbal Environments
Adults show little or no interest in children's activities because they are in a hurry, busy, engrossed in their own thoughts, or tired.	Adults verbalize affection and sincere interest in students and their interests.
Adults pay superficial attention to what children have to say. Instead of listening attentively, they fail to maintain eye contact or cut children off.	Adults send congruent verbal and nonverbal messages. Adults listen attentively to what children have to say.
Adults speak discourteously to children. Young children attend to the sarcastic tone of voice as much as the meaning of the words.	Adults speak courteously to children. They refrain from interrupting children, allowing them to finish what they say.
Adults use judgmental vocabulary in describing children to themselves and others (i.e., "He's hyper. She's a motor-mouth.")	Adults have spontaneous personal conversations with children throughout the day.
Adults rely on giving orders, directions, or making demands as their primary means of relating to children.	
Adults use children's names as synonymous with "no," "stop," etc. (i.e., "Tony!"). Using their name as a reprimand may cause children to associate this personal aspect of themselves with disapproval and rejection.	

Figure 2–1   Characteristics of Negative and Positive Verbal Environments.
Source: From "Children's Self-Esteem: The Verbal Environment," by Kostenlink, Stein, & White, 1988, Childhood Education 65*(1), pp. 29–32. Used with permission of the publisher.*

LEARNING OUT LOUD 2–1

Keep a journal for one day, paying close attention to the verbal and nonverbal messages you are sending when you communicate in daily interactions. Discuss your day with another student or in small groups of three or four peers.

Understanding How Student Talk Influences the Verbal Environment

Student discourse within an elementary or middle school classroom plays a significant role in shaping a student's sense of self-worth. When students receive messages from the teacher that convey a negative verbal environment, the result is a classroom discourse of unhonored voices, one that allows certain students access to power and privilege. Within a negative environment, a teacher leaves diverse student needs unattended. Students who are "different" from the teacher may unintentionally receive messages that their voices don't count. Vivian Paley (1992) described her efforts to reinforce a discourse of shared responsibility for creating a positive verbal environment. In her kindergarten classroom, she reinforced the norm that "you can't say you can't play." Paley wrote the following about her kindergarten class:

You can't play suddenly seems too overbearing and harsh, resounding like a slap from wall to wall. How casually one child determines the fate of another… Must it be so? This year I am compelled to find out. Posting a sign that reads YOU CAN'T SAY YOU CAN'T PLAY, I announce the new social order and, from the start, it is greeted with disbelief" (p. 3).

The important message that can be adapted appropriately for different grade levels is that every child is valuable and valued. Of course, it will take persistence and practice to encourage children to believe this is a value that is possible to promote.

As students interact within the classroom environment, they are constantly getting feedback that either affirms or disconfirms their developing sense of self. *Disconfirmation* is communication that denies a person's significance. One function of healthy interpersonal communication is that it is "person building" because who you are as a person depends, in many ways, on the kinds of communication you experience (Stewart & D'Angelo, 1993). In our everyday interactions, we place a great deal of self-worth on the kinds of interactions we have with peers and significant adults. George McCall (1976) describes how individuals' identities are formed based on interactions with others: *my me* is my view of myself; *my you* is my image of the person with whom I am communicating; and *my your me* is my view of the way you see me.

In the classroom, you can use children's literature as a vehicle to explore these concepts in action (Stanulis, 1999). In Kevin Henkes (1996) book *Chrysanthemum*, a little girl's sense of self-worth is affected negatively when children in her school make fun of her name. Before attending school, Chrysanthemum believed that her name was "absolutely perfect" (p. 6). Chrysanthemum's *my me* included a view of herself as special. She felt fortunate to have such a beautiful name. However, as she progressed throughout the first day of school, her *my you* saw other children whose name fit on their name tags, whose names were shorter than half of the alphabet, and who were not named after flowers. This image of others was constructed directly from Chrysanthemum's developing *my your me*. Chrysanthemum's *my your me* began to significantly affect her *my me* as she listened to children make fun of her name (Figure 2–2). When students on the second day of school said, "*She even looks like a flower… let's pick her… let's smell her*" (p. 15), Chrysanthemum became even more upset. Throughout her days at school, the author describes how "*Chrysanthemum wilted. She did not think her name was absolutely perfect. She thought it was absolutely dreadful.*" (p. 15)

It is evident that Chrysanthemum needed confirmation from someone at school—someone who could provide a positive *my your me*. Although Chrysanthemum was supported and nurtured at home, she dreaded coming to school each day. Then Chrysanthemum met the music teacher, Ms. Twinkle, who confirmed her *my your me*. As the children began once

My Me	My You	My Your Me
I wish my name could be Jane.	Your names all fit on a name tag.	You don't like me because I have a funny name.
I don't like being different.	You are not named after flowers.	You make fun of me.
	You all fit in.	

Figure 2–2 Chrysanthemum During the First Days of School Before Ms. Twinkle Intervened.
Source: Adapted from Chrysanthemum, *(pp. 6, 15, 26), by Kevin Henkes, 1991, New York: HarperCollins Publishers. Used by permission of the publisher.*

again to make fun of Chrysanthemum's name, Ms. Twinkle responded that her name would scarcely fit on a name tag, and that she was named after a flower. She said, *"My name is Delphinium Twinkle. And if my baby is a girl, I'm considering Chrysanthemum as a name. I think it's absolutely perfect"* (p. 26).

Understanding How Student Self-Talk Influences the Verbal Environment

Bradley, Joshua, and Chrysanthemum, like all students, have basic needs that must be satisfied for them to achieve optimal success in the classroom (Glasser, 1990). The ways that each of these characters talk to themselves illustrate a time when they felt alone and unsupported in their classroom environment:

> BRADLEY: "He understood it when the other kids were mean to him. It didn't bother him. He simply hated them. As long as he hated them, it didn't matter what they thought of him. That was why he had threatened to spit on Jeff. He had to hate Jeff before Jeff hated him." (p. 8)
>
> JOSHUA: "… he sat down… wishing he could erase the whole last year and return to the time when he was a regular third-grade boy with a reputation as an athlete and not a problem in the world except cavities." (p. 42)
>
> CHRYSANTHEMUM: "… that night Chrysanthemum dreamed that her name was Jane. It was an extremely pleasant dream." (p. 13)

As teachers, you can intervene to support student development and practice of constructive self-talk. First, it is necessary to help students bring their own metacognitive, unhelpful and helpful self-talk to a level of awareness. Grounded within a Vygotskian theoretical framework, it is believed that language and self-talk are critical to the development of self-regulation, as "finally, the child develops the capability for socioemotional expression—the use of self-verbalizations before an action in order to regulate performance" (Harris, 1990, p. 37).

As illustrated in chapter 1 with the example of the fourth-grade teacher Oppong, you can demonstrate ways that you talk to yourself throughout the school day that are helpful or unhelpful. In addition to providing this sustained modeling, you need to provide multiple opportunities for students to practice talking to themselves and others in positive ways that reinforce success, and coach students to guide themselves through frustrations.

Finally, you can help students recognize the significant role that self-talk plays in creating our sense of *my me*, and help students recognize and apply helpful, positive self-talk in their daily lives. For example, as Sachar (1987) describes ways in which Bradley develops confidence in his friendship with Jeff and others, Bradley begins to exhibit some helpful self-talk about his progress in relationships and task productivity at school. He thinks to himself, *"I'm going to be good… and then, when everybody sees how good I am, they'll know I'm not a monster"* (p. 95).

Learning Out Loud 2–2

What are some self-talk statements that you regularly say to yourself in inner or private speech that reinforce your image of yourself?

Krista Arnn, a kindergarten teacher, adapted the words to a song called "I Think I'm Wonderful" (original words/music by Red Grammar, from the tape *Teaching Peace*) to read as follows:

I Think I'm Wonderful

(Chorus)
I think I'm wonderful—when I say that to me,
I feel wonderful—as wonderful as can be!
It makes me want to say the same thing to somebody new.
And by the way, I've been meaning to say,
I think you're wonderful, too!

When I practice this phrase in the most honest way,
I find something special in myself each day.
I can light up the world one heart at a time.
It all starts by saying this one simple line…

(Repeat chorus)

When I feel important inside,
I'm loving and giving and glad I'm alive.
Oh, what a difference I can make in each day.
All because I decided to say…

(Repeat chorus)

Figure 2–3   Self-Reinforcement Song.
Source: Used with permission of Krista Arnn.

Teachers can and should play active roles in promoting norms that reinforce positive self-talk and other-talk. For example, one practicing teacher who took a class from us adapted words to current songs to sing with her children in elementary school (see Figure 2–3).

The purpose of integrating concrete examples of ways to reinforce ourselves is to help students learn to guide their speech toward helpful self- and other-talk, and to help students learn realistic and honest ways to reinforce their work, their effort, and their character. Manning, White, and Daugherty (1994) found that students rarely use self-reinforcement in their talk to self. The primary reason that reinforcing self-talk does not occur spontaneously is because students do not have adult models to demonstrate how to appropriately reinforce oneself. For example, if parents and teachers are verbalizing speech that is ordinarily private and saying phrases like, "I worked very hard on that science unit. I'm proud of what I accomplished!" or "I knew I could get through this test because I studied hard and read all the material," students would be more likely to practice similar ways of reinforcing themselves about task performance. The key is to connect reinforcement with effort.

Therefore, there is an inherent caution about simply promoting the singing of a song like "I'm Wonderful" in that students could develop an unrealistic sense of themselves and their achievements. If students develop an unrealistic sense of themselves, they may develop high self-efficacy toward a task that is unwarranted. Within this song, Krista Arnn qualifies that we "practice this phrase in the most honest way." Thus, as teachers, we need to understand the delicate balance of helping children celebrate how "wonderful" they are with specific examples and specific self-directed rewards for task performance. If students can learn to regulate the ways that they talk to themselves, including important talk to self that is reinforcing, researchers predict that task performance will improve (Manning, 1988, 1990b, 1991; Manning, White, & Daugherty, 1994). Instead of continuing to talk to themselves in ways that are self-defeating, Bradley, Joshua, and Chrysanthemum could learn ways of talking to themselves that promote task performance and block distractors. They could learn to

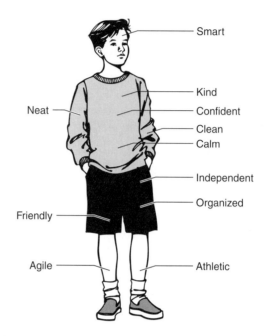

Figure 2–4   Ricardo

reinforce themselves in realistic ways, in ways that they earned legitimately through diligent effort and serious persistence. In order for this to occur, a positive teacher model must scaffold the process with knowledge, persistence, and concern for students.

Some teachers combine visual and verbal methods of teaching children about self- and other-reinforcement. One of our favorite class activities involves Ricardo, a boy who begins his day feeling good about himself (adapted from Canfield & Wells, 1976). The primary objective of this class activity is to help teachers and students understand how the environment plays a large part in determining how we feel about ourselves. Both teachers and students need to realize that a person's self-worth can be affected adversely, or even destroyed, by the words of others (Manning & Payne, 1996). We believe that a teacher who reflects on *why* he is acting a certain way is better positioned to thoughtfully monitor whether he *should* carry out a particular action. The activity begins as students receive a paper Ricardo that lists adjectives that describe Ricardo's feelings of self-worth before others deconstruct his sense of self (see Figure 2–4). We then read a script (adapted from Canfield & Wells, 1976) that details Ricardo's day. Beginning at home in the morning, where Ricardo's mother is yelling because Ricardo is always late and never cleans his room; to his bus ride when no one wants to sit next to him; to his classroom where he doesn't have the proper reading materials for learning and he has to redo his mathematics assignment because it was messy, Ricardo talks to himself in self-defeating ways such as, "I can't remember anything at all." As our teachers listen to this story, we ask them to tear a piece of the paper Ricardo each time someone makes a comment that is negative about Ricardo, or Ricardo says a negative statement about himself. When we are finished, there is little left of Ricardo.

One of our students uses an adaptation of Ricardo in her class. At the beginning of the school year, she introduces a paper cut-out in the shape of a person called "Crinkle." She allows the students in class to say mean things to Crinkle. As students call out negative descriptors, she begins to crinkle the paper. Then the class discusses what it means to "crinkle someone's feelings." She then posts Crinkle with a slogan cue, "Let's All Be Crinkle Free," as a cultural norm of the classroom, reminding students to be kind and thoughtful to others.

Recognizing the Impact of Nonverbal Behavior in the Classroom Environment

Nonverbal behavior in the classroom plays a key role in developing and maintaining a healthy, productive environment where children are ready to take responsibility for learning. The way a teacher maintains eye contact, controls facial expressions, and smiles sends messages of approval or disapproval. Tone of voice, posture, touching behaviors, and gestures are also important nonverbal behaviors that you need to be aware of and monitor and adjust constantly. It is vital that teachers be introspective, bringing to a conscious level of awareness the nonverbal cues that they are sending. These nonverbal cues reflect beliefs and biases that you, as teachers, hold. Because of Mrs. Goodwin's affirming nonverbal and verbal cues, the students in the class where Joshua was repeating third grade thought that Joshua *"obviously… was smart… because Mrs. Goodwin needed his help with the other children… Everybody wanted to sit next to him in music and art class, where there was a choice of seats… By October no one in third grade cared a bit that Joshua Bates had flunked"* (p. 46).

Nonverbal communication involves the ways that we use our body and voice to communicate a message and is a part of every human communication transaction. In fact, research shows that the nonverbal component of communication often overshadows the verbal portion of the message (Gorden & Nevins, 1993). As Burgoon, Buller, and Woodall (1989) state, nonverbal communication is trusted. This means that if a verbal message of "Good work, Bradley" is sent with no eye contact, no smile, and in a monotone, Bradley would probably not believe that Mrs. Ebbel's comment was sincere. When there is a contradiction in the message sent, people tend to believe nonverbal cues rather than verbal cues. Teachers need to be aware that, even unintentionally, they are continually sending signals to students that indicate degrees of interest, enthusiasm, and engagement (Neill, 1991; O'Hair & Ropo, 1994). Because nonverbal behavior is often difficult to control, teachers must ensure that their nonverbal and verbal cues match.

Because of the power of nonverbal communication, Burgoon, Buller, and Woodall (1989) advocate that nonverbal communication be discussed with K–12 children. They say:

> Despite the emphasis placed on communication skills in elementary school, attention is devoted almost exclusively to reading and writing—in other words, to verbal communication. Ideally, nonverbal communication should be interwoven into all communication study from preschool forward as an integral part of the communication system (p. 10).

O'Hair and Ropo (1994) also emphasize a need for introducing prospective and practicing teachers to fundamental knowledge of nonverbal communication. They argue that effective classroom communication involves not only an awareness of nonverbal communication, but also a sensitivity to demonstrating appropriate nonverbal behaviors that are congruent with diverse environments. We recognize that it is not easy to simply "be open" to diverse students, but it is a habit of mind one can strive for with awareness and practice. As Roxanne Henkin (1998) writes:

No one would argue against diversity and multiculturalism. We all want our children to get along with many different kinds of people. We want our children and our students to be able to think about complicated issues and see many points of view. The problem arises when we try to live within our belief systems. Even though we *say* that we embrace complexity, we still yearn for simple solutions (p. 19).

Throughout this book, we challenge you to look beyond "simple solutions" as you examine your beliefs and practices and prepare to teach culturally diverse students.

Students of all ages can be introduced to nonverbal communication by studying its major functions. According to O'Hair and Ropo (1994), nonverbal communication primarily serves four functions: (1) expressing emotions, (2) conveying interpersonal attitudes, (3) presenting one's personality, and (4) accompanying verbal communication.

Expressing Emotions

Teachers have much power to send messages of interest or dismay. Through voice, gestures, and body position, a teacher can convey enthusiastic approval of student behavior and actions. Similarly, a teacher can convey his dismay for a student by closed body positioning, lack of eye contact, and personal space distancing. Teachers express emotions to students through their nonverbal cues. Note the ways in which a teacher can handle the following situation:

Scenario: The whole class is involved in reading a Big Book while gathered on the carpet. Aaron is stumbling over the words.

Helpful Self-Talk: Just be patient, he will get it. He needs this practice to learn how to read. I need to show him that I am interested so he will gain confidence. Be sure to look at him, give him smiles of encouragement, and show with your posture that you are being patient.

Unhelpful Self-Talk: We've practiced these words over and over. How can he still be having trouble? I am so frustrated with him. I don't have any patience left. I can't help but scowl at him and close off my posture, I just want him to finish!

Constructive Behavior: I will nod my head and smile at Aaron, I will silently mouth the words to let him know that I am supporting him, and I will give praise and murmur encouragement. I will not cross my arms or frown.

Destructive Behavior: Sighing, looking at the clock, rolling my eyes, or quickly calling on someone else. Showing my impatience and frustration will further keep him from feeling success in reading.

Conveying Interpersonal Attitudes

Teachers can learn a lot by observing the nonverbal behavior of their pupils during the school day. If a student enters the classroom with slouched posture, little eye contact, and stiff gestures, a teacher would be alerted that something might be troubling the child. Teachers must be sensitive to diverse cultural norms to interpret nonverbal attitudes correctly. The following classroom scenario illustrates how teachers can learn from nonverbal messages that students send. Note the ways in which an attentive teacher can constructively involve students in problem solving:

Scenario: A sixth-grade teacher is teaching a science lesson. The students are normally excited about science, but they seem to be disinterested, sluggish, and daydreaming. Many have their heads down, are doodling, or talking to their neighbor. The students are avoiding eye contact and have slouched posture.

Helpful Self-Talk: I wonder what is wrong? I can tell by their facial expressions and posture that they are not interested in this lesson. What can I do to get them more engaged?

Unhelpful Self-Talk: It's their problem if they don't learn this lesson. Why are they frowning at me? I try the best I can to make this interesting. It really makes me angry when they daydream.

Constructive Behavior: I will tell the students that they are sending nonverbal messages that they are not interested in the lesson. I need to be specific in identifying these behaviors and acknowledging that I see this behavior. I want to understand why the students are not ready and eager to learn. I will use positive eye contact and animated facial expressions to communicate to them that I want them to learn.

Destructive Behavior: Continue the lesson, angry and frustrated at the students. Do not acknowledge their nonverbal cues. Send your own nonverbal cues of anger and dismay.

Presenting One's Personality

We form impressions of others based in large part on the presentation of nonverbal behaviors, including tone of voice, gestures, facial expression, touch, and personal space comforts. Cultural, racial, and gender norms are very context-specific and nonverbal norms will differ among individuals based on family and environmental experiences. Some students may cringe when touched, whereas others see touch as encouragement. Some students feel safe only when provided a large personal space zone, whereas others gain comfort from close proximity. In addition, you are constantly presenting your personality to students, parents, and administrators. Nonverbal communication helps shape the message that is sent about a teacher's personality:

Scenario: It is the end of the school day, and students are called to board the buses. The students are pushing to get to their bookbags and coats. You are trying to get them to clean up and pack up. Someone announces on the PA "Sam is riding bus 6," but you didn't hear the message and the student already left on another bus. Just then, a parent comes in unexpectedly and wants to have an immediate conference. The parent becomes impatient while waiting for you. You also realize that an important faculty meeting is scheduled to begin in 15 minutes.

Helpful Self-Talk: Focus on one thing at a time. Try to appear calm. Be sure that the parent feels welcome in my classroom as I explain that I have to attend to the children first.

Unhelpful Self-Talk: I can't believe she is just showing up like this again. Why does she keep popping in and expecting me to drop everything? I don't have time for this now.

Constructive Behavior: I will take 1 minute and gather my thoughts before I talk with this parent. I need to be sure that I am making her feel important and valued for coming to talk to me by maintaining direct eye contact, close proximity, and animated facial expression. I can let her know that I don't have much time to talk now without shutting down communication.

Destructive Behavior: Tell the parent that I have limited time now, with an irritated tone of voice, turning away, rolling eyes, sighing, and having closed posture.

Accompanying Verbal Communication

According to O'Hair and Ropo (1994), nonverbal communication can (a) reinforce what is said verbally, (b) regulate verbal behavior, (c) complement verbal communication, (d) substitute for verbal behavior, and (e) even contradict a verbal message. Every time a teacher speaks, she is sending nonverbal messages alongside her verbal message. If these messages contradict, the nonverbal message is often believed. You need to be aware of the nonverbal cues that accompany verbal communications:

Scenario: The teacher asks a question and is waiting for the directed student to answer.

Helpful Self-Talk: Maybe I didn't word this question very well. How can I restate this in another way? I need to show that I am patient and that I want to wait for her to have a chance to answer the question.

Unhelpful Self-Talk: She never knows the answer. I can't help it, I just naturally show my frustration with her. I know that I should have called on someone else. How long do I have to wait before I call on someone else?

Constructive Behavior: I will smile, nod affirmatively, or wink at the child to let her know that I am encouraging her to take her time. I will stay in close proximity so she feels supported.

Destructive Behavior: Roll my eyes, cross my arms to close off my body, look at my watch, and sigh.

LEARNING OUT LOUD 2–3

In dyads, review the four functions of nonverbal communication. Visualize one of the four and write a one- to two-paragraph response about how you might improve this nonverbal communication within a classroom setting.

Teacher-Student Relationships

Understanding the Teacher's Role in Balancing Support and Challenge

Harry Allard and James Marshall's (1977) children's book, *Miss Nelson Is Missing*, provides an effective example of the fundamental elements many pupils desire in a teacher-student relationship. Research indicates that the nature of the teacher-student relationship correlates positively with academic and affective achievement. Yet, providing a caring environment that is not accompanied by high standards of rigor can be unproductive as well. At the beginning of the story, Miss Nelson is a caring teacher who talks to her students in a very sweet voice. When she would ask the class to settle down, the students did not listen. So Miss Nelson dressed up as a "witch" and pretended to be the substitute teacher, Miss Viola Swamp. In an unpleasant voice, she hissed her expectations to the students. "*Right away she put them to work. And she loaded them down with homework. 'We'll have no story hour today,' said Miss Swamp. 'Keep your mouths shut,' said Miss Swamp. 'Sit perfectly still,' said Miss Swamp.*" The children were begging for Miss Nelson to return to class. And when she did, she no longer had disruptive problems. Her students realized that they needed a caring teacher, and that a caring teacher deserves respect.

Support HIGH	Challenge LOW	Student is not challenged to achieve higher development.
Support LOW	Challenge HIGH	Student is likely to withdraw from learning.
Support LOW	Challenge LOW	Student will not likely change.
Support HIGH	Challenge HIGH	Student will make the most substantial progress.

Figure 2–5   Balancing Support and Challenge in Teaching.
Source: From Effective Teaching and Mentoring *(pp. 32–33), by L. Daloz, 1986, New York: John Wiley & Sons, Inc. This material is used by permission of John Wiley & Sons.*

Different amounts of support and challenge certainly can have a significant effect on learning. Daloz (1986) studied mentoring relationships and described the delicate balance between support and challenge (Figure 2–5). Daloz believes that when support is high but challenge is low, the learner will feel confirmation but will not be challenged to achieve higher development. When support is low but challenge is high, it is likely that the learner will withdraw from learning. When support and challenge are both low, the learner will not change. Finally, when support and challenge are both high, the learner will grow and make the most substantial progress. Daloz (1986) describes a theory of learning wherein the teacher, as mentor, plays a pivotal role in the growth and development of her students. He wrote:

> If we are serious when we assert that education is most successful when students "grow," that it is intellectual development we are about rather than simply knowledge acquisition, then the evidence is strong that emotional engagement must be a part of the learning process. The recognition that passion is central to learning and the capacity to provide emotional support when it is needed are hallmarks that distinguish the good mentor from the mediocre teacher (pp. 32–33).

Developing Effective Teacher-Student Relationships

Educators such as Thomas Gordon, known for his work in teacher effectiveness training (1974), believe that a positive teacher-student relationship is paramount for learning. He believes that the relationship between a teacher and a student is good when it has the following components:

1. Openness or transparency, so each is able to risk directness and honesty with the other
2. Caring, when each knows that he is valued by the other
3. Interdependence (as opposed to dependency) of one on the other
4. Separateness to allow each to grow and to develop his uniqueness, creativity, and individuality
5. Mutual needs meeting, so that neither's needs are met at the expense of the other's needs (p. 24).

It is important for you to recognize examples of teacher-student relationships that foster both healthy self-esteem and challenging learning. One way to achieve this goal is for you to observe current classroom teachers and find a personally meaningful critical incident or well-remembered event (Carter, 1994). The well-remembered event (WRE) is a mechanism used to foster analysis and reflection on a teaching episode.

A well-remembered event "is an incident or episode a teacher observes or experiences in a school situation and considers, for his or her own reasons, especially salient or memorable"

(Gonzalez & Carter, 1996, p. 40). Building on the belief that teacher knowledge is event structured, the well-remembered event provides novice and expert teachers an opportunity to comprehend, interpret, and predict classroom events more effectively. Research shows that there are differences in how expert and novice teachers interpret such events, so it is important for you to talk to classroom teachers about the event you observe to gain a more accurate understanding of the event. Observation and analysis of a WRE can help you understand complex teacher-student relationships. Figure 2–6 provides directions for writing about a well-remembered event. This is followed by Learning Out Loud 2–4, in which you will have an opportunity to read and analyze one of Stanulis's teacher's WREs. You may also wish to write a WRE of your own following the guidelines provided in Figure 2–6.

During your field experience, you will observe your mentor teacher many times as she interacts with children in one-to-one, small-group, and whole-group sessions. You will observe how she begins and ends each day, how she uses transitions to move between activities, how she teaches in a variety of content areas, and how she adapts instruction to meet learner needs. You will also observe your teacher as she helps her class understand the routines, rules, and procedures of the classroom at the beginning of the school year, and how she reinforces these expectations throughout the school day.

From the myriad of opportunities that you have to observe your teacher, choose two occasions to think about and write about in detail. The decision is yours: you need to choose what critical incident in your mind is a *well-remembered event*—one that you learned something from that either confirms your philosophy or that you would handle differently. You need to be able to describe the event and explain why you selected this observation as a well-remembered event.

An important component of learning about teaching is talking with the teacher about the decisions she made. Because you have limited teaching experiences from which to draw, it is difficult to understand some teaching decisions because of all the complexities of classroom life. After each WRE, ask to meet briefly with the teacher within 24 hours of the observation, and ask respectful questions about decisions she made during that event that will help you understand her perspective.

The Write-Up

Write a two- to three-page description and analysis after observing your cooperating teacher in a teaching area of your choice. The paper should contain four sections: (1) a description of the teacher event that you observed, (2) a summary of the teacher's perspective on the event, (3) a statement of the issue and issues this event raises (teacher/student relationship, motivation, content pedagogy, management), and (4) a statement of what sense you made of the event for your own learning-to-teach process. (What did I learn from observing and reflecting on this event?)

The WREs are private and do not need to be shared with your mentor teacher. You need to feel comfortable being honest in your reflections, but do be careful that you are making informed comments based on theoretically based reflections, and are not focusing on judging the teacher's actions.

	Points Earned	Comments

Description (10 points)
• Identifies a single event
• Describes event
• Tells what was observed

Analysis (10 points)
• Discusses the significance of the event
• Analyzes the event according to theories read about and discussed in the course
• Analyzes the event according to the teacher's rationale

Reflection (10 points)
• Reflects upon the sense you make out of the event as someone learning to teach
• Discusses what you learned about teaching as a result of observing the event

Written Presentations (5 points)
• The four sections are distinguishable
• Spell-checked and grammatically correct

Total   **35 points**

Figure 2–6   Writing About a Well-Remembered Event.

LEARNING OUT LOUD 2–4

Consider the following example from one of our students who observed this event during her field experience in a third-grade classroom. Then, in small- or large-group discussion, analyze the presence or absence of the five components of a healthy relationship between a teacher and a student (Gordon, 1974). If present, discuss the benefit in this particular situation. If absent, discuss how adding the component(s) would have enhanced healthy relationships.

Elisa Crittenden (1998), Early Childhood Education Student, Well-Remembered Event

One day when I was walking around reading journals as everyone was coming in and beginning to sit down and write, a little boy came up to me with much excitement in his eyes. He handed me a story that he had written the night before. This student was not one who typically gets excited about writing, and because of his nationality, writing was not the easiest thing for him to do. I was very surprised at his willingness to write at home and also very excited. I took his story and began to read it. It was different from any other piece of writing I had ever seen him do, and grammatically, it was perfect. I asked the little boy about the writing and he said that his brother had helped him. So, in my cynicism, I asked my classroom teacher to read it. After she read it, she smiled and said, "This looks like a retelling of The Ant and the Grasshopper." *She went over to her bookshelf and pulled out a copy of the book. She told me to read it and tell her what I thought. After realizing that she was right about this, I asked the boy if that is what he was writing about. He said that he had never read that book. My classroom teacher advised that I sit down with him and read the book to him. Then we should talk about the similarities of the stories, but in no way should I discourage him because of the mere greatness of him wanting to write at home. She also discouraged me from saying anything about his brother helping him, because we did not know exactly how much he had helped. So, I did all these things by the end of the day. The result was a tremendous growth in an excitement for writing and in his writing itself. During my lessons, I gave them much time to write and this boy wrote some of the best pieces I had ever read from a third grader. Although his spelling was very poor, when he read his pieces to me, they were wonderful. From this I concluded that his brother had helped him a lot with spelling but probably did not help him a lot with the actual writing. My teacher made a very wise decision in not discouraging him, even if she did have suspicions.*

When asked about this, my classroom teacher said that we must always give the children the benefit of the doubt and they will surprise us so many times. There was no clear evidence that the child had not written the story, except that his spelling was perfect. Considering that children are encouraged to ask others for spelling help, this was no grounds to accuse him. She figured that we should always encourage students if they are taking the time to do something like that at home.

This event shows me that my teaching was trying to set up a positive verbal environment in her classroom. She did not want me to discourage him, but rather, to listen to him and allow him to tell me about writing the story. She wanted him to know that he was cared for and valued and that what he had written was important. She also wanted to encourage that interdependent relationship between the student and me. This means that he could write a story to show me the next day in class and not need me to initiate the writing. Also, by my teacher's desire to see the student grow on his own and explore writing outside of class, she was encouraging separateness (Gordon, 1974). Also, in this, she was providing a good balance of support and challenge for me as a student intern. She was guiding me in solving the problem and giving me suggestions,

(continued)

Learning Out Loud 2–4 (continued)

but she also challenged me in that I had to do it myself. It would not have been the same if she had just taken the story and dealt with it on her own (Stanulis & Manning).

The most important thing I learned about children is that they need to be given the benefit of the doubt. I should not ever think they are trying to "pull a fast one" on me unless there is substantial evidence to prove this true. The way that my teacher encouraged me to handle this was definitely the best thing I could have done for this child. She knew the child and knew that writing was not something he was normally excited about. If I had discouraged him, it would have taken a long time to undo that damage. This tells me that I need to know my students well and also to always be an encouragement to them in writing (Calkins, 1994). If I had discouraged this child he might not have ever produced those beautiful works that he did during the rest of the time that I was there.

We can learn much about the ways in which caring is manifested in the classroom by observing and describing teacher-student relationships. This is an important piece in helping you develop your own philosophy of caring.

Learning Out Loud 2–5

Think about one of your favorite teachers. What are some personal or professional qualities this teacher displayed? What qualities do you believe you displayed?

Responsible emotion management for both teachers and students is critical to healthy verbal classroom environments and positive teacher attributes. If teachers lose their emotional control (e.g., screaming, crying), they immediately become poor role models for their students. Such overt emotions can render teachers helpless as problem solvers. Of course, feeling our emotions is legitimate and even necessary to sound mental health. However, the behavior resulting from unmonitored emotion has the potential to damage and even destroy healthy classroom environments.

Verbal Mediation to Promote Healthy Classroom Interactions

Students deserve a healthy, well-adjusted teacher who is fully capable of moving them forward academically, socially, emotionally, cognitively, and metacognitively. Those of us who share a passion for teaching and learning understand the excitement we feel when our students learn, excel, cope, and make progress.

Nevertheless, teaching inherently creates multiple opportunities for teacher frustration, stress, and anxiety. From chapter 1 of this text, we know teachers make decisions at the rate of about one every 2 minutes, (Clark & Peterson, 1986) they have 1,000 face-to-face interactions per day (Jackson, 1968), and they lose approximately 55% of their classroom time to disruption (Gottfredson, May, 1989, personal communication). No wonder teaching is

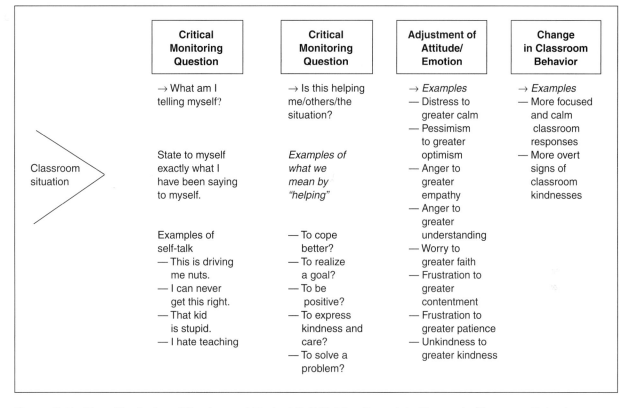

Classroom situation	Critical Monitoring Question	Critical Monitoring Question	Adjustment of Attitude/ Emotion	Change in Classroom Behavior
	→ What am I telling myself?	→ Is this helping me/others/the situation?	→ *Examples* — Distress to greater calm — Pessimism to greater optimism	→ *Examples* — More focused and calm classroom responses
	State to myself exactly what I have been saying to myself.	*Examples of what we mean by "helping"*	— Anger to greater empathy — Anger to greater understanding	— More overt signs of classroom kindnesses
	Examples of self-talk — This is driving me nuts. — I can never get this right. — That kid is stupid. — I hate teaching	— To cope better? — To realize a goal? — To be positive? — To express kindness and care? — To solve a problem?	— Worry to greater faith — Frustration to greater contentment — Frustration to greater patience — Unkindness to greater kindness	

Figure 2–7   From Monitoring of Teacher and Student Self-Guiding Speech to Change in Classroom Behavior.

considered a stressful profession. There is little doubt that the teacher-student scenario of simply being in one (often small) classroom for 6 hours or more per day, with at least 25 pupils is one that is ripe for provocation. This potentially volatile situation requires constant self-monitoring and adjustment of teacher emotions, attitudes, and behaviors.

Talking Through Provocation in the Classroom

As discussed in chapter 1, it is not easy to monitor and adjust emotions, attitudes, and behaviors. In fact, we contend that lasting change, as such, will not occur unless we give concentrated attention to the self-guiding speech that underlies and affects our emotions, attitudes, and behaviors. Figure 2–7 illustrates how you can begin to bring your current practices to a level of awareness, which, in turn, can lead to internalizing habits of monitoring, adjustment, and change. Such internalization can occur only through repeated practice, asking questions such as, "What am I telling myself?" and "Is this helping?" and repeatedly analyzing situations.

Without question, teachers who effectively use silent or audible self-verbalizations to calm, soothe, and de-stress are much more likely to be exemplary teachers: those whom we would want teaching our own children, in control of their emotions, attitudes, and behaviors. With this teacher model in the classroom, it is much more likely that students will be guided toward greater self-regulation. Likewise, students can be taught and can learn awareness and regulation of their own self-guiding speech and, subsequently, their classroom behavioral reactions. Figure 2–8 presents classroom scenarios that offer realistic

These situations and accompanying teacher and student self-talk of adjustment can be read, role-played, or used to help you generate examples of your own.

Classroom Situation 1

FIRST

Teacher's Impulsive Reaction   Teacher shouts at the students.

Student's Impulsive Reaction   Student A pushes student B during transition between subjects.

SECOND

Mediated Adjustment

Teacher's self-guiding speech used to effectively mediate emotional outbursts that are too strong:

I'm just tired. I need to control my outbursts. What kind of example am I setting when I scream at them.? My screaming may be the reason that students have been shouting at each other lately. I better watch out!

Student's self-guiding speech used to effectively mediate emotional outbursts that are too strong:

I know that pushing is against the rules and doesn't help me keep friends. Sonja hurt my feelings. We need to talk this over today. Pushing won't help!

THIRD

Teacher's Reflective Reaction   Teacher calmly addresses the students.

Student's Reflective Reaction   Student A tells student B that they need to talk after class.

Classroom Situation 2

FIRST

Teacher's Impulsive Reaction   Teacher punishes the whole class because one student forgot her homework.

Student's Impulsive Reaction   Student sulks and won't look at the teacher.

SECOND

Mediated Adjustment

Teacher's self-guiding speech used effectively to mediate emotional outbursts that are too strong:

I know better than this. It is demoralizing to punish everyone when only one person is at fault. This does not create a climate of healthy communication. I need to rethink this.

Figure 2–8 Examples of Classroom Situations.

LEARNING OUT LOUD 2–6

Document your own use of self-instructions to manage anger in your daily interactions following the steps outlined in Figure 2–9. After reviewing these steps and the reflective talk, discuss reader reactions. Ask questions such as, "How familiar does this sound? Can I relate to this? If so, how? If not, why not?" Make suggestions for adding other "Reflective Talk" statements and questions to thinking before, during, and after anger. Share these ideas in small groups. Each small group may want to choose the most authentic example and relate the situation that prompted anger and its accompanying reflection to the whole class.

Reversing Unhelpful Teacher and Student Self-Guiding Speech

Classroom life carries a price tag of some frustration, stress, and anger. Use of strategies that alter teacher and student reactions seems a logical way to dilute the power and "hold" that these have over our lives. Self-monitoring and adjustment strategies also provide teachers and students with lifelong coping, correcting, directing, and reinforcing skills. Becoming adept at monitoring and adjusting unhealthy self-guiding speech also is a major influence on the type of verbal environment created in individual teachers' classrooms.

Lynn Williams, a fifth-grade teacher, decided to implement some of the strategies learned in a graduate course that she took from both of us. She was interested in helping her fifth-grade students learn ways to use helpful self-guiding speech to control anger. Following is an example of one of her lesson plans about verbal mediation. Before she taught this particular lesson, she provided students a foundation of what self-talk is and ways to use helpful self-talk in daily interactions. She decided that the students were ready to move to discussions of anger control.

Before students could be taught to manage their own anger positively, they had to first be made aware of how they could recognize when they were angry. Lynn began with a basic introduction to prompt students to think about situations that provoke anger. She stressed three important aspects about their anger: (1) they create their own anger; (2) they can use their anger to hurt others or self or they can use it to help others or self; and (3) anger warns them that they have a problem to solve. She then posed the question: How do you know when you're angry? The fifth graders responded: teary eyes, red face, heavy breathing, flared nostrils, sweaty hands, see colors (like red and white), and your face tightens. Lynn then had her students work on the "Do I Get Mad?" activity (Figure 2–10) to help them think about constructive ways to use self-talk for anger control.

The second lesson consisted of students actually practicing using self-talk to handle conflict. Students individually recorded times that they were angry, how they responded to that anger, and how they could have responded in a more positive manner. Lynn modeled a few examples first. Then students had an opportunity to practice by discussing with a partner what they had written on their sheets. Lynn created a skit to illustrate one of the problems. The first skit dealt with the problem in a negative manner, one in which she did not use positive self-talk to calm herself, but addressed the problem through anger. In this first example, Lynn did not use verbal mediation, which involves words spoken to oneself to reconcile between stimulus and response (Manning, 1991). The second skit focused on the same problem, but used self-talk statements that calmed her before she actually addressed the problem. In this model, the students could see how verbal mediation helped calm the person down before responding to the stimulus. Then the class held a whole-group discussion on the differences between the two ways of handling the same problem. The students concluded

Complete the following sentences. After you are finished, discuss your responses with a partner.

1. It made me mad when

_____

_____

What I did:

_____

_____

What I could have said to myself to control my anger:

_____

_____

2. It made me mad when

_____

_____

What I did:

_____

_____

What I could have said to myself to control my anger:

_____

_____

3. It made me mad when

_____

_____

What I did:

_____

_____

What I could have said to myself to control my anger:

_____

_____

Figure 2–10   Do I Get Mad?

Source: Adapted from by L. Williams, C. Lowe, R. N. Stanulis, & B. H. Manning, 1999, "Cognitive Self-instruction: The Key to a More Positive Me." Unpublished manuscript.

that with the self-talk statements, the problem was solved with no hard feelings, while in the other skit, the problem never really got solved and everyone remained angry. Once Lynn was sure that students had gained an understanding of what their jobs were, she told them to get into small groups and come up with skits that demonstrate self-talk to solve problems.

Understanding Opportunity versus Obstacle Thinking

Manning recently worked with a group of teachers on a school improvement project. During a discussion, one teacher proudly announced that she was so much happier in her profession since she dropped out of the "Ain't It Awful, Ain't It Horrible Club." The other teachers laughed, and more explanation followed. The teacher confided that among some of her colleagues, the way to gain peer approval was to moan, groan, and complain about students, the principal, other teachers and staff, parents, and the school environment. This is a clear example of obstacle thinking (Manz, 1992). Teachers who engage in "yes, but" for almost all interactions and "focus on reasons to give up and retreat from problems" (p. 24) are engaging in *obstacle thinking.*

LEARNING OUT LOUD 2–7

Take a few moments to discuss classroom situations and/or individuals (no names, please) in your life who are negative, about many situations. Assess their personality and attitude. How much time do they waste? How productive and effective are these people? List five self-statements or questions to replace the negative self-talk you usually hear in these situations or from these people.

On the other hand, individuals who "focus on constructive ways of dealing with challenging situations" engage in *opportunity thinking* (Manz, 1992, p. 24). Research indicates that opportunity thinkers make a much greater effort (Nech & Manz, 1992; Seligman, 1991).

Nech and Barnard (1996) provide very helpful suggestions for becoming an opportunity thinker. We have addressed all three in this chapter—internal dialogue (self-talk), mental imagery (visualizations), and beliefs and assumptions—but we are reminded of their importance again.

The way you talk to yourselves impacts your attitude, health, self-esteem, interpersonal relations with others, and stress levels. Therefore, there are direct and indirect influences of teacher self-talk on the climate and learning in a classroom. For example, the teacher's interpersonal skills are manifested overtly to students. The verbal environment in the classroom is directly influenced by the constructive or destructive ways teachers talk to themselves throughout the day. On the average, teachers engage in approximately 55,000 self-talk utterances per day and, unfortunately, approximately 75% of these utterances are counterproductive to one's personal and interpersonal variables (Helmstetter, 1986). Obstacle self-talk can cause us to snap at a child, lose patience quickly, or rush ourselves and our students. Virtually everything we do and feel is regulated by our self-guiding speech, including the verbal environment we create, as teachers, in our classrooms on a daily basis.

Visualization of our goals aids the accomplishment of these goals (Maltz, 1960). Therefore, in addition to opportunity self-talk, teachers need many experiences that visualize a healthy, constructive classroom in which the verbal environment is warm, inviting, and engaging—a place where students are safe to learn, grow, make mistakes, and experience many successes.

Numerous researchers emphasize the importance of acknowledging, monitoring, and adjusting our beliefs and assumptions about classroom life (e.g., Burns, 1980; Ellis, 1977; Nech & Barnard, 1996). For example, if we believe that teachers are responsible for setting the positive tone in the classroom, we will assume active roles to ensure that the verbal environment is healthy. On the other hand, if we assume that students will always behave in loving ways, that it is exclusively their responsibility to set the positive tone in the classroom, we, as teachers, will not assume a major role in monitoring and insisting on a healthy verbal environment. Practice of helpful self-talk, clear, constructive images of a healthy verbal environment, and responsibility-oriented beliefs can have dramatic impact on changing negative school environments to positive places to learn.

Summary

There are many ways to develop a healthy, productive verbal and nonverbal classroom environment. This chapter addressed three main topics: (1) the verbal and nonverbal environment of the classroom; (2) teacher-student relationships; and (3) verbal mediation to promote healthy classroom interaction.

The influences on the verbal and nonverbal environment of the classroom include teacher talk, student talk, and teacher/student self-talk.

The all-important teacher-student relationship so critical to healthy classroom environments is illuminated by understanding the teacher's role in the tedious balance between supporting and challenging his or her students. A caring learning environment develops that includes the positive dispositions of teachers revealed through verbal and nonverbal expression.

The verbal mediation information and activities to promote healthy classroom interaction in this chapter facilitate productive steps for handling provocation in the classroom, managing classroom anger effectively, and reversing unhelpful teacher and student self-guiding speech. Integral to these steps is understanding opportunity versus obstacle thinking and incorporating such positive, helpful attitudes, emotions, and behaviors into classroom teaching and learning.

Chapter 3

Promoting Social Responsibility and Productive School Work Habits

Self-Questions

Knowledge: Identify the five considerations related to reconciling care and order in the classroom.

Comprehension: Differentiate prevention from intervention strategies.

Application: Provide two examples of logical consequences and two examples of natural consequences that a classroom teacher might use.

Analysis: Elaborate on the three components of transactional analysis and discuss the relationship between each component and classroom guidance.

Synthesis: Argue for and describe an approach that integrates responsibility components for each prevention model.

Evaluation: Critique Manning's cognitive self-instructional approach to foster student responsibility.

Introduction

Chapter 2 discussed ways to create a healthy and productive classroom environment for optimal learning. Building on this theme, chapter 3 provides classroom guidance prevention strategies that foster self-regulated, autonomous learners and aim to prevent problems from occurring. These methods will help you reconcile the need for both care and discipline in the classroom. Classroom discipline is a national challenge, requiring powerful intervention techniques and calm, dedicated teachers who are well-informed and well-prepared. This chapter provides classic and recent information, as well as classroom activities, that will prepare you for the awesome responsibility of guiding your own students. Intervention strategies that deal with existing classroom problems will be addressed in chapter 4.

Prevention Strategies for the Most Efficient Classroom Functioning

A teacher who carefully chooses prevention strategies is taking a proactive approach to maintain a healthy classroom where major management problems can be "prevented." Management techniques, such as carefully creating classrooms (including rules and procedures), are an important aspect of prevention strategies. Excellent interpersonal skills and pedagogical expertise are also important. The interaction among management, interpersonal skills, and pedagogy (Weinstein, 1998) is aimed at the goal of striving to promote responsible, self-regulated students. Teachers who promote self-regulated students must exercise self-regulation strategies themselves, such as self-questioning. For example, when teachers tell their students to be quiet, they should consider the following questions:

- Why am I requesting quiet?
    a. To address my needs as a teacher (e.g., I like to work in a quiet room)
    b. To address the needs of my students (e.g., the noise is making it difficult to concentrate)
    c. To address school policies (e.g., the administration values a very quiet school)
    d. Combination(s) of a, b, and c
    e. Other reasons

- Does this noise interfere with or promote learning?
- Is this noise likely to end soon or be inconsequential?

Without sufficient and appropriate teacher self-questioning, you may, as a beginning teacher, accept arbitrary school and/or traditional rules as "the law." Such unquestioned acceptance may not necessarily promote optimum learning—indeed, it may prevent learning. Always remember that a quiet classroom does not necessarily mean that your students are learning. You, as the teacher, will have responsibility for determining (a) how to foster, and (b) what constitutes an optimum learning environment. Keeping a balanced, inclusive, and varied approach to classroom guidance to foster optimum learning is the approach offered in this chapter.

Reconciling Care and Order in the Classroom to Optimize Learning

Caring teachers can and do have orderly classrooms where great learning occurs. However, many novices struggle to find the balance between care and order. For her article, "I Want to Be Nice, but I Have to Be Mean," Weinstein (1998) surveyed 141 teacher education students about their conceptions of caring and order. She found that many prospective teachers created a false dichotomy between caring and order, polarizing them as opposites that do not overlap or coexist. For example, one student teacher, Mollie, whom Weinstein supervised, clearly positioned care and order at opposite ends of a continuum. Mollie's students ignored her and walked out of the classroom at the rate of one student every 3 minutes under the pretense of going to the restroom. When Mollie and Weinstein conferred after the lesson, Mollie's response to the chaos was, "I want to show the children that I care about them." Similarly, in Stanulis (1995), a student teacher despaired as she moved from "being nice" to "being a witch on the broom." Teachers often think of caring in the classroom as exclusively showing affect (e.g., smiles, hugs, rapport, accessibility, words of encouragement) and conversely conceptualize classroom order as exclusively managing (e.g., establishing rules and procedures, dealing with discipline problems, time out). Teachers often polarize care and order and believe these two are not compatible.

We agree with Weinstein and others who argue that by teaching well, care *and* order can coexist. Caring teachers provide strong interpersonal skills important to developing a stable classroom community. Caring teachers provide a structure where children feel safe and secure and are ready to learn. This structure can be equated with order. Some rules, routines, and expectations for behavior are necessary for a safe environment to prosper. Drawing on Weinstein's (1998) study, Figure 3–1 offers a model for reconciling care and order in the classroom that includes the components of pedagogy, interpersonal skills, and management activities. Figure 3–2 provides five major considerations for promoting optimal learning in the classroom through reconciling care and order.

LEARNING OUT LOUD 3–1

Discuss what it means for teachers to care. Everyone in the group should read and take notes on the following Weinstein article and one of the four other readings. Divide into groups of four. Make sure each of the four members has read carefully one article from the list so that all four articles are represented in a group. Discuss each reading in light of reconciling care and order in the classroom. Develop a one-page summary of the connection(s) among caring, order, and learning in the classroom. What part does teaching responsibility play in these connections? Discuss your summaries with the whole class.

Outstanding Readings on Caring and Teaching/Learning

Cohn, M. M., & Kottkamp, R. B. (1993). *Teachers: The missing voice in education.* Albany, NY: State University of New York Press. (Read only sections related to care and order.)

(continued)

LEARNING OUT LOUD 3–1 (CONTINUED)

Hargreaves, A., & Tucker, E. (1991). Teaching and guilt: Exploring the feelings of teaching. *Teaching and Teacher Education, 7*(5/6), 491–505.

McCall, A. L. (1989). Care and nurturance in teaching: A case study. *Journal of Teacher Education, 40*(1), 39–44.

Rogers, D., & Webb, J. (1991). The ethic of caring in teacher education. *Journal of Teacher Education, 42*(3), 173–181.

Weinstein, C. S. (1998). I want to be nice, but I have to be mean: Exploring prospective teachers' conceptions of caring and order. *Teaching and Teacher Education, 14*(2), 153–163.

PEDAGOGY

Description: Emphasis is on students' academic/cognitive learning; preparing lessons; presenting material; encouraging participation; fostering creativity.

Examples: Presenting material in a creative way; making learning fun; encouraging active participation; maintaining pace so students won't get bored; showing relevance of material to real life.

INTERPERSONAL SKILLS

Description: Emphasis is on students' social/emotional/ affective development; establishing rapport with students; creating positive relationships; creating an atmosphere of trust, caring, affection, and respect; fostering self-esteem; enhancing feelings of affiliation; affection; and nurturance.

Examples: Establishing a good rapport; taking an interest in students' lives; making students aware I am there for them; showing students I care about them; showing understanding and empathy; treating students with respect; showing I'm a person; showing levity, humor; learning students' names.

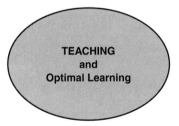

TEACHING
and
Optimal Learning

MANAGEMENT ACTIVITIES

Description: Emphasis is on creating order; establishing rules and routines; expectations for behavior, establishing authority as a teacher; creating an orderly; organized environment in which students can learn.

Examples: Setting rules down; being consistent; establishing rewards; establishing consequences; speaking in a loud, stern voice; having a time-out chair; rewarding good behavior.

Figure 3–1   Model for Reconciling Care and Order in the Classroom.
Source: Reprinted from Teaching and Teacher Education, 14*(2), C. S. Weinstein, "I Want to Be Nice but I Have to Be Mean," pp. 153–163, © 1998, with permission from Elsevier Science.*

CONSIDERATION 1:	Students may be at a learning disadvantage and can be physically unsafe in out-of-control classrooms, although nurturing care may be present.
CONSIDERATION 2:	An expansive, inclusive view of teaching more closely approximates the complex and interactive nature among pedagogy, interpersonal, and management activities.
CONSIDERATION 3:	Teacher candidates tend to polarize caring and order in the classroom and believe they are incompatible characteristics.
CONSIDERATION 4:	Some teacher candidates define caring and order in less disparate ways and believe they are not only compatible, but also are interdependent.
CONSIDERATION 5:	Students in classrooms often view caring teachers as those who help them learn and stay safe.

Figure 3–2 Five Major Considerations: Reconciling Care and Order to Promote Optimal Learning in the Classroom.

LEARNING OUT LOUD 3–2

Read two of the following articles to learn more about how scholars describe aspects of management in the classroom. Describe how the findings support active independent responsibility rather than only supporting students toward a goal of obedience.

Boostrom, R. (1991). The nature and functions of classroom rules. *Curriculum Inquiry, 21*(2), 193–213. (elementary and middle grades)

DeVries, R., & Zan, B. (1995). Creating a constructivist classroom atmosphere. *Young Children, 50*(3), 4–13. (early childhood and elementary)

Dinwiddie, S. A. (1994). The saga of Sally, Sammy, and the red pen: Facilitating children's social problem solving. *Young Children, 49*(5), 13–20. (early childhood and elementary)

Gareau, M., & Kennedy, C. (1991). Structure time and space to promote pursuit of learning in the primary grade. *Young Children, 46*(4), 46–51. (early childhood)

Grosser, S. (1992). Managing the early childhood classroom. *Young Children, 47*(2), 186–191. (early childhood)

Lasley, T. J. (1994). Teacher technicians: A new metaphor for new teachers. *Action in Teacher Education, 16*(1), 29–40. (elementary and middle grades)

Morine-Dershimer, G., & Reeve, P. T. (1994). Prospective teachers' images of management. *Action in Teacher Education, 16*(1), 29–40. (elementary and middle grades)

Ross, D. D., & Bondy, E. (1993). Classroom management for responsible citizenship: Practical strategies for teachers. *Social Education, 57*(6), 326–328. (early, elementary, and middle grades)

Short, R. J., & Short, P. M. (1989). Teacher beliefs, perceptions of behavior problems, and intervention preferences. *Journal of Social Studies Research, 13*(2), 28–31.

Solter, A. (1992). The disadvantages of time out. *Mothering*, 38–43. (early childhood)

Rules and Procedures in the Classroom: A Self-Regulated Teaching Approach

One of the earlier cautions prevalent in the literature (e.g., Brophy & Evertson, 1976; Cusick, Martin, & Palonsky, 1976) is to limit the number of rules in a classroom. Gaddy (1988) states that "many approaches to external order that consist of the heavy-handed application of rules and regulations may foster a superficial order that is detrimental to the ultimate aim of self-discipline" (p. 513). Many experts in teacher education believe that too many rules stifle students' initiative and responsibility for their own learning.

The Dichotomy of Teaching and Disciplining

Finkelstein's study (in Boostrom, 1991) of 19th-century teaching indicated another false dichotomy—the division of teaching practices into two categories: instructing and disciplining. Finkelstein wrote in *Governing the Young* (1960) that "Teacher behavior can be studied by focusing on the two important functions which the teacher performed: instructing and disciplining" (p. 37). However, just as many teachers today do not separate instruction from management or discipline strategies, many 19th-century teachers did not seem to view these two as disparate functions of teaching. Excellent teachers in the past, easily blurred the lines that artificially separate teaching from disciplining. Nevertheless, the predominant view of the relationships between teaching and disciplining was then, and is currently, dichotomous and even contradictory. For example, Metz (in Boostrom, 1991, p. 197) reflects this dichotomy, perhaps unknowingly, in the following way: "Public schools have a paradox at their very heart. They exist to educate children, but they must also keep order" (p. 243).

LEARNING OUT LOUD 3–3

Consider the following categories:

Class Rule   Learning   Order   Self-Regulated Learning

Determine a class rule that you believe is important to classroom learning, order, and self-regulation. Then describe a classroom scenario in which this rule has the potential to promote learning and order as opposed to chaos, and self-regulated learning as opposed to mere obedience. This activity can be done as a whole class, in small groups, or as an individual activity with the whole class sharing when the activity is finished.

The goal of education in a democracy has been defined as the shaping of "self-disciplined, responsible persons who never blindly comply with the demands of an authority figure" (Render, Padilla, & Krank, 1989, p. 627).

LEARNING OUT LOUD 3–4

Read the definition of the goal of education in a democracy out loud several times. Do you agree? Why or why not?

Defining the Nature and Function of Classroom Rules

Boostrom (1991) claims that classroom rules "embody a way of life and also give structure to the intellectual life." He steps away from the common view that classroom rules simply create order in a classroom (e.g., Ross & Bondy, 1993). Instead, Boostrom believes that class rules direct the understanding of classroom life:

> This broader vision of rules brings together the means and ends of classroom life, making it possible for teachers to reflect on what they are about. Rather than ignoring the significance of much of what they do, they can attend to it. The problems of regimentation and mechanical practices lie not in the acts of obedience, but in what the students are obedient to (p. 214).

The separation of classroom management from teaching and learning is an artificial and, perhaps, detrimental practice. Some educational researchers (e.g., Martin, 1997; Weinstein, 1998; Weinstein, Woolfolk, Dittmeier, & Shanker, 1994) have emphasized the importance of the integration of classroom management with learning and the interpersonal characteristics of the teacher. It is possible to have order, learning, and lots of caring simultaneously. These classroom components need not be discrete entities; in fact, they should not be. Students have a much greater chance of becoming self-regulated, lifelong learners in a classroom environment in which discipline is not dominated by teachers' doling out rewards and consequences.

LEARNING OUT LOUD 3–5

Consider the following words of Darlene (from Richardson & Fallona, 2001) and discuss your agreement or disagreement with her positions on (1) responsibility for self and (2) responsibility for everyone's learning in the classroom

Responsibility for Self: Third Grade

In today's math lesson I said, "Today, I'm not looking at anything you do. You have total responsibility. You can decide you're not going to learn at all and I can't guarantee we'll get another opportunity to learn this. Or, if you want to learn it, here are some steps you could follow. This is the goal and here are some steps you could follow to learn it today." They're just real responsible, but that's what I think this whole process is about: having to take responsibility for their own learning. The reason I do it is because I didn't have a clue until about 7th grade.

Responsibility for Others: Third Grade

The other thing I like to do is to make sure that every child in the room feels responsible for the learning of everybody else. Not that they have to teach them, but that they have to set up an environment and be a part of a community that allows children to be comfortable in making the mistakes that you have to make when you take the risks you have to take. So, those are the two magical musts (responsibility for your own and for others' learning) in the classroom as far as I'm concerned. And so, consequently, already in every classroom I've ever been in you will hear kids saying, "Nice try, though!" or "It's okay, we'll help you" or "Shh! He needs awake time." Those kinds of comments where they're helping each other.

Source: From "Classroom Management as Method and Manner," by Richardson, V., & Fallona, C. A., 2001. Journal of Curriculum Studies, 33(6), 705–728. Reprinted with permission of author.

First Proposition:	Rules are instrumental. Their importance lies in how they enable a teacher to manage a classroom and to maintain discipline.
Second Proposition:	The relationship of rules to instruction and learning depends entirely on the contribution of rules to orderliness in the classroom.
Third Proposition:	Too much attention to rules undermines the instructional aims of schooling by inhibiting the development of self-discipline.

Figure 3–3   Three Propositions Related to Rules.
Source: From "The Nature and Functions of Classroom Rules," by R. Boostrom, Curriculum Inquiry, 21*(2), p. 196. Reprinted with permission of John Wiley and Sons.*

Viewing teaching as a two-phase process (i.e., first order, and then learning) has motivated educational writers to focus on classroom rules as a characteristic of the first phase—"a feature of a teacher's management technique, as part of the program for discipline and deportment, as an instrumental mechanism" (Boostrom, 1991, p. 196). Such a view places rules in classrooms as "incidental and their influence on learning indirect" (p. 196). The rules appear arbitrary. Further, Boostrom (1991) provides three propositions about rules that may be helpful to you as a teacher (Figure 3–3). These propositions should be considered carefully to break down the assumption that classroom order is an end, rather than an important means to the development of rich opportunities for optimal learning within a community of learners. These propositions build on one another and highlight the dichotomous view of teaching and disciplining. In the reality of the classroom, students learn to be quiet when their peers are talking so that they (1) treat their peers with respect and kindness (social responsibility) and (2) heighten the likelihood that they may learn something of value from their peers (academic advancement). In this reality, the rule of quietness is not separate or contradictory from the goals of social responsibility or academic advancement. The dichotomy between classroom order and classroom learning does not and should not exist. And, in fact, in many classrooms of outstanding teachers across the nation, order promotes learning and learning promotes order.

As you develop as a classroom teacher, you will become more and more proficient at managing your classroom, using rules to foster and structure the meaning that you and your students construct in your classroom environment. Management and learning will become one, like a beautiful marriage.

Three Examples of Management Skills

Lasley (1994) proposes three skills needed by beginning teachers to build in-depth understanding of and proficiency with a small number of management skills. These skills are matched to the developmental level of beginning teachers. Lasley's premise is that these foundational skills are "necessary preconditions for successful beginning classroom practice" (p. 13). Exemplary classroom management to foster optimal learning is acquired later through on-the-job staff development and graduate education. Lasley's examples will introduce you to three important areas of classroom management. These sample skills are based on an extensive body of classroom-based literature (e.g., Brophy & McCaslin, 1992; Everston, Emmer, Clements, & Worsham, 1994).

Figure 3–4 explains the three technical skills offered by Lasley as appropriate for beginning teachers. You need opportunities during your field experiences to implement these practices and to receive supportive feedback from more experienced teachers and teacher education faculty about your performance, related to an in-depth understanding of and high-level proficiency in the execution of such strategies. Only Lasley's first technical skill

---

Technical Skill 1   An ability to develop and implement specific classroom rules.

Differentiate specific, workable rules such as "Raise my hand to contribute ideas during large group instruction," from abstract, unworkable rules, such as "Be polite." Know the difference and use the specific, workable rules in your classroom.

Teach the rules using the process of explanation, rehearsal, and feedback. Be sure to emphasize the connection among rules, order, and optimal learning.

Technical Skill 2   An understanding of when and how to use both low- and high-profile desists in dealing with student misbehavior.

Low-profile desists are less intrusive to classroom functioning than high-profile desists. Low-profile desists include proximity, eye contact, and subtle gestures that are intended to redirect or stop student misbehavior without calling class attention to the misbehaving student or his/her misbehavior. Conversely, high-profile desists are teacher reactions intended to stop misbehavior that bring class attention to the misbehaving students' antics. In so doing, learning is disrupted.

Balance low- and high-profile desists, keeping in mind that a disproportionate, larger number of high-profile desists will create too much teacher policing, less time on task, and a climate of negativity. In addition, high-profile teacher attention can inadvertently reinforce undesirable classroom behaviors, increasing their frequency.

Realize that there is a time and a place for the use of both low- and high-profile desists. Try to aim for more low-profile, but know that if these correction/redirection strategies are not working, a high-level desist may be more appropriate, depending on the classroom situation.

Technical Skill 3   An ability to use parents as a resource in dealing with chronic, severe misbehavior.

Many authorities in the area of classroom management believe parents are the most underused, but most effective and appropriate resources to redirect disruptive, misbehaving students in the classroom (e.g., Georgiady, Sinclair, & Sinclair, 1991; Lasley, 1994).

Be very specific when talking to parents about their child's misbehavior in the classroom. Document dates, times, and places of misconduct before calling the parent, and describe the misbehavior using objective language (e.g., Sally talked out loud to her friend Angela 12 times during mathematics class yesterday even though I asked her not to do so) instead of subjective language (e.g., Sally is rude to me in mathematics class.) See parents as partners, a positive option, instead of a last resort.

Figure 3–4   Lasley's Three Technical Skills.
Source: From "Teacher Technicians: A New Metaphor for New Teachers," by T. J. Lasley, Action in Teacher Education, 16(1), 14–17. Copyright 1994 by Thomas J. Lasley. Reprinted with permission of the author.

addresses a prevention strategy (i.e., an ability to develop and implement specific classroom rules). The last two skills (i.e., using low- and high-profile desists in dealing with student misbehavior and using parents as a resource in dealing with chronic, severe misbehavior) are intervention strategies that will be revisited in chapter 4 when we discuss intervention/discipline strategies. Following are a few other important points to consider.

Developing and Teaching Rules and Procedures

1. Write rules in first person, present tense.
2. Use only a small number of rules, especially for younger students. A general guideline is two or three rules for grades K–1; three to five rules for grades 2–4; five to six rules for grades 5–6; and six to eight rules for grades 7–8.
3. Write rules in positive, active voice rather than negative, passive voice. Tell what should happen (e.g., "Raise my hand to contribute during large group discussion") rather than what should not happen (e.g., "Do not speak out").

Carefully planned rules and procedures are a "must" in every well-organized classroom. Developing such rules and procedures prevents misbehavior. Evertson, Emmer, and Worsham (2000) differentiate rules and procedures: Rules "identify general expectations or standards for behavior" while procedures "are usually applied in a specific activity, directed at accomplishing something rather than prohibiting some behavior or defining a general standard" (pp. 19–20). Example rules developed in first person, present tense, include the following:

Rules

I work quietly.

I keep my hands, feet, and objects to myself.

I listen carefully.

I raise my hand and get a signal to speak.

I walk quietly and calmly in the halls.

I use good manners at all times.

Example procedures include tasks that become a part of the routine, including collecting student work, turn taking, using the restroom, and so forth (Evertson et al., 2000). Evertson and her colleagues (2000) have a checklist for teachers to consider when planning their procedures. These procedures provide excellent stimuli for your mental deliberations. In addition to thinking about and writing your procedures for (1) classroom use, (2) individual work and teacher-led instruction, (3) transitions into and out of the room, (4) small-group instruction, and (5) general procedures (e.g., distributing materials), it is very helpful to write examples of self-questions and self-statements or both as a metacognitive checklist for yourself. In this way, you are learning to be proactive, rather than simply being reactive. Figure 3–5 provides some examples.

You will need to go beyond merely thinking about the various aspects of classroom procedures and establishing a set of rules. In most cases, you will need to model the rule/procedure so that your students will understand more clearly. After sufficient teacher and peer modeling, the next step is to have your students practice the procedures or rules, if appropriate. This practice can be accomplished via planned role-play (e.g., a skit on respect for property) or simply executing the procedure on-the-spot. Another part of practicing is to monitor how many students are actually following the rule or procedure. If many students are not following the rule or procedure, you will need to reteach with additional modeling, practicing, and cueing (Manning, 1991). The final aspect of teaching rules and procedures is to cue the students with age-appropriate reminders. For example, you can prompt your students to raise their hands during class discussions, to listen attentively to you and to their peers, to wait turns, and to stay seated when appropriate.

I. Transitions
  A. Beginning the school day
    1. What do I want students to do when they arrive at school and enter our classroom?
    2. I want them to become engaged, but not overwhelmed with busy work.
    3. What activities will I be responsible for and what activities will the students do (e.g., taking attendance)?

II. Procedures during Group Activities
  A. Expected behavior in the group
    1. How will I know they are on task in each small group?
    2. Having a product from their work together will hold them accountable.
    3. Will I need a leader and scribe in each small group?

Figure 3–5   Sample Self-Talk Statements/Questions.

Preventing Discipline Problems With Cognitive/Metacognitive Strategies

Research with elementary students (Manning, 1988, 1990, 1991; Manning, Glasner, & Smith, 1996, Manning & Payne, 1996a; Manning, White, & Daugherty, 1994) in K–8 classroom settings indicates that students assume more responsibility for their learning and behavior if they are taught cognitive/metacognitive strategies. One approach that has proven beneficial is cognitive self-instruction (CSI). Manning applied CSI to help students with mild conduct problems regulate their own classroom behavior. Manning's CSI uses the three learning processes of modeling, practicing, and cueing.

Cognitive Self-Instruction*

Cognitive self-instruction (CSI) is defined as instructing yourself using your own cognition. The cognition is usually in the form of audible and/or inaudible self-talk. Talking to yourself in order to question, guide, cope, correct, and reinforce your own learning and behavior is a set of subskills that comprises cognitive self-instruction. Students are likely to have a head start on the educational process if they have had significant adults in their lives who modeled, explicitly taught, and/or demonstrated such skills. They will be more knowledgeable about how, when, where, and why to facilitate their own learning. However, even these students can profit from instruction aimed at improving and increasing the use of their self-instructional skills or both. In addition, your classrooms will be filled with students who have experienced impoverished social/linguistic environments, where models of cognitive and metacognitive self-instruction are wholly lacking. Such students will be more likely to lack knowledge of when, how, what, where, and why to use self-instructional language and strategies.

Manning's cognitive self-instruction is used to optimize students' school work habits and social responsibility and, thus, prevent misbehavior in the classroom (Figure 3–6) This approach has ample evidence to trust its use with K–8 students, gifted students, and reluctant learners. Manning's CSI can be used to prevent classroom disorder that interferes with learning. CSI can also be used with students as intervention strategies to improve school work habits such as problems concentrating, focusing attention, following through with assigned tasks, and finishing schoolwork accurately and promptly. (See chapter 7 for examples.)

Modeling.   Modeling of CSI is essential because of the abstractness of thought processes. It is much easier to teach overt behaviors than to teach metacognitive thinking strategies to regulate overt behaviors. Students need to hear first-hand how teachers and productive peers guide themselves verbally to regulate behavior. Do not assume that all students understand and can spontaneously use CSI—it appears to occur very naturally and easily for some individuals and not for others.

CSI modeling can be presented spontaneously by adult or peer models, or presented as audiotaped or videotaped modeling. Students should hear CSI models during school work habits (e.g., concentrating, staying on task) and during social responsibility (e.g., waiting turns, sharing materials). The CSI self-talk categories that need to be modeled explicitly for students are problem defining, attention focusing, self-guiding, self-coping, and self-reinforcing. (Refer to Figure 3–6 for the modeling component.)

---

*Pages 65–80 of this text were first published in Manning, 1991 and were later reprinted in Manning & Payne, 1996a, pp. 115–132. Reprinted with permission of Allyn & Bacon.

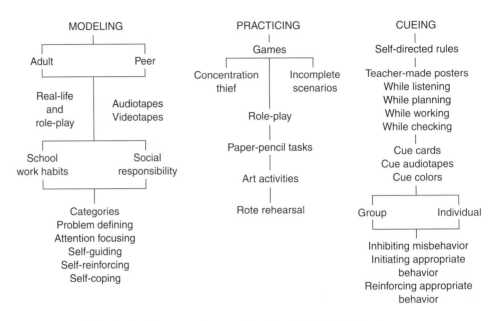

Figure 3–6   Manning's Classroom Approach to Cognitive Self-Instruction.
Source: From "Application of Cognitive Behavior Modification: First and Third Graders Self-management of Classroom Behaviors," by B. Manning, 1988, American Educational Research Journal, 25*(2), pp. 193–212. Copyright 1988 by the American Educational Research Association. Reprinted by permission of publisher.*

Teacher modeling is a viable way for students to learn. Optimally, teacher modeling needs to occur on four levels: (1) spontaneous teacher use of CSI for teacher need (e.g., self-guiding speech to correct the situation when the overhead projector will not work); (2) role-play CSI for teacher need (e.g., staying calm while being observed by the principal); (3) spontaneous teacher use of CSI for student need (e.g., teacher sees some students looking on other students' tests and he models on-the-spot the choice between cheating and not cheating), and (4) role-play CSI for student need (e.g., after several days of students pushing in the line for water, the teacher subsequently sets up a role-playing situation in which she models self-talk for waiting in line for water even when students' thirst is great). Figure 3–7 provides examples of each level.

After spontaneous teacher or other adult modeling, review with the students "what," "why," "how," and "when" CSI needs to be employed. Ask students questions such as, "Did anyone notice what I was doing when the overhead would not work? Why was I talking to myself? Sometimes I do this aloud and sometimes I do it inside my head. Either way, it helps me to plan what I need to do." Ask students if they ever talk to themselves. "When? What kinds of things do you say to yourself?" List their responses on the board or a poster. "Why do you use this self-talk? When I was talking to myself about cheating, what did I say to myself? Who remembers something I said?" Continue and prompt if necessary until students have named most or all of your self-talk and have discussed the benefits of guiding themselves verbally. Because the self-talk occurs spontaneously and is used as a teaching tool after the fact, this modeling will most likely not be available on tape.

Role-playing sessions of CSI can be used for instruction just as any role-play situation can. Prepare the students. Describe the scenario and the self-talk script they will hear. Tape the session. Show the self-talk sessions and teach directly the CSI categories of problem defining, attention focusing, self-guiding, self-coping, and self-reinforcing if you deem that

Level 1—Spontaneous Teacher Use of CSI for Teacher Need

Categories	*CSI*
Problem defining	Why won't this overhead turn on?
Attention focusing	Let me see. I'll try all the switches again.
Self-guiding	This arrow points to the right. Did I turn left or right? Try again.
Self-coping	It is easy to get frustrated. Take a deep breath and relax. There must be a solution.
Self-reinforcing	Success: Hey! I stuck with it and found the outlet is faulty. I'll try this other outlet. It works!
	No success: I've tried all I know. I'll either show you this information by putting it on the board or call the media specialist to help fix the machine. Which would be the fastest?

Level 2—Role-Play CSI for Teacher Need

Categories	*CSI*
Problem defining	Why am I getting so uptight about being observed?
Attention focusing	Now put a lid on this. Stop panicking myself. Calm down.
Self-guiding	Count slowly. Concentrate on the students. Forget the principal is here.
Self-coping	I may make a few mistakes. It won't be the end of the world even if I do! Things will be fine.
Self-reinforcing	Success: I knew I could get through this observation calmly.
	No success: My heart never stopped pounding and I didn't teach my very best. Next time I'll be better prepared so I can stay calmer. Learn something from this.

Level 3—Spontaneous Teacher Use of CSI for Student Need

Categories	*CSI*
Problem defining	I forgot to study for my test. Should I look at my friend's test?
Attention focusing	I can see her paper easily. But is that right?
Self-guiding	Just do my best. I'll feel better about myself if I don't look.
Self-coping	This is hard. I know some of my answers are wrong. That's okay. I've done the best I can. Next time I won't leave my book at school.
Self-reinforcing	Success: I'm glad I didn't take answers that didn't belong to me. I feel good about that!
	No success: I looked at someone else's answer. I feel terrible. I'll just turn in my paper and tell the teacher. I hate this feeling. I'm too important to treat myself this way. Make better choices next time.

Level 4—Role-Play CSI for Student Need

Categories	*CSI*
Problem defining	What if I push in line or jump in front of someone? How can I follow the rule to wait my turn when I'm so thirsty?
Attention focusing	Look, everyone else is thirsty, too. They don't want to wait either.
Self-guiding	Just think about something else. There are just three more people and Mrs. Dollard is moving people along quickly.
Self-coping	I don't like to wait. But who does? I can do it.
Self-reinforcing	I'm proud of myself. I didn't push and I didn't jump in line. I can wait my turn. I like that about me.

Figure 3–7   Teacher Modeling Levels.

this type of direct instruction is appropriate for your group of learners. We do not recommend teaching the categories to most kindergarten groups.

Peer modeling of CSI logically follows teacher modeling. It is important for students to experience how their productive classmates guide themselves verbally at school. There are numerous ways that teachers can use peer models of CSI.

In our previous research, we have been impressed with students' positive reaction to videotapes of elementary school children their age or older using self-instruction to guide on-task classroom behaviors during seatwork. The students participating in our research studies internalized and used similar CSI after viewing and discussing the tapes for only 2 weeks, twice per week for 50 minutes. Teachers can easily make their own videotapes. First, film your class during independent seatwork time or, for older children, during study sessions. Write a script of self-talk (after interviewing students about what they were saying to themselves) and audiotape the self-talk script using male and female readers to coincide with male and female students on the screen. Dub the self-talk over the original audio soundtrack. Following are some examples of self-talk from a videotape we have used:

Problem-defining CSI

What am I supposed to be doing?
Was I supposed to be sitting in my seat paying attention?
Let's see, what was I going to put there?

Attention-focusing CSI

Mrs. Bowersett is telling me what to do. I need to listen carefully.
I better get back to this writing if I want to finish.

Self-guiding CSI

Let's turn back and see if I can get some help from the directions.
I need to be careful while cutting this.

Self-coping CSI

This is a lot of work today, but I'm going to go slowly.
Oops, I made a mistake, but that's okay. I need to slow down.

Self-reinforcing CSI

Yeah! I think I'm getting it.
I did that problem well. No one had to help me.

As students become proficient at identifying categories of self-guiding speech, they are able to supply their own self-talk needs in each of the categories (e.g., student identifies frustration over a task and then identifies the need to use self-coping statements: "I'm having trouble here, but I can figure this out if I take my time").

LEARNING OUT LOUD 3–6

Students' Categories of Cognitive Self-Instruction
Directions: Listen to one student talk to himself or herself during independent school-work. Younger children (ages 4–7) may talk to themselves aloud spontaneously while working on an assigned task or at home while playing alongside a peer. With children older than 7, you may have to request that they think aloud as they work or play. In either instance, record and/or write at least 20 self-talk utterances (a word, phrase, or sentence spoken aloud to self, separated by a 3- or 4-second pause). Then classify each of the 20 utterances into one of the following categories. After you collect the data, share your

results in groups of three or four. In this way, if you have a category with no representative utterances someone else may have an example in that category. As a class, make a graph of how many utterances were recorded for each of the five categories.

1. Problem definition (e.g., What did the teacher say to do next?)

   _____

   _____

2. Focusing attention (e.g., Now get back to work on this math.)

   _____

   _____

3. Self-guiding (e.g., Watch carefully here.)

   _____

   _____

4. Self-coping (e.g., Even if I do not get all the answers correct, I will do my best.)

   _____

   _____

5. Self-reinforcing (e.g., Good, I remembered to wait my turn.)

   _____

   _____

Practicing.   It is not enough to just model CSI for students, even if a large amount of modeling occurs and creative development of modeling episodes are used in the classroom. Students need to practice CSI themselves to internalize the processes. Practice is crucial for transfer and maintenance of such strategies. Students must create their own metacognitive reality—they need to experience CSI for themselves. Students must be directly involved in practicing and must experience enough repetition to incorporate self-guidance into their present way of thinking about school behavior.

The following sections present practice examples for students that were provided by individual teachers. Practice strategies include games, role-play, paper-pencil tasks, art activities, and rote rehearsal (refer to Figure 3–6). These examples have worked well for the teachers who developed them, but may require modification in your classroom. We hope that these "starter suggestions" will spark teacher creativity and motivation.

Games.   Three games have been tried and endorsed by teachers: Concentration Zapper, Incomplete Scenarios, and Can We Play? In Concentration Zapper, the teacher initially (and later, a student) goes around the room attempting to break students' concentration on an academic task. Students often do not understand what it means when the teacher says, "Concentrate on your work." After students are given a certain school assignment to complete, they are told to concentrate on the assignment, which means, "Keep my mind on my work." As the students repeat aloud with or echo after the teacher, "Keep my mind," they point with their fingers to either side of their head; "on my work," they point down to their papers. The kinesthetic, tactual experience of moving hands from the head to the work seems important in helping young students understand the concept of "concentration." Students are directed to say to themselves in a whisper or silently, "Concentrate on my work." The game itself helps them to understand the role they must assume to ensure the quality of their own concentration. The Concentration Zapper carries a pretend container, a "concentration bucket," and tries to take away (zap) somebody's concentration. The teacher (zapper) walks among the students making noise, rattling papers, tapping students on shoulders, whistling, laughing, dropping books—trying in any acceptable manner to cause a distraction. If a student looks toward the zapper or away from his work, or laughs, that student has just lost his concentration to the zapper. The zapper says, "I just zapped your concentration; you'll have to ignore me next time, which means don't look at me, think about your work." Students still remaining when time is up (time set by teacher) are designated "Great Concentrators" and a new zapper is chosen from among them. In the busy classrooms of today, filled with many interruptions, children have to be able to help themselves concentrate on the task at hand and selectively ignore distractions. A game such as Concentration Zapper teaches them to do this.

In addition to the game, some teachers use cue cards (explained in detail later in this chapter) during Concentration Zapper. Teachers give each student a laminated index card that says, "Concentrate on my work." Students are instructed to read the cue card to themselves when the Concentration Zapper is trying to distract them. In this way, students remind themselves to concentrate even during distractions. One teacher, Susan Jones, developed a catchy slogan that she uses as a visual reminder to children to concentrate: "I am as busy as a bee, the concentration zapper won't get me!!!" The last time we were in Susan's classroom, this slogan was displayed prominently. Mrs. Jones's young students know how to concentrate.

The second game, Incomplete Scenarios, is geared more toward school/social responsibility. The teacher describes a situation such as, "Your class has just come in from recess. It is a very hot day and the line for water is long. The teacher has talked to you about waiting your turn, but she is nowhere in sight. Your best friend is next to get water and she offers to put you up in line. What will you say to yourself?" After children respond to the incomplete scenarios, role-play can be used with an emphasis on the five categories (e.g., self-coping) of self-talk. The focus is on self-guidance of appropriate choices. The following self-talk utterances were developed for this scenario by Dagley (1988, p. 163). They are written in large letters on a comic-strip bubble, accompanied by the students' favorite fictitious character, looking as if the character is saying these self-talk statements. This display appears in the hall over the water fountain and serves to remind students to verbally guide themselves in an appropriate manner. Teachers say this display has really helped to decrease pushing in line and other inappropriate behaviors at the water fountain.

"I wait patiently in line for my turn at the water fountain."

"I stand quietly at the water fountain."

"I do not push and shove while waiting my turn at the water fountain."

"It's hard when I am so thirsty to wait patiently. But I can do it."

"I am happy with myself when I wait my turn."

"My teacher is proud of me when I stand quietly and wait patiently at the water fountain. Good for me!"

Another example of an incomplete scenario (Dagley, 1988) is focused on lunchroom behavior. Billy wants to get Tim's attention. Tim is sitting several spaces down from Billy. Billy says to himself, "I think I'll yell at Tim, or even better, I'll throw my roll at him to get his attention." What can Billy say to himself to help in this situation?

"I need to eat my food while in the lunchroom."

"After I eat my lunch, I talk quietly to those people sitting beside me."

"I eat my food quietly in the lunchroom."

"I do not play with my food."

"When I want to talk, I talk quietly to my neighbors."

"The lunchroom is a nicer place to come to when I eat my food and talk quietly."

"I feel better when I eat my food slowly and don't rush through my lunch."

"I am proud of myself when I eat my lunch quietly."

A third game is called Can We Play? This game was adapted from Markman (1977, 1979). The teacher instructs the students to ask themselves (self-questioning) three questions: "Does this make sense to me?" "Is there any thing missing?" "What else do I need to know?" The teacher writes these questions on the board or poster and displays them as a stimulus/reminder. Students are given sets of complete and incomplete directions for games and activities. They play the game (with incomplete directions) when they can supply the missing instructions. Any usual classroom games (e.g., Dog and the Bone, Five Up) can be used by simply omitting essential parts of the directions and then asking the students, "Can we play?" "Why or why not?" Remind students to ask themselves the three questions on the board.

Role-Play.   The focus here has changed from modeling in a role-play situation to practicing CSI in a role-play situation. Any of the incomplete scenarios might be used as a stimulus to practice the use of CSI through role-play. For example, students can role-play walking to the lunchroom appropriately using a silent self-talk statement (e.g., "As I go to lunch, I won't disturb others") before they actually go to lunch for the first time in a given school year. Any school procedure (e.g., fire drill) needs practice, with *accompanying CSI*, to facilitate cooperativeness and a healthy school climate.

A form of role-play that is more appropriate for older students is called Soliloquy, a sociodrama technique (Torrance & Myers, 1970). A volunteer subject is asked to speak aloud her thoughts about a school-related problem to aid problem resolution via CSI. The setting for this particular soliloquy is as follows: "You have a test in social studies tomorrow. You are really uptight about the test. You know when you get like this you don't make very good grades. Talk to us about what you are saying to yourself about this problem." Other students listen for self-talk categories (e.g., self-reinforcing).

Student's Soliloquy

"Well, I've been really paying attention in social studies, but did I go over my questions every day? Sometimes I don't ask the teacher questions about the things I don't understand. Why do I do that? I need to ask right then, but the others would think I was a dummy. Well, I better start studying. But I don't know where to start. Do I have in mind what to study? Guess I better call Samantha; she always makes high marks. Maybe she'll tell me what to study. Why do we have stupid old tests anyway? They make my stomach hurt. My mother thinks I'm lazy. I am not very smart in social studies. Did I bring my book home? What if I make a zero and everybody finds out? I'm really going to have to think hard tomorrow. I wish my teacher wouldn't call out everybody's grade. Don't worry so much. I can't study if I worry, and I'll make a zero if I don't study. I better call Samantha. I can do this if I will first calm down, stop saying horrible things to myself, get organized and *study*. I'm just wasting my time. Get with it. Do the best I can—that's all anyone can ask for or do! I feel better. I can do this. I trust myself."

Paper-Pencil Tasks.   These tasks include such things as self-talk journals, CSI booklets, cartoon characters, and handwriting.

Assignments that require students to keep *self-talk logs* or journals can be varied to fit age level and specific student needs. Students have a tendency to describe external events instead of describing their internal talk, unless the teacher spends quality time preparing them. In classrooms where teachers have been using many CSI strategies, promoting metacognitive skills as vital to learning, students are more apt to find self-talk journals a natural, creative outlet. Students write in first person what they have been saying to themselves during math class, recess, or during morning work, or any time agreed upon by students and/or teachers. During or after these classes once every day, or at least once per week, students write down their self-talk. Many follow-up activities can occur at the discretion of the teacher based on "knowing the students." For example, students can classify their self-talk entries for their math lessons after 1 month in one or more of the following ways:

1. Positive-neutral-negative
2. Helpful-unhelpful
3. Adult-parent-child
4. Problem defining, attention focusing, self-guiding, self-coping, self-reinforcing
5. Task relevant-task irrelevant
6. On task-off task

As a result, students and teachers gain insight into student frustration, apathy, motivation, and boredom. Teachers can learn a great deal about students through self-talk logs that they may not discover in any other way. Also, students may convert some of their negative self-talk into neutral, positive, task-relevant self-talk. In essence, they learn new, more helpful ways to guide their own learning. The greatest challenge to the teacher will be to get the students to externalize internal thoughts into written journal entries. It can be done with persistence and a creative teacher's touch. We know a wonderful kindergarten teacher who has her students (in the last half of the year) use their invented spellings and drawings to convey their inner thoughts about various assignments. Readers would be impressed with what these young children have learned about verbal expression of their own thought.

The next paper-pencil example is to have students make a *CSI booklet*. One teacher asked students to make CSI booklets to emphasize when to use CSI across the school curriculum. Manning (1984a, 1984b) designated four school uses of CSI. Teachers spend the majority of each day engaging students in academic work. To increase their achievement in academics, students of all ages must *listen* well, *plan* effectively, *work* efficiently, and *check* their work accurately. These four school uses of CSI—listening, planning, working, and checking—are identified and discussed in Manning 1984a and 1984b. The booklet is centered around students learning, reinforcing, and extending these four uses of CSI. On the cover of the booklet, the students write *WHEN TO USE CSI* and draw themselves with a balloon caption (comic bubble) over their heads saying something helpful to themselves at school (e.g., "Do I have all my materials together to start my assignment—a sharpened pencil and paper?"). Each of the next four pages of the booklet is devoted to listening, planning, working, and checking. Each page is labeled with a word, (e.g., *LISTENING*) to aid students' association with the corresponding self-talk for listening times at school. Depending on students' ages, they draw or cut out pictures of people or they write examples of self-talk for each "time to use CSI." Over each person's head they draw a bubble and write a task-relevant, helpful, self-talk message. Some teachers have modified this activity by using familiar cartoon characters first, then magazine cut-out people, then self-portraits or their own school pictures (movement from an external to an internal focus). The booklet familiarizes students with appropriate school times to remember to use CSI. Following are some examples from a second-grade class:

Listening

What is she saying?
Do I understand?
Does this make sense?
I need to listen carefully.

Planning

Do I know what to do?
What should I do first?
I'll do my best on this.
Let's get going.

Working

I need to slow down.
This looks sloppy. I can do better.
I need to quit staring out the
    window and get back to
    this work.
Looking better.

Checking

Does this look good to me?
Did I skip anything?
Can I do it a better way?
I have all the sentences.
I'm proud of this work.

Another paper-pencil task is to use commercial comics and ask children to rewrite them, based on what the characters are saying to themselves rather than to each other. This requires monitoring by the teacher and students to make sure they are using private speech and not social speech. This is not an appropriate written activity for K–1 students—this activity can be modeled for them as a discussion of the cartoon characters' self-talk, with a follow-up language experience story using self-talk as the focus. In addition, even second- to fourth-grade teachers have reported that their students respond best to this activity when they begin with a comic strip that has only one character per frame—it makes more sense that the character is talking to self, rather than to someone else. However, it is a fun activity for students to write in self-talk when there are two or more characters per frame—it is a challenging and usually humorous activity. Students enjoy sharing their creations. Begin by cutting out comic strips that appeal to you. Cut out white paper bubbles to glue over the original captions or "white out" the original words and photocopy the cartoon for students. Laminate about 40 of these for a classroom set. Try to select cartoons with one character per frame to use at first and then progress accordingly. Each student receives a strip on which to write the character's self-talk. This activity can be completed in dyads or small groups. One teacher uses an opaque projector for follow up discussions of each self-talk cartoon.

Another activity is provided by a first grade teacher who places a set of questions (Figure 3–8, Example 1) at each work station in her classroom. The teacher reports that these questions cause students to reflect on their own school tasks as they practice metacognitive thinking.

Another paper-pencil task that reinforces CSI is to ask students to make written posters for the class. These posters can include anything related to CSI that the teacher and students want to display in the room. One example is to have four groups of students make a helpful poster for each of the four school uses of CSI. Each group is assigned one of the times to use CSI (i.e., listening, planning, working, and checking). They write a draft list of task-relevant, helpful questions and statements-to-self for each of the four areas and propose this list for acceptance. The drafts are evaluated by members of the other three remaining groups to validate the helpfulness of each self-talk entry. If an entry is considered unhelpful or task irrelevant by a majority of students, that entry is deleted. The remaining self-talk entries are written neatly on a poster and displayed as a CSI bulletin board. The next page shows four posters developed by a fifth-grade class.

In a final example, the teacher writes a language experience story (to be used later as a handwriting lesson) illustrating how students are successfully using CSI. The story, using the students' names for characters, illustrates examples of how the students were able to maintain concentration on their school assignments even in the midst of classroom

Example 1

Taking Care of My Business

Name _____   Date _____   Work Station _____

Listening   Yes or No
  _____ Does this make sense to me?
  _____ Is there anything missing?

Planning and Working   Yes or No
  _____ Am I ready to begin?
  _____ Do I have all of my supplies?

Checking   Yes or No
  _____ Did I stay on task?
  _____ Is this my best work?
  _____ Is my work complete?
  _____ Is my name on all my papers?

Note: Students respond by writing "yes" or "no" in the blanks and hand in this sheet along with their morning work is completed.

Figure 3–8   Paper-Pencil Task.

Poster 1	**Poster 2**
While Listening:	While Planning:
1. Does this make sense?	1. Do I have everything together?
2. Am I getting this?	2. Do I have my friends tuned out for right now?
3. I need to ask a question now before I forget.	3. Let me get organized first.
4. Pay attention.	4. What order will I do this?
5. Can I do what he's saying to do?	5. I know this stuff!
Poster 3	**Poster 4**
While Working:	While Checking:
1. Am I working fast enough?	1. Did I finish everything?
2. Stop staring at my girlfriend and get back to work.	2. What do I need to recheck?
3. How much time is left?	3. Am I proud of this work?
4. Do I need to stop and start over?	4. Did I write all the words? Count them.
5. This is hard for me, but I can manage okay.	5. I think I'm finished. I organized myself. Did I daydream too much?

conversation, and other activity. The focus is on the students' self-talk. On one day, "Concentration" may be the theme; on another day "CSI for Listening" is the theme. Other themes may include "CSI for Planning," "CSI for Working," "CSI for Checking," "CSI for Completing Tasks," and so forth. The students are more motivated to practice handwriting if it is personalized. In the meantime, their CSI skills are positively reinforced.

Art Activities.   Refer back to Figure 3–6 to locate where we are at this time on the CSI model. Art activities are used here to ensure that students practice the CSI strategies they have heard and seen modeled for them previously. Art activities and CSI are integrated because students often enjoy expressing themselves through art. They are motivated by the drawing, painting, and so forth, while CSI is infused into the art activity as reinforcement and practice of CSI strategies. Classroom teachers use art activities to practice cognitive self-instruction. Students draw self-portraits with a cartoon bubble over their heads that illustrates a CSI statement: "I will remember to wait my turn." Students can also paint their portraits and add a touch of self-talk. Students can be divided into four groups to illustrate on four different murals the four school times to use self-guiding statements (i.e., listening, planning, working, and checking). These murals usually consist of drawings or paintings of students in a school environment with a bubble over each head, with the self-talk written with magic markers. These make beautiful wall displays in the room. One principal was so impressed that she asked to use them in the school foyer for everyone to enjoy.

Another activity is to divide a sheet of drawing paper into four sections: "Listening," "Planning," "Working," and "Checking." Students are asked to draw themselves for each section and write a CSI statement-to-self or question to self.

Rote Rehearsal.   The last practicing component is rote rehearsal. In this activity, students practice the modeled CSI, following Meichenbaum and Goodman's steps (1971). For classroom use, students practice self-statements aloud, softly, and silently to themselves to internalize the process. Meichenbaum and colleagues were successful in improving students' impulsivity and promoting creativity when subjects were taught helpful, facilitative self-talk. However, it is inadequate to stop after teachers or peers have modeled CSI statements. Instead, the three steps of student practice in sequence are: (1) students practice CSI speaking aloud, (2) they whisper CSI statements to themselves, and finally (3) they silently rehearse the statements-to-self. Teachers should use judgment in the application of these three steps because some children do not need this much repetition—students who already have efficient self-guiding language often become bored and frustrated. On the other hand, some students are severely lacking in a battery of self-regulated learning strategies and will, therefore, require a great deal of repetition. This process can be conducted with the whole class, in small groups, or individually. Meichenbaum used CSI with individuals to reduce impulsivity.

One example of rote rehearsal is an activity called Hallway Behavior. For example, the class has just returned from lunch, and students are excessively noisy, pushing each other, opening doors to other classrooms, and running over smaller children in the hall. The sixth-grade teacher decides to use a CSI strategy. She begins by expressing her dissatisfaction with students' hallway behavior using "I-messages." Next, she describes her expectations clearly:

> As you go down the hall tomorrow, I'd like you to do five things. They are (1) walk, don't run; (2) remain silent, don't talk; (3) stay together, don't leave the group; (4) stay in a line, don't run into others; and (5) keep your hands and feet to yourself, do not touch another. I am going to talk about each one of these separately because they are very important. We must stop disturbing the whole school each time we leave this room. I'll talk to myself as if I were one of you going down the hall. First I'll talk about the need to walk, instead of running. Please listen carefully. Tell yourself to listen to every word I say. If I were you I'd talk to myself like this: "I walk quietly down the hall. When I run, I endanger my own safety and those I may meet. Sometimes I forget this safety rule. I will, remember to walk, not run. I'll monitor my feet by saying, 'Walk feet—no running feet allowed'. I can do it!" Now, class, I'd like you to repeat each one of the statements I

just said to myself. I'll write them on the board. We will repeat all the statements aloud together, then I want you to whisper all the statements, and then say all of them silently to yourself. The first one is "I walk quietly down the hall." Starting with this one, and reading down the list, repeat aloud together until we finish the last one, which is "I can do it." All together, now.

The students repeat the statements together using all three forms: aloud, whisper, and silent self-talk. The same process is repeated for the other four rules for hallway behavior that the teacher described to the students. After each hallway rule is verbalized, following Meichenbaum and Goodman's (1971) steps, the students and teacher return to the hall and practice using CSI statements for hallway behavior.

Students often do not follow class procedures and rules because the procedures and rules are not specific, nor have they been explicitly taught by the teacher, modeled by the teacher or peers, and practiced by the students with accompanying self-guiding speech. You may be saying, "Too time consuming." It isn't too time consuming if you observe how much time you spend policing, nagging, and pleading with students to behave. Recent statistics revealed that teachers lose approximately 55% of their instructional time to disruption (Gottfredson, May, 1989, personal communication). In addition to being less time-consuming over the long run, explicit instruction allows students to learn a means for life-long self-control via quality exposure to a "self-talk" role model. We believe strongly that if all teachers took time at the beginning of the school year to teach and model self-talk, and to provide for practice of all classroom rules and procedures, classroom discipline problems would no longer be the number one or number two problem in our nation, as they have been for the past 20 years.

For each school location (e.g., lunchroom, hallway, bathroom, water fountain) that requires teacher planning and deliberation about procedures, teachers should also do something resembling a task analysis. The sixth-grade teacher model for hallway behavior (presented earlier) represented this kind of thought. The behaviors the teacher required in the hall were (1) walking, (2) keeping quiet, (3) staying together, (4) staying in line, and (5) keeping hands and feet to self. Therefore, her task analysis of hallway behavior consisted of these five behaviors. If teachers will take the time to (1) analyze other procedures in their classroom, (2) conduct a task analysis to decide what they really mean by appropriate behavior (e.g., in the lunchroom), (3) articulate these behaviors clearly, (4) model accompanying, facilitative self-talk, (5) ensure practice from students using the three forms (aloud, whisper, and silently), (6) role-play the procedures, and then (7) monitor and encourage the use of CSI, a great improvement in classroom management should result. But better still, they foster a means for self-control.

Cueing.   Referring again to Figure 3–6, the last component of Manning's approach to CSI is cueing. Students have experienced teacher and peer modeling of self-management. They have had first-hand practice of self-management. Now students may need prompts and reminders to ensure continued and sustained use of CSI. Prompts can take the form of posted class rules written from a self-management orientation rather than the traditional other-control orientation, posters, group and individual cue cards, cue audiotapes, and other cueing signals.

The first suggestion is to write classroom rules and procedures in first person, present tense. For example, instead of reading "Wait your turn," the rule reads "Wait my turn." This facilitates responsibility toward oneself. When the second person is used, it is not really a self-reminder—it is a reminder made by someone else. Young children, who view the world from an I-orientation, respond much better to rules stated from their own perspective rather than from an external directive. When young children read the rule "Wait your turn," they often read it literally to mean that "You should wait your turn, but I don't have to." When the rule reads "Wait my turn," young children are more likely to realize that the rule includes them as well. Also, older children respond more personally to self-directed rules, using "I" and "my" in place of "you" and "your." In addition to using first person, teachers should write rules in present tense: "I raise my hand" or "Raise my hand." Future tense rules, such as "I will raise my hand" foster futuristic thinking and may cause students to postpone adherence to a later date. Many of our creative student teachers have developed outstanding thematic rules that accompany units of study. In one example, in a first-grade animal unit, the teacher posted the rules on paper climbing monkeys. One monkey had the rule "I don't monkey around," written on his stomach; another monkey had "I go bananas over finishing all my work" written on his. The students were very motivated to follow the "monkey rules" stated in a self-directed manner. Following is another example of self-directed rules, using pictorial cues to accompany the rules. These picture rules are very helpful for nonreaders or young learners.

Written Class Rule	**Cue Picture**
I raise my hand.	Picture of a student with hand raised
I listen.	Picture of a large ear
I wait my turn.	Drawing of two students, one waiting for water while the other is drinking water
I stay in my seat.	Picture of a student sitting quietly, working on a task at desk

The teacher-made posters for the four school uses (listening, planning, working, and checking) are similar to the posters made by students to practice CSI statements-to-self. In this place on the model (see Figure 3–6), these posters serve a cueing role to remind students to use CSI. Teachers are encouraged to use student-made posters to represent the best self-talk examples for cueing purposes. With younger students (grades K–2), teachers should introduce these posters one at a time and provide for practice of the targeted skill for approximately 2 weeks to 1 month before introducing the next poster. Teachers should use professional judgment in determining how fast older students (grades 3–12) can process the information effectively. One fourth-grade teacher puts all four uses on posters—with examples of exemplary CSI—over her chalkboard to guide the work habits of her students all year. Her posters contain the following information:

While Listening to Instructions

1. Goal setting: I will listen carefully.
2. Coping statements: I can understand if I don't daydream.
3. Guiding statements: She is telling us what to do first.
4. Self-questioning: What do I do when I finish?
5. Self-reinforcement: I know what to do now. Good for me!

While Preparing to Work

1. Goal setting: I will get everything organized.
2. Coping statements: I don't have all the crayons I need. What should I do about that?
3. Guiding statements: Put all my materials on my desk.
4. Self-questioning: Am I ready to begin?
5. Self-reinforcement: I have everything ready.

While Working

1. Goal setting: I want this to be my best workday.
2. Coping statements: This is hard for me, but I'm trying.
3. Guiding statements: Be careful—don't skip a line.
4. Self-questioning: Is this looking right to me?
5. Self-reinforcement: This is really looking super. I'm working hard.

While Checking Finished Work

1. Goal setting: I check over every paper.
2. Coping statements: I'm tired of looking over this. Just two more problems, though.
3. Guiding statements: Yes, that's right.
4. Self-questioning: Where do I put these?
5. Self-reinforcement: I finished all my work and checked over it once. Good for me!

Cue cards can remind students to use CSI strategies. In the regular classroom, almost every child has some behavior that needs improvement. Each week, students may decide individually what behavior they wish to address via a cue card reminder. Of course, the regular classroom is not conducive to students talking aloud to themselves all at once. The students are instructed to whisper the self-instructions or to read them to themselves silently. Examples of cue cards might be, "Stay seated now," "Don't daydream—concentrate," "Try to answer." Cue cards can be individualized to meet the needs of each class member. One teacher uses a clear, plastic shoe bag in which she puts categories of behavior reminders on laminated index cards. All are stat ed from an internal perspective (e.g., "Finish all my work"). The students are free to get a card when needed and tape it on their desk as a reminder. Occasionally this teacher will choose a cue card for a particular child; however, the emphasis is on child initiative for self-correction. For nonreaders, Palkes, Stewart, and Kahana (1968) training pictures may be worthy of consideration. In any event, the cue card serves as a stimulus/reminder to mediate behavior.

Cueing can be used in the form of small index cards for individual children, large posters, group cue cards, and other display methods. One teacher uses a large cue card that simply reads "I can try." This card is suspended from the ceiling on poster board. The teacher introduced the card because her first-grade children had begun the unfortunate habit of saying "I can't" even before they heard all of the directions. She reports that the card has been very effective in practically eliminating shouts of self-defeating "I can't! I can't!" When students say this, she points to the card. Further, some of the students point to the card for their peers. The group cue card reminds the children not to defeat themselves before they even attempt tasks. This works extremely well in changing attitudes about what children are able to accomplish and about the corresponding accomplishments themselves.

Individual cue cards are used to remind single students. This cueing system is used for three types of classroom reminders: (1) to inhibit inappropriate classroom behaviors, (2) to initiate, and (3) to reinforce appropriate behaviors. Depending on grade level and the students' maturity, teachers can introduce one of these types at a time. Students practice until they follow their own cues quite easily. However, teachers in third grade and above report that they introduce all three types at once. Some teachers make a set of cue cards for each type and give them to students who exhibit a need for them. Other teachers have asked students to make their own cue cards as needed. These are usually taped on the student's desk and used as a reminder (e.g., "raise my hand") until the students and/or teachers believe that students no longer need them. When the appropriate behavior has become automatic, the cue card should be removed. Of course, modifications of cue cards are often made by teachers to suit their own particular needs. Modifications of cue cards have included paper bracelets with cueing on the bracelet, group cue cards displayed in the classroom (e.g., "I try my best"), and cueing folders kept at desks to self-record appropriate behaviors at the sound of a buzzer or timer in the room (e.g., "Am I on task? If not, tell myself to focus on my work").

In most cases, students should work on only one behavior at a time. Therefore, only one cue card should be visible on the desk. A string of cue cards taped to the student's desk is inappropriate and will probably be unhelpful.

Cue cards can contain drawings of animals, stick figures, people, or imaginary characters demonstrating the target behavior the teacher wishes the student to perform (e.g., listening to others). Teachers sometimes draw their own cue cards or purchase commercial cut-outs. Cards are usually laminated and are the size of a 3×5 index card. Cue pictures can be reduced or enlarged. Drawings (e.g., a smiling face with one oversized ear to cue listening) can be used with or without a written prompt (e.g., "I listen well").

In addition to teacher-made cues, there are some commercial cueing techniques available. The Ralph Bear training figures in the Bash and Camp research (1975) are extremely popular with teachers, as well as the Palkes, Stewart, and Kahana training pictures (1968) mentioned earlier. Teachers like to modify and then enlarge these for bulletin boards and other learning displays. They also make excellent individual cue cards singly and collectively.

Long (1984) demonstrates teaching self-control and pro-social behavior by using therapeutic signs and sayings in classrooms for emotionally disturbed children. Some of these are adapted easily or used as they are in regular classrooms. Most are stated in the second person (e.g., "Listen to your controls") and should be changed to first person (e.g., "Listen to my controls"). Cue cards can be adapted for individual school needs. For example, one particular school's faculty was not satisfied with lunchroom behavior. Children were throwing food, screaming, and getting under the tables. The teachers and/or students made large, colorful cue cards, (written in present tense, first person) and posted them in the lunchroom; they prepared centerpieces for the tables containing cue cards; they made cue card placemats for the lunch tables; and they prepared reinforcement cards or buttons for children to wear when they demonstrated appropriate lunchroom behavior. They reported a great deal of improvement in their lunchroom atmosphere.

Cueing of CSI can also be conducted using teacher-made audiotapes. Hallahan, Lloyd, and Stoller (1982) compiled a very helpful manual for teachers to improve students' attention. The materials needed are a self-monitoring tape and a self-monitoring card. In self-monitoring studies, the Hallahan et al. method was found effective for increasing on-task behavior and academic productivity. Benefits continued even after students stopped using the tape. Individual children can use tapes with earphones; whole classes or small groups experiencing difficulty with attention and concentration can use tapes. We might call this a "Tape Cueing Activity" for the purpose of encouraging student(s) to concentrate throughout the day and to be aware of their own concentration abilities. The directions for making such a tape follow:

1. Prepare a 60-minute tape periodically recording the sound of a bell or melodious tone. Record the ringing of the bell or tone at different intervals throughout the 60-minute period. Vary the length of the intervals.
2. Play the tape throughout the day as needed.

3. When the students hear the bell or tone on the tape, have them ask themselves, "Was I concentrating or not?"

4. Supply each student with a record sheet. Have each student mark "yes" if he/she was concentrating and "no" if he/she was not concentrating. Beside the "yes" response, the student reads a self-reinforcement comment such as, "I was concentrating, that's good." Beside the "no" response, the student reads a self-guiding comment such as, "I need to pay attention to my work now. I can daydream later."

5. Continue this procedure until students' concentration improves (1–2 weeks). Use it periodically throughout the year if you so desire.

Teachers can also use color for cueing of CSI. Zentall and Kruczek (1988) found that placing color on a difficult-to-remember part of a word increased performance for hyperactive, nonattentive students. Color can be used to draw attention to relevant stimuli within tasks. Color can be placed strategically on difficult words in a passage or even near difficult-to-remember objects (e.g., bright yellow dot placed over the light switch to cue children to turn off the lights in their room). However, the use of color just to make a task more attractive can actually disrupt the performance of many students. In one classroom example, the teacher put a large, bright red circle over the classroom door to remind young children to wait at the door for further instructions before exiting. One teacher used a red dot to cue students, who were hopping up every few minutes, to stay seated for a reasonable period of time. She placed a cue card on the desk with a red dot, a picture of a student sitting at a desk, and the words "Stay seated" on the card. She also placed a large red dot on the floor where one child would turn her foot to get out of her seat. The child was instructed that when she felt the urge to pop out of her seat at inappropriate times, she was to touch and read her cue card in a whisper and to look down at the red dot on the floor. This child was soon regulating her own in-seat behavior and had developed feelings of self-efficacy.

Cueing is a method used to encourage students to remind themselves to bring their behavior under their own control. This frees the teacher from excessive policing and allows more time for academic pursuits. The teacher is not continuously reminding students to raise their hands to speak, to sit down, to wait their turn, to lower their voices, and so forth. Instead, a system of cueing is implemented whereby students prompt themselves. Cueing is never administered as punishment. Cueing, as with most management strategies, can be abused if teachers use it incorrectly to control students. The aim is just the opposite—it is a means to help children learn to control themselves. Cueing is nonpunitive self-reminders: As students learn to manage their own classroom behaviors, they need reminders. Self-reminder cue cards are nonpunitive tools for the promotion of the self-controlled, self-managed student.

CSI in Action

Figure 3–9 describes CSI in action with a student, Megan Kathleen who was exhibiting extremely poor school work habits. The model focused on school-assigned tasks, following through, and finishing tasks promptly and accurately (Manning, 1990b). Megan Kathleen's greatest challenge at school was her inability to concentrate. Manning worked with Megan Kathleen to help her focus her attention, follow through, and finish her work using the CSI model. Figure 3–10 includes the specific materials used to work with Megan Kathleen.

Seatwork Variables	CSI Model		
	Modeling	Practicing	Cueing
Focusing	Teacher models by talking aloud as she prepares to begin work (e.g., Do I have all my materials ready?). Teacher uses a prepared checklist to self-check for readiness. Teacher demonstrates use of the checklist. Student observes a videotape of peers talking to themselves as they focus attention (e.g., I need to get started right now).	Student role-plays how she will talk to herself aloud as she begins work. Teacher observes and helps supply appropriate self-statements, if needed. Student continues by whispering and then saying self-directives silently to self. Teacher monitors. In addition, student writes example of what she will say to herself to prompt her attention. This is done in a comic-strip bubble over a self-portrait of the student. The drawing should show her beginning work promptly.	Teacher and student make a set of cue cards to be used one at a time on the desk (e.g., Now it is time to work!). Student uses self-recording each day by marking "yes" or "no" for focusing attention. The student uses the same checklist the teacher modeled earlier.
Following Through	Teacher models self-talk aloud as she persists at a task (e.g., I'd like to stop now but I can work longer). Self-coping and self-reinforcement statements are emphasized (e.g., I'll keep working even if every one is not correct. I'm doing my best. Good for me). Peer models (video and audio) are used. A small poster is used as a self-checklist if student stops the task (e.g., Am I working too slowly? Why did I stop working? Can I get right back to my task?)	Teacher plays Concentration Zapper with the student. Student practices work persistence even when distractors are tempting her to break concentration. Teacher reinforces her and teaches her to reinforce herself when she is able to keep working when it would be easy to be distracted (e.g., interruption in the classroom). Student draws herself working amid confusion and writes in her self-talk.	Student wears headphones and listens to a tape that has been previously prepared with intermittent tones. When she hears the tone, the student marks whether she was on or off task. If she is off task, she either tells herself to get to work or reads a cue card (e.g., Let's get going, Megan Kathleen!) She uses the demonstrated self-checklist as a reminder.
Finishing	Teacher models talking aloud to complete the assignment (e.g., I've been a good worker today. It is such a good feeling to have everything finished). Peers model self-talk for completion of work (videotape) (e.g., Great! I finished the whole thing).	Student makes her own audiotape of self-statements that instructs her to complete all her work. She is paired with a younger student who is experiencing difficulty finishing seatwork. She models for the younger student and uses her audiotape to teach "finishing work" cognitive self-instruction. Student draws herself and writes her own words of self-congratulations for finishing seatwork successfully.	Student uses a strip of colored paper for each week. She punches a hole by each day's seatwork assignment that is successfully completed. She may use self-reinforcement cue cards (e.g., I'm so proud I finished my seatwork. I reminded myself to finish). She hands in a self-checklist with the day's work.

Figure 3–9 Application of Manning's Model of Cognitive Self-Instruction to Independent Seatwork Variables: Focusing Attention, Following Through, and Finishing Assignments.

Focusing Attention/Practicing

Sample Self-Portrait With Self-Talk

I must concentrate.

Focusing Attention/Cueing

Sample Cue Card

I'm "hopping" to get started on my work.

Sample Self-Record

1. Did I start right away?	Yes	No
2. Did I have all my materials ready?	Yes	No
3. Did I head my paper correctly?	Yes	No
4. Did I put my name on my paper?	Yes	No
5. Did I do the first one as soon as possible?	Yes	No
6. Did I start without the teacher reminding me?	Yes	No

Sample Self-Portrait Amid Distractors

Figure 3–10 CSI Materials for Classroom Application.
Source: Developed by Manning, 1995.

Following Through/Cueing

Sample Self-Record Rating

On/Off Task Self-Record

Directions: When I hear the tone I mark the right box. Circle the "on" or the "off." If I mark "off," I tell myself to get back to work. If I mark "on," I say to myself "Good for me" and I continue working.

	1	2	3	4	5	6	7	8	9	10
♫	On	On	On	On	On	On	On	On	On	On
♪	Off	Off	Off	Off	Off	Off	Off	Off	Off	Off

Sample Self-Checklist for Finished Work

1. Did I do all the assignments?	Yes	No
2. Did I do my best?	Yes	No
3. I was in control of finishing my work.	Yes	No
4. I reminded myself to finish.	Yes	No
5. I like the way my work looks.	Yes	No

Finishing/Modeling

Sample Teacher Model

"Wow! I'm almost finished—good for me! Look, just two more sentences. I have really made a lot of progress. I am a good worker. I concentrate by keeping my mind and my eyes on my work. I am not easily distracted because I want to finish. It is such a good feeling to have all my assignments finished. I have completed excellent work. I am very pleased with it."

Finishing/Practicing

Sample Self-Reinforcement

I am doing my very best work.

Figure 3–10 (*continued*)

Finishing/Cueing

Sample Assignment Sheet for Completion of Seatwork

Assignment/Completion

Monday
Spelling ♦
Reading
Mathematics ♦
Language Arts ♦
Social Studies ♦
Science
Other _____

(Repeat for Tuesday through Friday)

*Indicates successfully completed work

Sample Self-Reinforcement Cue Card

I did my best and I finished.

Sample Self-Checklist for Finished Work

1. Did I do all the assignments?	Yes	No
2. Did I do my best?	Yes	No
3. I was in control of finishing my work.	Yes	No
4. I reminded myself to finish.	Yes	No
5. I like the way my work looks.	Yes	No

Figure 3–10 CSI Materials for Classroom Application. (*continued*)

LEARNING OUT LOUD 3–7

In groups of three or four, write a skit based on a classroom situation you have observed or experienced related to organizing and guiding the learning of your students. Based on Manning's CSI approach, develop the components of teacher and peer modeling, student practice activities, and cueing activities. Use the following framework:

Classroom Organization and Guidance Skits

Write a classroom scenario that features teacher organization, classroom management, or guiding students' learning. Describe the situation as you observed or experienced it.

_____

_____

_____

_____

Develop modeling, practicing, and cueing activities based on Manning's (1991) approach to teach self-regulated learning to improve school work habits and social responsibility.

Modeling

Write a think-aloud that you would model aloud to your student[s].

_____

_____

_____

Practicing

Generate several activities in which the students engage that reinforce and internalize their continued use of the desired strategies.

_____

_____

_____

Cueing

Prepare several cue cards or other ways to remind your students to initiate, stop, continue, or reinforce appropriate classroom behaviors that promote optimal learning.

_____

_____

_____

LEARNING OUT LOUD 3–8

After each group has completed the skits from Learning Out Loud 3–7 and have ample time to practice their presentations, role-play your skits for your classmates. As each group presents, take notes on the quality of the cognitive think-alouds (modeling), students' practicing activities, and ways to cue/remind students to use these strategies to improve their school work habits and social responsibility.

Other Considerations: Classroom Management for Responsible Learners

Constructive classroom management is a means to an end—that end being an optimal learning environment. We all must remind ourselves frequently that excessive emphasis on classroom order and control of our students often blocks the accomplishment of other, more important educational goals and objectives. When we spend time organizing our classrooms, teaching rules and procedures, modeling, practicing, and cueing productive school work habits and social responsibility, it is critical to ask ourselves why we are spending time doing these things. Is it to foster more and better learning outcomes? Or, is it merely to foster compliance and obedience? Why is it important for you, as a future classroom teacher, to learn how to do these five tasks?

LEARNING OUT LOUD 3–9

In groups of three to five, develop a chart that answers the question, "Why is it important that I, as a future teacher, learn how to do the five tasks and do them well?

Valuing Responsible Citizenship

Teachers can facilitate students' productive school work habits such as focusing attention, following through with assigned tasks, and finishing accurately and promptly. It is equally important that teachers use precious classroom time to develop students' social responsibility—an integral component of responsible citizenship and a valued aim of our society.

Some teachers and administrators emphasize order and control at the expense of promoting values of responsible citizenship. Management that involves the learners helps students practice effective communication skills such as listening, expressing diverse opinions, cooperating, and collaborative problem solving (Ross & Bondy, 1993). Figure 3–11 lists Ross and Bondy's nine suggestions to foster socialization toward responsible citizenship.

---

1. Always provide a rationale for rules and routines.
   a. Explicitly state the rationale for rules emphasizing community values such as respect for others, fairness for everyone, etc.
   b. Use children's books to address values issues.
   c. Use current events activities to enlarge children's view of values to include societal ones.
   d. Use decision stories (i.e., "stories in which two important values conflict")
2. Give students opportunities to make decisions in the classroom.
3. Involve students in developing classroom rules.
4. Involve students in developing and revising classroom routines.
5. Whenever possible, use classroom routines that provide opportunities to make choices. Making choices is a critical component in promoting self-regulated learners.
6. View inappropriate behavior as an opportunity for collaborative problem solving.
7. Effective communication provides a basis for collaboration.
8. Class meetings provide opportunities for collaborative problem solving.
9. Collaborative planning and evaluation is the key to solving individual problems.
   a. Students need to learn how to role-take in order to understand how others feel. Therefore, teachers need to set up role-playing situations.
   b. Provide classroom time for students to interact over special projects, etc.
   c. Intervene if necessary to help students develop social skills when altercations or confrontations occur.

Figure 3–11   Developing Responsible Citizens.
Source: From "Classroom Management for Responsible Citizenship: Practical Strategies for Teachers," by D. Ross and E. Brady, 1993, Social Education, 57*(6), pp. 326–328. Reprinted with permission of National Council for the Social Studies.*

LEARNING OUT LOUD 3–10

Choose one of Ross and Bondy's suggestions in Figure 3–10, items 2 through 8. Provide three to five ways to accomplish this suggestion. Refer to items 1 and 9 for models—these suggestions were followed by classroom methods to address the suggestion. Put your ideas on a small poster to teach to others in your teacher preparation class.

Summary

Several classroom strategies promote student self-regulation of behavior. Teachers need to reconcile the need for both care and discipline in the classroom.

Classroom rules and procedures are instrumental. They enable a teacher to manage a classroom and maintain discipline. Too much attention to rules, however, undermines students' development of self-discipline.

Chapter 3 discusses cognitive/metacognitive strategies to prevent discipline problems in the classroom, including Manning's cognitive self-instruction (CSI) approach with its components of teacher/peer modeling, student practicing, and cueing strategies. CSI can be used in a classroom to foster the productive school work habits of focusing attention, following through on school tasks, and finishing accurately and promptly. It is equally important that teachers develop students' sense of social responsibility and citizenship.

Chapter 4

Learning About Multiple Models of Classroom Guidance

Self-Questions

Knowledge: Discuss the characteristics of (1) Relationship-Listening (RL), (2) Confronting-Contracting (CC), and (3) Rules and Consequences (RC) approaches to classroom discipline.

Comprehension: How are these approaches different from one another? Compare and contrast RL, CC, and RC in light of teacher power. Which is more likely to promote self-regulated learners?

Application: Choose one of the models discussed in this chapter (TET, TA, Social Discipline, Reality Therapy, Assertive Discipline) and describe how you will use this approach in your own classroom. Give specific examples.

Analysis: Take each of Glasser's 10 Steps to Discipline and discuss how each can or cannot foster self-regulated learners.

Synthesis: Build a self-regulation model from the RL models TET and TA that has some components of both TET and TA, but extends beyond both to self-regulation.

Evaluation: Convince a school principal who has told you that you are required to use Assertive Discipline that you have a better approach that will foster greater learning, improved school work habits, and a higher quality of social responsibility.

Introduction

Eclectic intervention strategies (Wolfgang, 1999; Wolfgang, Bennett, & Irvin, 1999) for discipline problems are used as the basis for the discussions in chapter 4. Wolfgang and his colleagues provide a teacher behavior continuum around four perspectives: (1) Relationship-Listening, (2) Confronting-Contracting, (3) Rules and Consequences, and (4) Coercive-Legalistic. These four perspectives will be discussed as we move from prevention to intervention strategies that promote optimal learning. Some of these models definitely do not promote self-regulated learning in our students. However, all the models are presented here because each is prevalent in today's schools. You need to have knowledge of the often-used models to determine which models, or their components, might be most useful to better foster self-regulated learning and which ones you should avoid.

In chapter 4, we will describe two models from Relationship-Listening (i.e., Teacher Effectiveness Training [TET] and Transactional Analysis [TA]); two models from Confronting-Contracting (i.e., Social Discipline Model and Reality Therapy); one model from Rules and Consequences (i.e., Assertive Discipline), and also identify some of the Coercive-Legalistic needs of today's classroom teachers. Wolfgang and his colleagues (1995) address in depth many more discipline models that you might be interested in exploring—Figure 4–1 offers an overview.

Relationship–Listening/Intervention

The ability of teachers to develop healthy relationships with students is an important aspect of classroom learning. We need caring teachers, like you, who take the time to really listen to students, especially troubled students who struggle at school. Often these reluctant learners, or learners who lack self-regulated learning skills, impose behavioral problems on the classroom learning environment that cannot be ignored. Ignoring discipline problems that are disrupting the learning of the troubled student and that of his or her classmates disrupts and prevents learning for both.

In the complex classrooms of today, using only one discipline technique will not get the job done. Teachers must be equipped with a broad range of options to meet the needs of a diverse population with diverse cultural backgrounds, differing learning styles, and various educational goals and needs. In chapter 4, we begin with the minimum-teacher-power side of the continuum: Relationship-Listening. As you read the specifics of two examples, Thomas Gordon's TET and Eric Berne and Thomas Harris's TA, keep in mind that these approaches may not be those you will need for every classroom discipline problem you experience. You will need to be familiar with other approaches that require applying more teacher power. However, one of the givens in classroom discipline from a self-regulated learning

	Teacher's Power			
	Minimum Power			**Maximum Power**
Category	Relationship-Listening Face	Confronting-Contracting Face	Rules and Consequences Face	Coercive-Legalistic
Process	Therapeutic	Educational and counseling	Controlling, rewards, and punishment	Restraining, exclusionary, and legal
Models	Gordon's *T.E.T: Teacher Effectiveness Training, Teaching Children Self-Discipline* Harris's *I'm OK—You're OK*	Dreikurs's *Discipline Without Tears* Albert's *Cooperative Discipline* Glasser's *Control Theory in the Classroom, Schools Without Failure, The Quality School* Gathercoal's *Judicious Discipline*	Madsen/Madsen's *Teaching/Discipline: A Positive Approach for Educational Development* Alberto/Troutman's *Applied Behavior Analysis for Teachers* Dobson's *Dare to Discipline* Canter and Canter's *Assertive Discipline: Succeeding With Difficult Students* Alberti's *Your Perfect Right; Stand Up, Speak Out, Talk Back* Jones's *Positive Discipline*	Nonviolent crisis management and arbitrary, preestablished administrative procedures leading to physical restraint, exclusion, and legal actions toward the student or family CPI (Crisis Prevention Institute)

Figure 4–1   Today's Discipline Models.
Source: From Solving Discipline Problems: Methods and Models for Today's Teachers, *by C. H. Wolfgang, ©1999, New York: John Wiley & Sons. This material is used by permission of John Wiley & Sons, Inc.*

perspective is to start with strategies that require the least amount of teacher intervention and get tougher if necessary. We want to give students as much freedom and flexibility as possible to allow for the growth of student responsibility. Nevertheless, do not be afraid to apply the strictest teacher power models should they become necessary to restore an optimum learning environment. Now, let's take a look at the first relationship/listening model.

Thomas Gordon's Teacher Effectiveness Training (TET)

Gordon's TET is based on the work of Carl R. Rogers and is represented in books such as *Client-Centered Therapy, On Becoming a Person*, and *Freedom to Learn*. Rogers's underlying assumption is that every human being is unique and rational; therefore, no one can really make decisions for or give advice to others. Through verbal articulation of problems, each student comes to her own solutions. At the core of TET is the need to process our lives and life's challenges, including classroom problems, via our own language with self and others.

The centerpiece of the TET approach is nondirective, open, and honest communication between teacher and student. When a problem occurs in the class, the student either needs to be heard seriously or the teacher needs to communicate via an I-message what problems need to be corrected. Whether the teacher listens (Language of Acceptance) or talks (I-messages) is dependent upon who owns the problem.

Therefore, when a problem arises in the classroom, you, as the teacher, must engage in self-questioning like the following.

TEACHER SELF-QUESTIONING WHEN CONFRONTED WITH A CLASSROOM PROBLEM

1. Who owns this problem—me or the student?
2. Is the student having a problem such as being left out by others or home difficulties? (Student problems are individualistic and are not disrupting the learning of others.)
3. Is this student's misbehavior having a direct effect on my attempts to teach others?
4. Is the student's misbehavior interfering with the learning, safety, or rights of others?
5. Is the student's misbehavior interfering with his or her own learning, safety, or rights?
6. Is the student too young or too cognitively limited to be capable of solving problems?
7. If the problem is student owned, when will I make time to use the Language of Acceptance?
8. If the problem is teacher owned—my problem—when should I express my feelings using an I-message?

One of the challenges of Gordon's approach is deciding problem ownership. This decision is not always clean and clear-cut. However, it may be worth considering and taking this time to help students toward self-regulation.

Student Owned Problems.   If you, as the teacher, decide the student owns the problem (e.g., other students will not work with him on a voluntary basis), then you should employ the Language of Acceptance, which includes both passive and active listening. Some teachers are critical of Gordon's approach because the Language of Acceptance requires individual, one-on-one time with the student who owns the problem—they feel this is far too time consuming. However, teachers who favor Gordon's strategies believe, in the end, they actually gain more time for instruction if students have had an opportunity to examine their own problems and to arrive at plans to accomplish their goals or to resolve their problem.

As discussed in chapter 2, Gordon (1974) believes the relationship between a teacher and a student is an excellent one when it is characterized by (1) *openness*, or *transparency*, so that each is able to risk directness and honesty with the other; (2) *caring*, when each knows that he is valued by the other; (3) *interdependence*, as opposed to dependence of one on the other; (4) *separateness*, to allow each to grow and to develop uniqueness, creativity, and individuality; and (5) *mutual needs meeting*, so that neither's needs are met at the expense of the other's needs.

Gordon's Language of Acceptance (LA).   In discussions with the student who owns the problem, the primary point is to allow the one with the problem to take responsibility for most of the talking. This is very difficult for most teachers because their natural impulse is to give lots of advice and to talk. After all, that is what we do most of the day—teach, give directions, monitor, redirect. However, in Gordon's Language of Acceptance, a major component is *passive listening*, which means the teacher remains quiet. A second component is *acknowledgment responses* (e.g., nonverbal communication of nods, smiles, gestures, leaning toward, etc.), which let the student know clearly that the teacher is indeed listening and listening well. Verbal messages like "hmmm" and "really" are also considered acknowledgment responses because, in and of themselves, they do not communicate meaning. They simply acknowledge the communication of the target student. In the third component, *invitations* are extended to the student to talk (e.g., "Would you like to talk about _____?" "What's on your mind?") and invitations are offered to continue talking (e.g., "What else happened?" "And then you said?" "Would you want to talk again tomorrow?"). Such invitations to share thinking are called *door openers*. The fourth component of Gordon's Language of Acceptance is termed *reflection and interpretation*. When students are discussing their problems, the teacher's role includes listening and acknowledging, inviting conversation, and also reflecting and interpreting. Reflection is simply mirroring back to the target student what she is saying.

REFLECTION EXAMPLE

Student: I am late to school because my mom oversleeps every day.
Teacher: So you're late because your mom does not get up on time.

Interpretation takes a step forward when the teacher attempts to add the feeling or affect component to what the student is really saying. Of course, there is danger in doing this in that a misinterpretation may occur. However, taking this as a possibility, it is worthwhile to attempt interpretation anyway. If, you, as the teacher, are on the wrong wavelength, the target student most likely will illustrate by facial expression, gesture, or verbal correction (e.g., "No, that's not how I felt."). Then you can invite the student to express the more accurate feeling. In chapter 2, we refer to interpretation as *paraphrasing*.

INTERPRETATION EXAMPLE

Student: And I hate to come in the room late. Everyone stares at me and I just want to hide.
Teacher: You feel embarrassed when you are late to school.

A major part of interpretation is the teacher's responsibility to listen carefully to increase the likelihood of greater accuracy in interpretation.

The purpose of Gordon's Language of Acceptance is to facilitate students' thinking and follow-through to solve their own problems. During this listening time, the teacher can encourage "thinking aloud" through the solution steps or other components of the problem. You should not see your role as being the individual who is responsible for solving all classroom problems. If you take over students' problems, you actually cheat them of the authentic experience of working through the necessary skills of problem solving that foster the kind of autonomy this book is all about—becoming self-regulated, fully-functioning citizens. Figure 4–2 views, in a consolidated form, the four components of Gordon's Language of Acceptance.

LEARNING OUT LOUD 4–1

In pairs, write a three- to five-sentence scenario in which one of you has a student-owned problem. One of you will play the role of the teacher and use the components listed in Figure 4–2 to listen to your classmate, who is playing the role of the student with a problem. The components are not ordered/sequential. Use them in a way that seems most natural and authentic.

Passive Listening—Teacher keeps quiet and listens intently to the student with a problem.

Acknowledgment Responses—Teacher illustrates listening by nodding, smiling, frowning, gesturing, leaning toward student, saying "hmmm," or "really," or "yes," etc.

Door Openers and Continuers—Teacher invites the student to talk about the problem or to continue talking about the problem should the student begin and stop prematurely. Examples of door openers include, "What is on your mind?" "Do you want to tell me about it?" "What's the problem?" "Do you want to talk?" Examples of door continuers include "What else?" "Do you want to say more?" "What if we talk about this again tomorrow?" "And then?"

Reflection—Teacher shows that she is listening carefully. In essence, the teacher simply reflects or mirrors back what the student has said. Following are a few examples:

> *Student*: I'm not sure what I should do.
> *Teacher*: You are uncertain what you should do next.

> *Student*: I hate my mother for saying that to me.
> *Teacher*: You are feeling as if you hate your mother for saying these things to you.

Interpretation—Another way the teacher shows that she is listening carefully and trying to understand the student's problem. The teacher now goes beyond reflecting the message to interpreting the message the student is sending. Following are a few examples:

> *Student*: I'm not sure what I should do.
> *Teacher*: You are frustrated about your next step.

> *Student*: I hate my mother for saying that to me.
> *Teacher*: You are angry at your mother right now.

Figure 4–2   Gordon's Language of Acceptance.

In Reflection, the meaning of the student's talk is not altered at all. The teacher attempts to play the role of a mirror. The underlying assumption is that if we can feel supported and "see our problems" through the eyes of a caring, listening teacher, we are better able to solve our own problems. In this rather indirect way, the teacher promotes self-regulated learning.

In Interpretation, teachers run the risk that they will misinterpret what the student means. However, this is acceptable because the student usually corrects what the teacher has said explicitly. And even if the student only corrects the meaning in his mind, he still feels that the teacher is working hard to understand and to assist. In most cases, when a teacher knows the student well and is listening very carefully, the likelihood of misinterpretation is rare.

Teacher-Owned Problems.   If you, as the teacher, determine that a student's behavior is interfering with your teaching or others' learning, rights, or safety, you should employ an I-message, according to Gordon (1974).

Teachers offer I-messages to communicate clearly the *misbehavior* in nonjudgmental, nonevaluative terms; to explain the *tangible effect* this misbehavior is creating; and to convey the *feeling* the teacher experiences because of the student's misbehavior. The teacher should always use the personal pronoun "I" to emphasize that he owns the problem. In essence, I-messages could be termed "responsibility messages" because the teacher strongly assumes responsibility for communicating his own feelings. The teacher who conscientiously and routinely uses I-messages is also serving as a positive role model for students. Teachers who have begun to use Gordon's I-messages report that students eventually also begin to communicate to the teacher and peers with I-messages. Figure 4–3 offers seven examples of teachers' I-messages. Figure 4–4 lists the components of I-messages.

Student's ACTION	Teacher's I-MESSAGES
Joe talks to Ryan while the teacher is lecturing. He talks loudly enough that he disturbs everyone listening to the story.	"When students talk while I am lecturing (behavior), I have a hard time speaking so everyone can hear (effect), and that makes me frustrated (feelings)."
Katy leaves her equipment scattered across the lab table when she returns to her seat and readies herself to depart.	"When students leave equipment out on the lab tables (behavior), I am fearful (feelings) that others will knock them over them and get hurt (effect), and I am responsible for keeping equipment and students safe."
When the school bell rings, Caroline runs at full speed through the door and down the stairs.	"When students run down the stairs (behavior), I am fearful (feelings) that people will fall and get injured (effect), and my job is to keep people safe."
Mary appears in front of the teacher and, with hysterical excitement and rapid-fire delivery, begins to talk so loudly and at such a pace that the teacher cannot comprehend.	"When students shout (behavior), I can't understand what is being said (effect), and I am disappointed (feelings) that I can't help."
The teacher is talking to a parent when Carlos interrupts her and starts talking.	"It makes it hard for me (feelings) to understand two people who are talking to me at the same time (behavior), and I become confused (effect)."
Mark deliberately pushes Tim while lining up at the water fountain.	"When students are pushed (behavior), it is dangerous (effect), and that frightens me (feelings) because I am in charge of safety."
Ali and Chris fight over a book, pulling it back and forth.	"When books are pulled (behavior), I am afraid (feelings) that they will get damaged and destroyed and we will not have them anymore (effect)."

Figure 4–3   I-Messages.
Source: From Solving Discipline Problems: Methods and Models for Today's Teachers, *by C. H. Wolfgang, © 1999, New York: John Wiley & Sons. This material is used by permission of John Wiley & Sons, Inc.*

1. Misbehavior

2. Tangible effect

3. Feeling

Figure 4–4   I-Message Components.

LEARNING OUT LOUD 4–2

Read carefully the following classroom example. Then change the five you-messages to I-messages. Finally, write an I-message of your own. Write a personal I-message that you really want to give to a family member or a close friend or write a more school-based I-message to give to your future students. Another option is to write one personal I-message and one professional I-message.

Components of I-Messages

Nonjudgmental Description of;

Behavior—Usually begins with *When* and is what you don't like, are concerned about, etc.

When paper is left all over our classroom…

Effect on You—Most difficult part and often left out; okay if it doesn't seem to really be a tangible effect

I have to stay after school to pick it up and…

Feeling You Have—As a result

I get really frustrated and feel imposed upon.

Changing You-Messages to I-Messages

You-Messages	*I-Messages*
1. You make me so angry!	1. _____
2. You are 20 minutes late!	2. _____
3. You are going to get really sick!	3. _____
4. If you say that again, I'll hit you!	4. _____
5. Your answer is stupid!	5. _____

Write an I-Message

Nonjudgmental Description of Behavior   _____

Effect on Me   _____

Feeling I Have   _____

Anger as a Secondary Emotion.   I-messages should reflect primary emotions such as hurt, fear, worry, embarrassment, panic, and annoyance. Teachers should not speak from anger for many reasons, such as poor role modeling and negation of the positive verbal environment. Additionally, anger follows another emotion—some other feeling fed the angry reaction, according to Gordon (1974). Before you begin to protest with examples of anger, ask yourself these questions: "What did I feel before I noticed I was angry? Was I afraid, hurt, or annoyed before I became angry?"

LEARNING OUT LOUD 4–3

In pairs or triads, read the following situations and identify the primary emotion in each.

Classroom Situation	*Primary Emotion*
1. Student is late meeting the bus at the designated time for a field trip.	_____ ?

2. Student calls you, the teacher, "an
   ugly old hag."   _____?_____
3. Students are whispering to each other
   and pointing to your example on the board. _____?_____

Gordon might say we would claim anger as the primary emotion in each of the class-room situations in Learning Out Loud 4–3. However, did an emotion really precede the sec-ondary anger? Could situation 1 be worry or fear that something has happened to the student? Perhaps the student name calling in situation 2 might first embarrass or hurt your feelings. In situation 3, you might also feel hurt, embarrassed, or at least annoyed by the students' whispering and pointing prior to the moment you noticed the feeling of anger. The next time you are angry, ask yourself if another, more primary emotion came first. And, so what if it did? The point is we, as teachers, need to speak to our students from the primary emotion rather than waiting until we are angry. Speaking in I-messages from primary emo-tions represents an honest, yet vulnerable way to communicate with our students. This brings us to another disadvantage of Gordon's approach—the vulnerable position we as-sume with I-messages. Unless there is a reasonably strong relationship underlying the teacher-student interactions proposed by Gordon (1974), students may not care sufficiently to respond, as we might hope, to an honest, open communication system.

LEARNING OUT LOUD 4–4

Consider the following list of advantages and disadvantages of Gordon's (1974) Teacher Effectiveness Training (TET). Add others to the list based on your opinions, class discussions, and readings of Gordon's work.

Advantages	*Disadvantages*
1. Builds good relationships	1. Very time consuming
2. Honest, direct, clear messages	2. Younger children won't get it!
3. _____	3. _____
4. _____	4. _____
5. _____	5. _____

Eric Berne and Thomas Harris's Transactional Analysis (TA)

The second example in the Relationship/Listening approach to solving discipline problems is called *Transactional Analysis* (TA). TA is based on Freud's work in psychoanalytical the-ory. Perhaps you studied Freud's constructs of the id, ego, and superego. The *id* represents our basic drives, instinctual needs, and basic selfishness. The *superego* represents the re-straint imposed on us to keep these basic drives in check and under control. The *ego* is the mediator or the monitor between too much id and too much superego.

In a classroom example, a student decides to steal a classmate's new pen (id), but says to herself, "Oh, I can't do that. The teacher would punish me; my parents would get a call and I'd be so embarrassed" (superego). So then, the student might say, "I'll ask my mom if she'll buy me a pen like that or I could save my allowance and buy it for myself" (ego).

Transactional analysis was first offered in the books *Games People Play* by Eric Berne (1964) and *I'm Okay, You're Okay* by Thomas Harris (1969). Later, books were written for adults to work with children, such as *Born to Win* by (Muriel James and Dorothy Jongeward

(1971), *TA for Tots (1973) and TA for Kids* (1971) both by Alvyn Freed, and *Games Students Play* by Ken Ernst (1973).

In TA, three aspects of our personhood are apparent: child, parent, and adult. These aspects parallel Freud's id (child), superego (parent), and ego (adult). Based on our past history and experiences, our child, parent, or adult aspects are manifested. For example, stored-up memories of our childhood keep vestiges of our childishness alive forever. Likewise, memories of the authority figures in our lives, usually our parents, can repeat themselves in our interactions with others. The "adult" reactions are based on those objective, rational past experiences that enabled us to problem solve and make good decisions without the burden of emotionalism. Every one of us has these stored-up tapes from our past that we use in our interactions with others, according to TA.

The central core of TA is the social transaction of language. The transactional stimulus is the speaker's message, while the transactional response is the reaction of the listener to the stimulus. When we combine the idea of stored-up verbal tapes that are played in response to environmental stimuli, we can account for why individuals parent the same way they were parented (e.g., Nancy Friday's book *My Mother, Myself* [1977]) or why teachers teach the way they remember having been taught (e.g., John Goodlad's book *Teachers for our Nation's Schools* [1990]). Therefore, understanding TA can be your first step in breaking the cycle of reflex response. Your responses, as a classroom teacher, need to be based on deliberative, reflective thought (e.g., self-regulated teaching)— not merely replaying the tapes of your parents and former teachers. Thus, let's take a quick look at TA with the hope that you will read more about it on your own.

According to TA, the brain is a recorder. It has recorded every experience we have ever had. Siegel's (1986) book, *Love, Medicine, and Miracles*, documents that the brain records experiences even without our conscious awareness. For example, people under anesthesia record what is being said around them, and this affects their physical reactions. Siegel believes this experience can affect a patient's recovery. In addition, he believes that we can heal ourselves through optimism, self-talk that helps us reach our goals, and by imagining ourselves as healthy and disease-free.

Berne (1964) observed overt behaviors as individuals played their internal tapes from these stored-up experiences. Stored experience is quite similar to Vygotsky's (1978) idea of internalization. Children are first regulated by significant others' verbalizations. Children then internalize these parent verbalizations, which subsequently constitute the children's self-guiding language and verbal self-regulation of their own actions. TA proponents are saying the same thing when they talk about replaying the stored-up tapes from our past.

Three Voices of TA.*

1. ***Child***   This aspect comes from our recordings of our feelings and sensory input throughout our lives. There are three different, identifiable parts to the child ego state. The "natural child" is the part of us that expresses spontaneous feelings of happiness, love, and joy—the giddy, light-hearted kid in all of us. The "adapted child" is the part of us that collects bad feelings such as anxiety or depression. This part often plays the victim or the persecuted (e.g., "Everyone is always picking on me"). The "rebellious child" is that part of us that is defiant and stubborn.

2. ***Parent***   This state contains both the good and bad remembrances of our parents and other authority figures. We have two aspects of this state: the critical parent and the nurturing parent. The critical parent voice is often blaming, criticizing, punishing, hurting others,

*Manning & Payne, 1996, pp. 7–8.

Adult	Parent		Child		
	Nurturing	Critical	Natural	Rebellious	Adapted

Figure 4–5   Voices of Transactional Analysis.

or being aggressive toward others. Verbal clues to this voice are "never," "always," "should," "must," "have to," "don't," "ought to," or "you will." The nurturing parent voice soothes, calms, and comforts others (e.g., "Everything will be okay").

3. *Adult*   As children move from the toddler stage, they begin to store rational information for use in later events. The adult state is rational, emotionless, processes data objectively, and solves problems. Verbal clues include the "W" questions: who, what, when, and where, and also how. Other examples are "in my opinion," "let's take a closer look," and "in conclusion."

When viewing the three states of child, parent, and adult, the balance among the three is the important point. For example, too much child can lead to irresponsibility; too little child can lead to a lack of creativity and spontaneity. Too much rebellious child can cause us to lose friends, but too little rebellious child can cause us to be passive wimps that people run over. Too much nurturing parent causes "smothering" and too little causes "coldness." Too much adult causes us to be boring and nonfeeling, and too little causes us not to know how to solve problems and look after ourselves. Balance among the three is the key to healthy social transactions.

The premise of TA is that all individuals need to feel adequate. If the child state holds the greatest influence of all three states, individuals have an attitude of "I'm not okay, but you are okay." If the parent state holds the greatest influence of the three, the individual's attitude is "I'm okay, but you are not okay." If the parent and child are in conflict with very little rational adult intervention, we see an attitude of "I'm not okay and you're not okay." Figure 4–5 shows the three voices of TA. Complete Learning Out Loud 4–5 to see if you understand the three stored-up voices of TA.

LEARNING OUT LOUD 4–5

Read each verbal message and decide who is speaking from the following list:

1. *Adult*   rational/objective (uses words like *who, what, when, where, how*)
2. *Parent*
    2a. *Nurturing parent*   cares for others (uses words like *yes, it's okay*; good, caring, love, support),
    2b. *Critical parent*   criticizing others/judging/evaluating (uses words like *never, no, should, must, have to*)
3. *Child*
    3a. *Natural child*   excited, joy, enjoys life (uses words like *oh boy, cool, great, love it!*)
    3b. *Rebellious child*   temper tantrums, acting-out behaviors (uses words like *I hate this! No way! won't;* screams)

(continued)

LEARNING OUT LOUD 4–5 (CONTINUED)

3c. ***Adapted child*** whining, plays the victim (uses words like *why me? Everyone picks on me. Poor me!*)

CHOOSE A TA VOICE

EXAMPLE 1:

Teacher: What's number five? _____
Student: It's Commutative Property of Addition. _____

EXAMPLE 2:

Student: Ms. Sullivan, do you want today's assignment by Friday? _____
Teacher: Be quiet! Not now! _____

EXAMPLE 3:

Student: Oh, no! I've lost my assignment. My mom forgot to sign it! The teacher will make me stay in. _____
Teacher: It's okay. Don't cry. You can bring your paper in tomorrow. _____

EXAMPLE 4:

Ms. Adams: Students are so rude and irresponsible these days. No manners. _____

Mr. Bailey: I know—I've got a lot of whiny, spoiled brats. _____

EXAMPLE 5:

Teacher: I've had it with your rude behavior! Get out of my class right now! _____

Student: Oh, sure! You aren't my boss! Just try and make me do that. I'll sue you! _____

EXAMPLE 6:

Anthony: Cool! that was a fun class. I loved it! _____
Bob: Wow, that's super! Hearing that makes me feel happy. _____

EXAMPLE 7:

Teacher: Sarah, you should know better than that. Now don't let me catch you speaking out again. You know better! _____
Student: [crying and whimpering] I'm sorry [sniff, sniff] please, I'm sorry. I just forgot! _____

EXAMPLE 8:

Ms. Carson: Your shoes are beautiful! Why, I saw a pair just like them at a yard sale the other day. _____
Ms. Dellwood: Thank you. Your hair color is so pretty ... is it your own? _____

LEARNING OUT LOUD 4–6

Read the following classroom scenario. Write a classroom scenario similar in length and follow up by writing an adult, parent, and child question and an adult, parent, and child statement. Share these scenarios in small groups of four to five students.

TA Classroom Scenario Example

Mr. Alford, a fourth-grade teacher, turns to find three students removing their tennis shoes during mathematics class. Fred, the boldest of the three students, continues untying his laces while smirking at Mr. Alford. The other two students go back to their mathematics assignment while Fred kicks his first shoe off with a loud whoop and a look of challenge on his face. Mr. Alford catches himself before he follows his immediate reflex to order Fred from the classroom with the words, "Get your books and get out of here right now, you smart aleck!" Instead, he remembers the Transactional Analysis he has been studying. He realizes that Fred's behavior indicates he is being the *rebellious child*, acting out overtly with a challenge. Mr. Alford knows that if he screams at Fred to get out, he would simply reinforce the *child* in Fred by assuming the voice and behavior of the *critical parent*. Instead, he wants to speak as the rational *adult*, and by doing this, increase the likelihood of bringing forth the *adult* in Fred, as well. Therefore, Mr. Alford takes a deep breath, smiles at the two girls who decided to return to their mathematics assignment, and says to Fred, "Fred, this mathematics is pretty hard today, but you are smart enough to figure it out. Who would you pick to help you with the first problem?"

List three questions and three statements that Mr. Alford might have said.

Questions:
What in the world got into you, Fred? (parent)
Who do you want to help you? (adult)
Why are you always acting up in my class? (child)

Statements:
You never pay attention to what you are supposed to do. (parent)
The mathematics is hard, but you can handle it. (adult)
I'm really pissed off at you, you bad boy. (child)

Confronting–Contracting/Intervention

The next two discipline models move us more toward a teacher-centered approach, with an emphasis on teacher-student interactions. On a continuum (see Figure 4–1), these two Confronting-Contracting models are approximately midway between student-centered and teacher-centered. Dreikurs's Social Discipline Model (1964, 1968, 1972) and Glasser's Reality Therapy (1975, 1992) will serve to ground you in two frequently used models in today's classrooms.

Dreikurs's Social Discipline Model

Dreikurs's work is based on that of social psychologist Alfred Adler. Adler's basic premise is that we are social beings and need primarily to belong and to be accepted. If you wish to read more about this model, you should consult books written by Dreikurs and his colleagues: *Children: the Challenge (1964), Discipline Without Tears (1972), Logical Consequences (1968), Psychology in the Classroom (1968)*, and *Encouraging Children to Learn (1963)*.

Other researchers have continued to emphasize Dreikurs's work and expand upon it. For example, Albert (1989) has provided many strategies and suggestions for classroom teachers in her book *A Teacher's Guide to Cooperative Discipline: How to Manage Your Classroom and Promote Self-Esteem*. Dinkmeyer has spoken more to parents in his book *Systematic Training for Effective Parenting* (Dinkmeyer & McKay, 1976).

Dreikurs (1964, 1972) believed the primary reason for misbehavior is a lack of social acceptance. Also, all behavior is purposeful and directed toward achieving a goal or goals, according to Social Discipline philosophy. The teacher's role, therefore, is to assist misbehaving students to identify their mistaken goals and to provide more acceptable ways to obtain what everyone craves: acceptance by others. This awareness is metacognitive in nature—the misbehaving students think about their reasons for misbehaviors as the first step to alter rationally those behaviors. The four mistaken goals that cause misbehavior are (1) attention, (2) power, (3) revenge, and (4) helplessness. The following sections discuss each goal and provide teacher self-questions to help identify which goal is motivating the target child's misbehavior, and example strategies from Albert (1989).

Attention Seeking.   You will soon know and be able to describe the students in your classes who are constantly seeking attention. They consistently attempt to belong and receive recognition. When they are not able to get teachers' and/or peers' attention through socially acceptable means, they resort to unacceptable ways to gain incessant praise or criticism.

Teacher self-questions that indicate a student's mistaken goal of attention seeking include: (1) Do I feel annoyed by the student's misbehavior? (2) Am I mildly frustrated or agitated? (3) Do I feel I need to focus on someone else's behavior? (4) Is this student taking more than her fair share of my attention? (5) How well is this student accepted by others in the class?

The teacher moves from his self-questioning to ask the misbehaving student if she wants to know why she is misbehaving. If the attention-seeking student does not say "no," the teacher asks the following Dreikurs question: "Could it be that you want special attention?"

If the student provides evidence (Dreikurs calls this a recognition reflex), the teacher is on the right track. The student's recognition reflex can be a smile, a laugh, or a nod, or she may look at the teacher with a "yes," shrug her shoulders slowly, or show other such affirmations. If one or more of these indicators happen, the teacher can apply one of the strategies suggested by Albert (1989) and listed in Figure 4–6.

Power and Control.   This mistaken goal is used by students who not only feel left out, but also feel inferior and unable to measure up to others' expectations. This can be real, such as a physical or cognitive limitation, or perceived, such as a false perception of inferiority. The effect is the same—the power-motivated student tries to boss others, get his own way, brags or clowns, or forces himself into the inner circles of other groups or cliques.

Teacher self-questions that indicate the mistaken goal of power and control include: (1) Do I feel intimidated? (2) Do I feel more than just annoyed? (3) Do I want to respond like a child? (4) Is this student bossing others in the class? (5) Is this student well-liked and included?

The teacher moves from her self-questioning to ask the misbehaving student if he wants to know why he is misbehaving. If the power-driven student does not say "no," the teacher asks the following Dreikurs question: "Could it be that you want your own way and hope to be the boss?"

As with the attention-mistaken goal, the teacher looks for the recognition reflex to verify accuracy of her identification of the power-mistaken goal. If this verification is made, the teacher attempts some of the strategies suggested by Albert (1989) and listed in Figure 4–7.

Revenge.   If a student is unable to gain acceptable attention or power, she may move on to seek revenge for the hurt she feels. This student externalizes the hurt she feels and also desires to hurt others in the same way she has been mistreated. This student goes beyond a desire for attention or power, and even beyond the desire to boss and dominate. She achieves recognition by insulting others with cruelty, unkindness, and humiliation.

Teacher self-questions that indicate the mistaken goal of revenge include: (1) Do I feel wronged? (2) Do I feel hurt? (3) Do I feel like behaving as a critical parent? (4) Do I want to act out toward this child? (5) Do other students avoid and/or despise this child?

As with attention seeking and power, the teacher moves from self-questioning to questioning students about why they are misbehaving. The teacher asks the Dreikurs question for the student seeking revenge: "Could it be that you want to hurt others as much as you feel hurt by them?"

Student's Motivation	Behavior Characteristics	Teacher's Feelings
Attention getting	Repetitively does actions to make herself the center of attention. When asked to stop, she will comply, but will start again later.	Annoyed

Techniques to Use With the Attention-Getting Student

Minimize the Attention
    Ignore the behavior
    Give "the eye"
    Stand close by
    Mention the student's name while teaching
    Send a secret signal
    Give written notice
    Give an I-message
Legitimize the Behavior
    Make a lesson out of the behavior
    Extend the behavior to its most extreme form
    Have the whole class join in the behavior
    Use a diminishing quota
Do the Unexpected
    Turn out the lights
    Play a musical sound
    Lower your voice to a whisper
    Change your voice
    Talk to the wall
    Use one-liners
    Cease teaching temporarily
Distract the Student
    Ask a direct question
    Ask a favor
    Change the activity
Notice Appropriate Behavior
    Thank the students
    Write well-behaved students' names on the chalkboard
Move the Student
    Change the student's seat
    Send the student to the thinking chair

Figure 4–6 Nonsocially Adaptive Students: Attention Getting.
Source: From L. Albert. 1989. A Teacher's Guide to Cooperative Discipline: How to Manage Your Classroom and Promote Self-Esteem. *Circle Pines, MN: American Guidance Service, Inc., pp. 31–41. Reprinted with permission.*

If a recognition reflex is forthcoming from this child, including a possible breakdown of crying/reaching out, the teacher chooses appropriate strategies as suggested by Albert (1989). (See Figure 4–7.)

Helplessness or Inadequacy. This is the most serious goal because, at this point, the student has finally given up trying to be accepted. In fact, the helpless student has decided that indeed he is not worthy of social acceptance and no longer cares what happens. This apathy is often misinterpreted to mean the student is finally "behaving" at school because he is oftentimes quiet, passive, and withdrawn. These students feel unequal, uncared for, and incapable of doing anything—even misbehaving. One of your great challenges will be distinguishing the shy but happy, well-adjusted child from the helpless, withdrawn child who is very unhappy and apathetic to the world around him.

Teacher self-questions that indicate the mistaken goal of helplessness or inadequacy include: (1) Do I feel incapable of reaching the child in any way? (2) Do I feel powerless to

Student's Motivation	Behavior Characteristics	Teacher's Feelings
Power	Repetitively does actions to make himself the center of attention. When asked to stop, he becomes defiant and escalates his negative behavior and challenges the adult.	Intimidated
Revenge	Hurts others physically or psychologically	Hurt

Techniques to Use With the Powerful and Revengeful Student

Make a Graceful Exit
    Acknowledge student's power
    Remove the audience
    Table the matter
    Make a date
    Use a fogging technique:
        Agree with the student
        Change the subject
Use Time Out
    Time out in the classroom
    Time out in another classroom
    Time out in the office
    Time out in the home
    Enforcing time out
        The language of choice
        The "who squad"
        Setting the duration for time out
Set the Consequence
    Establish consequences
    Present consequences
    Guidelines for effective consequences
        Related consequences
        Reasonable consequences
        Respectful consequences
    Consequences versus punishments
    Choose the consequence
        Loss or delay of activity
        Loss or delay of using objects or equipment
        Loss or delay of access to school areas
        Denied interactions with other students
        Required interactions with school personnel
        Required interactions with parents
        Required interactions with police
        Restitution
          Repair of objects
          Replacement of objects
        Student response to consequences

Figure 4–7 Nonsocially Adaptive Students: Power and Revenge.
Source: From L. Albert. 1989. A Teacher's Guide to Cooperative Discipline: How to Manage Your Classroom and Promote Self-Esteem. *Circle Pines, MN: American Guidance Service, Inc., pp. 72–83. Reprinted with permission.*

help? (3) Do I feel rebuffed when I try to reach out? (4) Do I feel like saying, "You don't care so I don't care"? (5) Do other students see this child as invisible?

As with the other three mistaken goals, the teacher moves to ask the Dreikurs question for the student experiencing helplessness: "Could it be that you want to be left alone?"

If there is a recognition reflex to this question, the teacher chooses appropriate strategies as suggested by Albert (1989) and listed in Figure 4–8.

Student's Motivation	Behavior Characteristics	Teacher's Feelings
Helplessness	Wishes not to be seen; passive and lethargic; rejects social contact; refuses to comply or try most educational demands	Inadequate, incapable

Techniques to Use With the Attention-Getting Student

Modify Instructional Methods
Use Concrete Learning Materials and Computer-Assisted Instruction
    Attractive
    Self-explanatory
    Self-correcting
    Reusable
Teach One Step at a Time
Provide Tutoring
    Extra help from teachers
    Remediation programs
    Adult volunteers
    Peer tutoring
    Learning centers
Teach Positive Self-talk
    Post positive classroom signs
    Require two "put-ups" for every put-down
    Encourage positive self-talk before beginning tasks
Make Mistakes Okay
    Talk about mistakes
    Equate mistakes with effort
    Minimize the effect of making mistakes
Build Confidence
    Focus on improvement
    Notice contributions
    Build on strengths
    Show faith in students
    Acknowledge the difficulty of a task
    Set time limits on tasks
Focus on Past Success
    Analyze past success
    Repeat past success
Make Learning Tangible
    "I-can" messages
    Accomplishment albums
    Checklists of skills
    Flowchart of concepts
    Talk about yesterday, today, and tomorrow
Recognize Achievement
    Applause
    Clapping and standing ovations
    Stars and stickers
    Awards and assemblies
    Exhibits
    Positive time-out
    Self-approval

Figure 4–8 Nonsocially Adaptive Students: Helplessness (Avoidance of Failure).
Source: From L. Albert. 1989. A Teacher's Guide to Cooperative Discipline: How to Manage Your Classroom and Promote Self-Esteem. *Circle Pines, MN: American Guidance Service, Inc., pp. 98–104. Reprinted with permission.*

Dreikurs's Social Discipline Model has also been referred to as the Logical Consequences Approach (Dreikurs & Loren, 1968). Dreikurs differentiates between *natural consequences* and *logical consequences*. Natural consequences occur without teacher intervention: a student runs to the bus and falls. The teacher's role is to point out to students the potential for natural consequences. Sometimes, just stating the likelihood of a natural consequence in a nonaccusing, very objective, calm voice is all that is needed to redirect a student's misbehavior.

NATURAL CONSEQUENCES STATED BY TEACHERS— EXAMPLES

Running: If you run, you may get hurt and hurt others.
Leaning back in chair: If you tilt back your chair, you may fall and get hurt or at least feel embarrassment.
Wasting class paper: If you use up all of our paper, we will not have any left to draw beautiful pictures.

On the other hand, the teacher must impose logical consequences. She must take some action to apply a logical consequence, and this consequence should be related to the misbehavior. For example, if a student pushes in line to get to the front, the teacher removes the student from the front, placing him at the end of the line. Some examples of logical consequences and guidelines for applying logical consequences are as follows:

EXAMPLES OF LOGICAL CONSEQUENCES

1. *Student destroys art materials.*   Teacher will not allow the student to use art materials for 1 week.
2. *Student plays during mathematics class.*   Teacher requires the student to finish mathematics during play or free time.
3. *Student spits on others during lunch.*   Teacher removes the child from others' tables. Teacher eats with the student, or if appropriate, the student eats alone.

GUIDELINES FOR APPLYING LOGICAL CONSEQUENCES

1. Tell the misbehaving student calmly what will happen if the misbehavior continues. Provide one warning: Diane keeps poking Roger with her ruler. Walk over to Diane and calmly say, "Diane, rulers are for measuring, not poking. You are showing that you cannot use your ruler correctly. If that happens again, I will take your ruler."
2. If the misbehavior happens again, follow through immediately. Go over and take Diane's ruler.
3. Be sure that Diane understands the logical connection between her choice of misbehavior and the loss of her ruler. Ask her why she has lost her ruler.
4. Match the severity and duration of consequence to the developmental level and age of the misbehaving student. For example, if Diane is 6 years old, you can return her ruler the next day. If Diane is 12 years old, she may receive a 0 on the mathematics assignment that required use of her ruler, which she lost by choice.

5. Provide encouragement for the next time in a way similar to the following, "You will have another chance tomorrow to show that you can use your ruler correctly."

Dreikurs emphasizes the importance of using encouragement rather than praise. He urges teachers to emphasize a student's improvement rather than a perfect product. Be sure to criticize the student's actions, but not the student, with statements such as "I care about you, but I really don't like to see you spitting on others." Try to put misbehaving students with other students who tolerate them well and are willing to help, if this is in the realm of possibility. Find a peer friend if you can. Also, refrain from using competition as a way to motivate the misbehaving student, especially when this student has no chance of winning.

LEARNING OUT LOUD 4–7

The following lists provide examples of praise and encouragement. Develop three more examples for both praise and encouragement. Share these with three peers. From this sharing session, choose the top three examples you wish to share with the whole class. Dreikurs prefers encouragement over praise. Do you agree or disagree? Why?

Praise

1. I (teacher) like your poem.
2. Wonderful work! What a bright student you are!
3. You get a bonus point (free time) for doing that.
4. I'm going to tell your parents and other students how proud I am of this work.
5. _____
6. _____
7. _____

Encouragement

1. You are improving.
2. You must be so pleased with this effort!
3. It must be a good feeling to know you're learning so much.
4. You have many reasons to feel pleased about your work.
5. _____
6. _____
7. _____

Glasser's Reality Therapy

The second discipline model in Confronting-Contracting is Glasser's work (1990). Glasser is probably one of the first to espouse the merits of self-regulation. He believes that methods such as TET and TA promote dependence on others and do not hold individuals accountable for their actions. He believes we all must live in the real world with others. Therefore, the rights of individuals must not infringe on the rights of others, and if they do, certain consequences must result. Even children who are disturbed, dependent, impoverished, or delinquent are not excused from appropriate behavior. Glasser's book, *Reality Therapy* (1975), sends the message that we all must make a commitment to act responsibly toward ourselves and others.

Glasser's views may sound harsh and severe. However, he also advocates care and warmth as the support foundation that expects and demands responsible behavior from others. It is within this climate of trust and love that others become self-regulated.

Glasser's book *Schools Without Failure* (1969) caused educators to reevaluate the relevancy of school to children's lives. In his more recent books, *Control Theory in the Classroom* (1986) and *The Quality School: Managing Students Without Coercion* (1992), Glasser updates his language and modernizes his philosophical positions. However, his basic contributions to classroom discipline remain the same. Figure 4–9 lists Glasser's 10 Steps to Discipline.

Step 1:	What am I doing? (The teacher asks this question of himself or herself to gain an intellectual awareness of self, rather than a stereotypical reflex response involving a narrow set of predictable teacher behaviors that are not working and may be making things worse.)
Step 2:	Is it working? If not, stop doing it. (A directive by the teacher to himself or herself based on Step 1.)
Step 3:	Recognition. (The teacher should give the student "the time of day" and establish an informal relationship with the misbehaving student during the times the child is not misbehaving, in order to personalize himself or herself to the child.)
Step 4:	What are you doing? (This question is directed to the child, delivered without guilt, as a genuine request for the child to reflect cognitively on his or her behavior. If the child cannot remember, remind the student what he or she did.)
Step 5:	Is it against the rules? (The teacher asks the student this question, again for cognitive reflection.)
Step 6:	Work it out and make a plan. (The student is counseled on how he or she may act whenever this incident occurs again. The teacher and student now have an agreement on what the student's behavior will be in the future. The plan may be solemnized with a handshake or written out and signed by both parties.)
Step 7:	Isolate from the class: within the classroom. (Used only in elementary school—what Glasser calls "off to the castle" or to a chair at the back of the classroom.)
Step 8:	Isolate from the class: out of the classroom. (in-school suspension or a time-out room in the building.)
Step 9:	Send the student home.
Step 10:	Get professional help. (Ask parents to get psychological help for the child and possibly improve parenting skills through counseling for themselves.)

Figure 4–9   Glasser's 10 Steps to Discipline.
Source: From Solving Discipline Problems: Methods and Models for Today's Teachers, *by C. H. Wolfgang, ©1999, New York: John Wiley & Sons. This material is used with permission of John Wiley & Sons.*

Glasser is opposed to many of the everyday happenings in schools across America today, including the following:

Opposed to:	Because:
1. Grades	1. Decrease or eliminate students' motivation to learn
2. School curriculum	2. Most is irrelevant and unmeaningful to students' real lives
3. Top-down approach to running schools	3. Demoralizing to front-line educators
4. Mandated standardized testing	4. Not relevant and poor measure of success
5. Comparative scores, especially those published in newspapers	5. Disregard the learning that does take place in schools

This is not a complete list of Glasser's points of opposition. However, it provides a sampling of his perspectives.

A Discussion of Glasser's 10 Steps.   The first two steps are teacher self-questions. This reflection encourages teachers to explore what they are or are not doing in the classroom that may be contributing to the misbehavior. In Step 2, if teachers determine that their discipline plan or steps are not working, they should *stop* using them and develop a fresh, new approach. Glasser issues a very basic directive: if it isn't working, stop doing it!

In step 3, teachers show their human side to their students during the school day when misbehavior is not occurring. For example, the teacher might eat lunch with the group who were too noisy during science class, or she might ask Sam about his new baby brother. Actions such as these help teachers build relationships and build community with their students.

The *what* questions are the confronting part of Glasser's approach. Making strong eye contact with a student and asking, "What are you doing?" is one of the most powerful discipline questions we can use. Do not ask students, "Why are you doing that?" They either do not know why or will not tell you—you usually just receive the "raised-shoulder" response and a look of "I don't know, and even if I did, I wouldn't tell you." However, asking, "What are you doing?" usually elicits a response. Once the student has told you what he is doing, ask step 5: "Is it against the rules?"

If the student does not respond to your *what* question or gives you an inaccurate response about what he is doing, say to the student, "I see you are playing with the manipulatives in the back of the room." A sample narrative with steps 4–6 follows:

Yolando is playing with the math manipulatives in the back of the room during language arts writing time.

Teacher to Yolando:	*Yolando, what are you doing back there? (step 4)*
Yolando to Teacher:	*Oh, I'm getting my writing folder.*
Teacher:	*Your writing folder is at your desk. I see you are playing with the manipulatives. (step 4)*
Teacher:	*What are you supposed to be doing now? (step 5 modified)*
Yolando:	*Writing my story.*
Teacher:	*So what's your plan for getting your story written? (step 6)*

You may have noticed that the teacher did not use step 5, asking Yolando if her activity was against the rules, precisely as Glasser proposed. Instead, the teacher modified step 5 to: "What are you supposed to be doing right now?" If Yolando had been engaged in an activity that was against the school or class rules, such as calling out answers without raising her hand, the teacher could have asked, "Is it against the rules?" As teachers, you should make Glasser's 10 steps work for you, modifying them as needed. The intent of getting students to assume responsibility for their behavior or misbehavior in classrooms by verbally claiming it is the important point, not whether we ask Glasser's questions verbatim.

Glasser, in step 5, makes reference to "rules." The following example provides some of teacher's rules. (See also chapter 3.)

EXAMPLE RULES

1. ***I work quietly and until I am finished.*** I say this to myself when I am working to make sure I'm not bothering my friends and so I can be proud of myself when I finish all of my work.
2. ***I keep my hands, feet, and objects to myself.*** I say this to myself when I feel like I need to touch or hit someone, or when I see others fighting. It helps keep me out of trouble.
3. ***I listen carefully.*** I ask myself if I am listening carefully during lessons and when my teacher is giving directions to make sure I understand what she is saying. If I don't, I can ask a question.
4. ***I raise my hand and get a signal to speak.*** I say this to myself when I have something to share out loud so I don't talk out and interrupt my teacher or a friend. I also remember to do this when my teacher asks questions so my friends have time to think about the answer.
5. ***I walk quietly and calmly in the halls.*** This is what I say to myself when I am walking in the halls so I don't disturb others who are in their classrooms trying to work.
6. ***I use good manners at all times.*** I say this to myself when I am in the restroom or at lunch to make sure I am being polite.

In step 6, Glasser suggests writing a "plan." This plan is often called a *contract*, especially if it is written. Students should be held responsible for making written plans to commit to their own plan of action to improve or change their behavior. Figure 4–10 is a sample written plan.

My Problem-Solving Plan

What happened?

What can I do to make things better? (My plan is. . ..)

How am I using my plan? (I am. . ..)

Figure 4–10   A Sample Lower-Elementary Self-Plan.

My Goal Story Interview

1. What is one thing I really want and why do I want it?

_____

_____

2. What is my plan of action to get it? Write the plan on the lines below.

_____

_____

3. Name an obstacle that blocks my efforts to get what I want. What is the obstacle?

_____

_____

4. How can I alter my plan so I can overcome the obstacle and realize my dreams? How can I use my self-talk skills of reinforcing myself to obtain my goal?

_____

_____

_____

_____

5. If I cannot overcome the obstacle, how can I use my self-talk skills of coping to make myself feel better?

_____

_____

_____

Figure 4–11   A Sample Upper-Elementary Goal Story Interview.
Source: Adapted from Self-Talk for Teachers and Students *by B. H. Manning and B. D. Payne, 1996, Needham Heights, MA: Allyn & Bacon, pp. 192–193.*

For step 6, the goal story interview technique provides a way to prepare upper-elementary students for the achievement of goals and the blocking of our goals via self-talk skills of coping and reinforcing (see Figure 4–11). The goal story interview was first introduced by Goldman (1982) and modified by Manning (1991) to include a self-talk component.

Teachers of third through eighth graders find the goal-setting chart a useful tool in practicing self-regulated learning skills (see Figure 4–12). Students self-monitor whether they have successfully completed a goal, and have their parents sign the form after discussing it with them at the end of each week.

Glasser's steps 7 and 8 advocate isolation, which is more commonly called *time-out*. In step 7, time-out occurs in the student's own classroom. For step 8, the student is isolated in a peer teacher's room. Some schools have special rooms provided for time-out called in-school suspension (ISS) or opportunity rooms (ORs). Whether a student is timed out within or outside the regular classroom, the teacher should assign and review a student-developed plan (in writing) that must be signed by the parent.

Goal-Setting Chart

Name _____

You are responsible for monitoring yourself each week. At the end of each week, please bring home this chart, discuss your progress for the week, and choose a goal to work on for the next week. Be sure to have your parents sign the form and return it to school on Monday!

MY GOAL FOR THIS WEEK IS TO WORK ON: _____

MY GOAL FOR NEXT WEEK IS TO IMPROVE: _____

	MON.	TUES.	WED.	THURS.	FRI.
I have my materials ready.					
I have completed my homework.					
I worked independently.					
I did not disturb others.					
I worked well in a group.					
I listened and followed directions.					
I asked good questions.					
I used my time wisely.					
I talked to myself in helpful ways.					

Signatures:

Student _____   Parent _____

Teacher _____

Figure 4–12   A Sample Goal-Setting Chart.

In step 9, Glasser says simply, "Send the student home." This means that steps 1–8 have been implemented without success. Glasser's steps are ordered, and you should stop at the lowest number possible. Having attempted steps 1–8, the parents should now share in the responsibility for turning this child around toward appropriate social behavior in the classroom.

In the event that the parents are not capable or are unwilling to assist with their child's behavior at school, Glasser goes to his last step, step 10. Here, we move from family intervention to community intervention: Get professional help. Occasionally you will teach a student whose misbehavior is beyond your realm of expertise. This happens to all of us who teach for any reasonable period of time. When it does, know that it is okay to say, "This child's misbehavior is such that I must ask for support outside the school." Turn first to the parents (step 9) and then to the community resources (step 10). If you have gone through steps 1–8 and have kept your principal well-informed, do not hesitate to take steps 9 and 10.

Glasser's Classroom Meetings

Teachers everywhere use Glasser's structure for classroom meetings. Figure 4–10 lists several characteristics that distinguish classroom meetings ala Glasser. Within the problem-solving meeting, specific student problems that affect others can be raised for discussion. We hasten to add that careful steps must be taken in classroom meetings in which an individual student's problems are discussed. Wolfgang (1995) outlines the following typical problems.

1. Meetings are held (a) to deal with individual students' problems, (b) to revise the classroom organization, and (c) to develop curriculum.
2. There are three types of meetings:
   a. Open-ended—Students discuss divergent issues that concern them, such as: What are your dreams for the future? What will the world be like in 50 years?
   b. Educational/diagnostic—The teacher introduces a curriculum issue or topic to find out students' prior knowledge, gaps or misconceptions in knowledge, and areas of greatest interest related to the topic. This information is used by the teacher to plan curriculum units, projects, and evaluation.
   c. Problem solving—Students focus on authentic, classroom-based problems that affect the whole class. They define the problem carefully, supply missing information, come up with a solution, and agree upon a plan that they will all follow, including the teacher. Examples include: What can we do about cheating in the class? How can we stop hallway noise? How can we get started with class promptly?

Figure 4–13   Glasser's Characteristics of Classroom Meetings.
Source: From Solving Discipline Problems: Methods and Models for Today's Teachers, *by C. H. Wolfgang, ©1999, New York: John Wiley & Sons. This material is used by permission of John Wiley & Sons.*

1. The teacher asks each student to express openly what this target student has recently done to interfere with him or her personally. The students are asked to tell the target student, face-to-face, what those behaviors are and what effects they have had on them (emotionally and/or physically).
2. After all have had their chance to speak (including the teacher), the misbehaving student is given an opportunity to explain what others have done to interfere with him or her.
3. The teacher suggests that the class and the offending child may be able to offer some possible solutions to the problem— ones that would be agreeable to all. The teacher listens to all ideas and then asks the group to narrow down the alternative plan and ideas that were offered.
4. Finally, the target student is asked to select a plan and commit himself or herself to it. At the same time, the members of the class (including the teacher) commit themselves to carrying out any actions that will help the target student in implementing his or her plan.

Figure 4–14   Glasser's Steps for Conducting a Meeting About an Individual Student-Specific Problem.
Source: From Solving Discipline Problems: Methods and Models for Today's Teachers, *by C. H. Wolfgang, ©1999, New York: John Wiley & Sons. This material is used by permission of John Wiley & Sons.*

- A student who "hogs" the gym equipment (balls, bats, frisbees, and the like)
- A student who physically pushes other students around
- A student who constantly distracts others from working by making loud noises, talking, and so forth
- A student who takes items from others
- A student who plays cruel "tricks" on others (locks children in the closets, writes on others' homework, and so on)
- A student who tries to be boss all the time, who is always telling others what to do but will not accept any criticism of self

You may believe that having classroom meetings to address such issues is too harsh and risky. If fact, we recommend that you not use the specific student focus for topics in classroom meetings during student teaching or even in your first year of teaching. However, after your first year or so, you may feel comfortable enough to try this strategy if it seems appropriate. If you use individual student-specific problems, be aware of the guidelines listed in Figure 4–11 from Wolfgang (1999) and Figure 4–12. Again, this type of meeting is not held to embarrass, humiliate, blame, or punish a student. Instead, it is a way to let the target student know

1. Meetings are held regularly and no less than once per week for 30 minutes (grades K–4) or 45–60 minutes (grades 4–8).
2. It is best to have the meetings at the same time each week (e.g., before lunch on Fridays).
3. Back the meeting to a natural close because it is often difficult to stop a very active discussion (e.g., have right before PE, music, lunch, or dismissal).
4. The teacher must always meet with the group and take an active role to monitor in order to ensure that the meeting discussions stay within bounds of physical and psychological safety (e.g., no name calling or derogatory remarks are permitted).
5. The class always sits in a tight circle facing each other, usually on a rug, sometimes in chairs.
6. The teacher sits in a different location in the circle in order to vary who she or he sits next to and to continue sending the message that she or he is also a participant in the meeting, not the ruler of the meeting.
7. The topics can be suggested (perhaps in a class suggestion box) by any student or the teacher. Decide the topic in advance of the meeting and post the topic, if possible.
8. The teacher stresses the following game rules for classroom meetings:
   a. There are no wrong answers.
   b. Everyone should talk and feel free to express ideas, feelings, beliefs, and opinions.
   c. The teacher has the right to express his or her opinions, beliefs, feelings, and ideas in the same manner as each student. Teacher expressions carry no more weight than student expressions.
   d. Students are asked to keep conversation in the present or the future, rather than dwelling in the past.
   e. No one is allowed to disparage or insult when addressing others or speaking about others.
9. Students are not forced to speak if they do not wish to comment.
10. Students are not required to raise hands to speak, but should not interrupt each other. Younger students may enjoy throwing a big beach ball to the person who starts talking to help him or her learn the patterns of conversation. No one talks unless he or she is holding the beach ball and no one should hold the beach ball too long.

Figure 4–15   Steps for Conducting Classroom Meetings.

directly that her behavioral choices are violating the rights of others. This is the reality part of Reality Therapy. Beyond making the target student cognizant of her actions and their results, the meeting's purpose is to find acceptable solutions for all involved.

Rules–Consequences/Intervention

Another model in the psychological school of thought is called Rules and Consequences (Wolfgang, 1995; 1999). Canter and Canter's (1976) Assertive Discipline was chosen to represent this area because many of their ideas are prevalent in our schools today. However, from the perspective of this text (i.e., fostering self-regulated learners [SRLs]), the psychological models of Gordon's TET and Berne and Harris's TA in the relationship-listening area, and Dreikurs's Social Discipline Model and Glasser's Reality Therapy in the Confronting-Contracting area are more closely aligned to SRL. The Relationship-Listening and especially the Confronting-Contracting models appear best suited to foster students who are more motivated and equipped to engage in self-regulation for learning and school behavior. Therefore, we address only one model from Rules and Consequences to give the full spectrum of eclecticism for classroom discipline intervention techniques.

Canters' Assertive Discipline

In 1976, Lee and Marlene Canter introduced their book *Assertive Discipline*. The Assertive Discipline model was derived from assertiveness training from publications such as *Stand*

Up, Speak Out, Talk Back (Alberti & Emmons, 1975) and *When I Say No I Feel Guilty* (Smith, 1975). Three response styles to conflict include being *nonassertive* (passive, allowing others to take advantage of us), *hostile* (overly assertive toward others using harsh, loud, vindictive reprimands), and *assertive* (speaking up in a calm, rational tone of voice that objectively reports our rights and responsibilities).

The Canters applied these three response styles to the classroom context. They provided workshops, with packaged videotapes and workbooks, to "train" teachers. This exposure has been widespread. It is very rare for a teacher not to be exposed to the Canters' approach and materials. This is the main reason why we have included the approach in this text on self-regulated teaching and learning: to make teachers aware of this approach so they are not blindsided by it when they enter teaching.

The Canters' Assertive Discipline model is based on three value statements for classroom teachers. Canter and Canter (1992) assert that teachers have the right and responsibility to (1) establish rules that define limits of acceptable and unacceptable behavior; (2) teach students to consistently follow these rules, and (3) ask for assistance from parents and administrators when students are not following these rules.

Steps of Canters' Assertive Discipline

1. First, the teacher writes a discipline plan and has the principal approve it. The plan is informed by the Canters' suggestions for Assertive Discipline (see steps 4–12).

2. Next, the plan is sent home to the parents for them to read, provide any suggestions, sign, and return to the teacher. A final published copy is given to the principal, parents, and students.

3. The teacher posts the plan on the chalkboard and teaches it to the students through a "Say, Show, and Check" process. She explains the plan carefully, models and role-plays the plan, and double-checks that each student comprehends the plan.

4. The plan must include classroom rules that are posted in writing. The Canters provide suggestions for rules with the directions that these rules should be specific, observable, and relevant across the school day. They say students should be involved in making rules, if possible. However, in the end, the teacher has the final word.

This list provides some typical rules that are needed "to run" a classroom (Canter & Canter, 1992, p. 50):

- Follow directions
- Keep hands, feet, and objects to yourself
- No profanity or teasing
- No eating
- Walk in the classroom
- Do not leave the classroom without permission
- No yelling or screaming

5. Provide positive reinforcement and recognition through praise, positive notes sent to parents, marbles dropped in jars, or special privileges. Other positive relationship builders are suggested by the Canters, such as greeting students at your classroom door, making home visits, sending get-well cards to sick children, and inquiring about students' special interests.

6. The teacher must establish a clear set of consequences that will be applied if students do not follow the classroom rules. A sample schedule of consequences follows:

Consequences Plan

a. First time a student breaks a rule	Teacher issues a warning
b. Second time rule is broken	Student stays in class 1 minute after the bell
c. Third time rule is broken	Student stays in class 2 minutes after the bell
d. Fourth time rule is broken	Teacher calls parents
e. Fifth time rule is broken	Teacher sends student to the principal

7. Canters' Assertive Discipline Plan calls for a severity clause that the teacher can invoke at any time if the student's misbehavior becomes dangerous to self, classmates, or school property. Therefore, the teacher needs to publicly display the consequence plan, including a severity clause.

Severity Clause: Send to the principal

8. When students break the rules, teachers view this as the students' choice, and they assert their authority by repeating statements similar to the following: "Steven, you have chosen to break our no-running rule. Therefore, you have chosen to lose 1 minute of your time after class."

9. The teacher always has the right to teach and to expect students to follow the established, approved, taught, and posted rules.

10. The Canters revised their position of putting misbehaving students' names on the board with checks after them for offenses. Instead, they now recommend that misbehaving students' names should go privately in a discipline folder or gradebook. A Behavior Tracking Sheet can be copied if you buy the Canters' workbook.

11. When students are sent to the principal, it is not for corporal punishment. Also, the Canters recommend that time-out/isolation be used very cautiously and for only a few minutes for younger students and not in excess of 1 hour for middle school or high school students.

12. Use the Canters' Who-Squad after a rule has been broken for the fifth time. In the event a student refuses to go to the principal's office and is openly defiant toward the teacher, the teacher uses two previously written letters that are kept in his or her desk for easy accessibility. One of the letters is addressed to a peer teacher who is close by, while the other is for the principal. A well-behaved student is asked to deliver both letters. The letters ask both to come immediately to escort the rebellious student from the classroom. The peer teacher and principal come to the classroom, ask "Who?", and the teacher points to the target student. The target student is escorted from the classroom by the Who Squad (peer teacher and principal) to the principal's office for counseling and, perhaps, negative consequences.

13. Teachers should use the lowest level of teacher verbal commands to discipline the class or individual students. For example, they should not use a strong I-message if a hint will get the job done. Examples of each level of assertive authority are provided next. Begin with "a" and proceed to "d" as needed.

a. ***Teacher hint***   "Everyone should be working on his or her mathematics assignment."
b. ***Teacher question***   "Is everyone working on mathematics?"
c. ***Teacher I-message***   "I want all eyes on the math worksheet." Note that Canters' I-messages are very different from Gordon's three-component I-messages. Canter and Canter recommend that teachers begin I-messages with *I want*

(teacher directive) or *I need* (teacher directive). "*I want* quiet in this classroom now." "*I need* to hear total silence."

d. ***Teacher demand ("Broken Record" technique)***   Repeat for a maximum of five times what you want or need in the classroom, as the teacher, without allowing students' interruptions to distract you with their wants or needs.

14. In the Canters' later work (1992, 1993), they add suggestions for classroom practice that are similar to Jones's positive discipline approaches (Wolfgang, 1995, p. 264). These remind the teacher to *scan the room to praise students who are on task; circulate around the room* instead of staying behind the teacher's desk and, finally, *redirect students* by (a) "the look," (b) mentioning the student's name during the lesson, (c) proximity praise-praising the behavior of students who sit near the misbehaving student to alert him or her to the appropriate behavior and, finally, (d) praising the target student when he or she complies.

Many instructional media, books, and workbooks have been written by the Canters and their associates. For a comprehensive list, see Wolfgang, 1995, pages 265–269.

LEARNING OUT LOUD 4–8

Consider the 14 characteristics of Canters' Assertive Discipline. With two or three peers, generate a list of advantages and disadvantages to this approach. Would you use Canters' Assertive Discipline? If so, what components? If not, why not? Be prepared to debate, one team representing the advantages of the Canters' approach and the other team representing the disadvantages of Canters' Assertive Discipline.

Coercive–Legalistic/Intervention

If we refer back to Figure 4–1, which depicts many discipline models (Wolfgang, 1999) across the four categories of Relationship-Listening, Confronting-Contracting, Rules and Consequences, and Coercive-Legalistic, we can see the path taken in this chapter. The final discussion will be a short one—pointing out that teachers today and, most likely, teachers of tomorrow, need to verse themselves thoroughly in their legal rights and responsibilities. It is unfortunate that teachers must always be on guard for student violence, as well as other legally volatile situations. For example, teachers are required by law to make a reasonable attempt to break up fights. While today's schools are potentially places where students assault teachers and their peers, the education and safety of our children remain the primary focus of teachers. This has always been the case for exemplary teachers. However, alongside the commitment for outstanding curriculum and instruction that fosters the development of self-regulated learning is the need for back-up knowledge and skills to identify and manage violence toward you or your students.

It is beyond the expertise of the authors of this text and also beyond the scope of this book to provide you with a thorough grounding in the Coercive-Legalistic perspective. You may want to read Wolfgang's (1995) chapter 11, titled "Managing Student Violent Assaults and Breaking Up Student Fights" as a starting point. Another important resource is *Special Education Discipline Law* (2002) by Dr. John Dayton, professor, former attorney, and former public school educator.

LEARNING OUT LOUD 4–9

Divide yourselves into teams of four. Each team should identify a helpful reading for teachers related to the area of managing student violence and teachers' legal rights and responsibilities. This can be a book chapter or a scholarly article. Prepare a team presentation for your classmates. Fill out the form provided in Figure 4–13 called an RRR—Recent Related Reading. Make a copy for each of your classmates and your teacher.

Also, if possible, have each team invite an expert (e.g., a law professor well-versed in school law, a principal who has exemplary school guidelines to address school violence, etc.) to serve on a panel presenting information about the Coercive-Legalistic perpective.

Name

Title of Reading

Author(s)

Bibliographic Information

Main Purpose of Reading

Highlights/Key Points

Conclusions

Application Ideas

Recommendations for Other Teachers About This Reading

Figure 4–13   Recent Related Reading (RRR) Summary.

Summary

Chapter 4 discussed intervention strategies and discipline models. These strategies and models are organized around Wolfgang's eclectic approach (1999) to classroom discipline problems. Starting with minimum teacher power and more child-centered approaches, we begin with the Relationship-Listening category; followed by the Confronting-Contracting category, which sees the teacher taking a more active role in discipline strategies; followed next by the Rules and Consequences category in which teacher power is stepped up and teacher-centered approaches take center stage. Finally, we only nod at the Coercive-Legalistic, maximum-teacher-power perspective and recommend sincerely and enthusiastically that teachers educate themselves about these issues through self-assigned readings, resources, and outside experts.

We discuss in depth two models each for Relationship-Listening (RL) (i.e., Gordon's TET and Berne and Harris's TA); and for Confronting-Contracting (CC) (i.e., Dreikurs' Social Discipline and Glasser's Reality Therapy). We provide extensive treatment of RL and CC because these strategies are more closely akin to the self-regulated focus of this text. We overview briefly only one model for Rules and Consequences (RC) (i.e., Canters' Assertive Discipline) and point teachers in the direction of informing themselves about their legal rights and responsibilities, especially in the area of student violence.

This chapter serves as an introduction to the wide array of choices teachers must make about how they will develop the learning community in their classroom. We believe that the diverse classroom populations of today necessitate an eclectic approach to intervention techniques to foster the maximum learning. It is our hope, however, that you will be able to choose minimum-teacher-power models and strategies to foster the maximum student-centered regulation. In general, we believe too many discipline approaches neglect the central aim of education: to foster optimal student learning via self-regulated learning approaches. In fact, in most of the RL, CC, and RC approaches, student learning is not explicitly addressed. In chapter 5, the aim of each concrete application is explicitly connected to student learning and achievement.

From Teacher as Planner to Teacher as Strategist

Planning to Promote Learner Responsibility

Self-Questions

Knowledge: Provide examples of content standards for a particular lesson you are creating.

Comprehension: Explain the basic premise of service learning.

Application: Write a lesson plan, beginning by planning backwards to envision what students should know and be able to do by the end of your lesson.

Analysis: Analyze key elements of curriculum integration and service learning and show how the two models of learning overlap.

Synthesis: Design a self-assessment component of learning using components of effective lesson planning. Describe how this plan helps students fulfill goals of self-regulated learning.

Evaluation: Debate the pros and cons of curriculum integration.

Introduction

Effective planning involves critical decision making about what you want students to learn and why such learning is important. Classroom organization and management decisions should be an integral part of planning. Your philosophical stance about curriculum influences every aspect of instruction, so we believe it is important for you to analyze your beliefs about your role in curriculum development and implementation as you develop as a teacher.

While you consider each aspect of planning discussed in this chapter, we hope you will continually reflect on your views of learners and learning, about teachers and their power to design and implement curriculum, and ways to meet standards of learning that fit naturally with how a child learns.

This chapter introduces you to many components of planning and analyzing instruction in ways that promote learner responsibility in a responsive classroom. You will learn about developing lesson plans, writing goals and objectives, assessing learning, and creating curriculum. We examine curriculum integration and community service learning as methods to engage students in active learning that fosters responsibility. Additionally, we consider the importance of developing a strong home school connection in meeting student needs.

Planning

Planning Backwards

One approach to planning that emphasizes student learning is called *planning backwards*. McDonald describes this concept in a 1992 article published in *Teachers College Record*. The essence of the planning backwards model is that a teacher begins by envisioning what a student should know and be able to do at the end of a lesson or unit if he has gained an understanding of the material, and then asks herself or himself, "How do I help students get there?" As the teachers in the ETEP program at the University of Southern Maine continually think about the impact of lesson and unit activities on student learning, they maintain the mindset of "planning backwards" from the knowledge and habits of mind they envision students possessing to the orchestration of activities to help students reach these goals. Interns within the ETEP program are required to document steps they have taken to move their students forward based on formative and summative assessment data. Having practiced goal-directed accountability in their own preparation program, the ETEP graduates are more likely to include self-assessment in their practice and understand how self-regulated learning can improve motivation, reflection, and understanding.

For example, in a study of the ETEP program, Whitford, Ruscoe, and Fickel (2000) observed several ETEP graduates during their first year of teaching:

> During our observation, Mr. Fogg is showing his students how to complete self-assessments, which concerns items such as attitude, attention to task, homework completion and quality, and class participation. Each student is to rate the items from "needs improvement" to "very good."

Later, Mr. Fogg will review these evaluations and indicate where he disagrees with their assessments. If necessary, he will ask students for signatures from parents in order to alert them to potential problems.... As illustrated by the student self-evaluation exercise, Mr. Fogg emphasizes the importance of students accepting responsibility for their own learning—and getting parents involved where necessary. (pp. 186, 188)

As we continue to discuss elements of planning, consider how you can integrate the concept of planning backwards into your thinking about learning to teach.

Developing Lesson Plans That Are Logically Sequenced

Lesson plans can be viewed as a blueprint for instruction. Plans can help you think through the what, how, and why of a lesson (Riner, 2000). Usually, a lesson plan is created for a single lesson and can be combined with other lesson plans around the same topic or subject to form a unit (Eby, 1998). The value of a lesson plan reaches well beyond the one day it is used. Lesson plans can be shared with other teachers, administrators, and parents, and can serve as an excellent resource from year to year. As a beginning teacher, it is important that you make all of your instructional intentions explicit. As you construct detailed lesson plans, this "blueprint" can help you think through each important step of your lesson. The processes of sequencing the lesson, teaching the objectives, planning for materials and transitions, and checking for understanding are so imperative that it is essential for beginning teachers to convey these steps explicitly. After you gain experience teaching and you have internalized the process of planning, you may find it unnecessary to write so many details. While some teachers find detailed plans comforting in that they can refer to them throughout the lesson, other experienced teachers find that outlined notes or sketches of their lessons are sufficient.

It is no surprise, then, that the actual lesson plan form varies from teacher to teacher and year to year. However, most lesson plans contain similar elements. Figure 5–1 details suggested parts of a lesson plan and their intended uses.

LEARNING OUT LOUD 5–1

Observe a school or university instructor during a lesson. Can you identify the different parts of the lesson? What would a lesson plan for the instruction look like? What components of the lesson seemed to be adjusted or based on what happened during the lesson?

Figure 5–2 shows a lesson plan written and taught by Stanulis. The lesson plan reflects the format components outlined thus far.

By practicing writing lessons plans in a detailed format, you can internalize the process of planning. Soon you will automatically plan your lessons this way, each time thinking about the components of a lesson plan and how to best implement the plan in your class.

Goals

The goals of a unit are the broad objectives for the whole unit of curriculum. Goals help both teachers and students focus on what is to be learned. Goals help teachers direct their instruction, while they help students realize what they will be learning during the course of study. Because they are not specific to a particular lesson, it may take several lessons to accomplish a particular goal. Teachers may have just one goal in mind for a unit, or several (Wood, 1997).

Objectives:
Objectives should reflect depth of content and both higher- and lower-level thinking skills.

Content Standards:
Each lesson plan should be based on helping students achieve the learning standards outlined by county, state, and national professional organizations.

Materials:
List the materials you will use in each activity. Be sure to include copies of the materials if possible (e.g., activities, student edition pages, word lists, game directions) and describe material that cannot be included with the lesson plan.

Introduction (include time estimate):
The introduction is a quick, focusing activity that describes how you will start the lesson. How will you explain its purpose to students? You should plan a stimulating, motivating introduction to help ensure students' attention to the lesson. How are you conceptually connecting the lesson to other lessons? How are you involving students in creating and/or knowing the lesson objectives?

Procedures (include time estimate for each activity):
This section describes lesson activities that help students develop the knowledge and skills you have envisioned they might have by the close of the lesson. Plan backwards to check that the activities *do* connect to the objectives, content, and assessment. Be sure to include enough activities per objective to increase the likelihood that students will learn the material. This is the bulk of the lesson plan.

Closure (include time estimate):
This is a brief summary of the lesson provided by you or the students to check for understanding, make connections, raise further questions, and draw lesson to a close. It may also include (if appropriate) a transition to the next lesson. Closure typically occurs at the end of the lesson, but may be done at the end of group work before students go on to work on individual projects, or before a whole-group session breaks into small-group work.

Assessment/Evaluation:
Describe how you and the student will know if the student has achieved each objective. Describe indicators of achievement. Assessment may be on going (formative) or may occur at the end of the lesson (summative).

Modifications:
Describe the adaptations in materials, procedures, or assessment you will make for students who have differing needs.

Reflections:
This section is completed after the lesson plan is implemented. Discuss what you learned from teaching the lesson. What went well? What unexpected things happened and how well did you handle them? What evidence do you have that students learned? Write specific examples of student learning. How could the lesson be improved? What would you do differently?

Figure 5–1   Sample Lesson Plan Format.

For example, Tiffany House, a second-grade teacher designing a unit on dinosaurs, identified one broad goal that she wanted to accomplish with her unit: *The students will develop a greater knowledge base and understanding of the dinosaurs and the period of history in which they lived.* Notice how her goal identified the overall purpose of the unit from a long-term perspective. By looking at just the unit goals, it would be unclear as to what each individual lesson would address, but we do know that by the time the unit is completed, Ms. House's students will have a good understanding of the dinosaurs and the time in which they lived.

Wood (1997) identifies three types of general goals: content, attitudinal (affective), and process objectives (Figure 5–3). Each type of objective has a different purpose, although all point to an overall goal of the entire unit.

Objectives

Objectives are more specific than goals and are typically accomplished within one lesson. You can think of the objective of the lesson as answering the questions "Why?" and "What?" in your lesson plan. *Why* should the students learn the material? *What* should

Objectives:
1. The learners will identify different things that the wind can and cannot do.
2. The learners will demonstrate concrete examples of how moving air (wind) is part of weather.
3. The learners will perform their own interpretation of the story.
4. The learners will respond to a story's content.

Content Standards:

Speech Communication Association—Third-grade oral communication competencies
Demonstrate the ability to dramatize a story
Demonstrate the use of pantomime as a means of nonverbal communication

National Science Education Standards—Weather changes from day to day and over the seasons. Weather can be described by measurable quantities such as temperature, wind direction and speed, and precipitation.

Planning Backwards—How I envision the learners by the end of the lesson:

General—I hope to see students swirling around the room with their wind scarves, demonstrating understanding of wind through performance and discussion.

Specific—I want the third-grade students to build upon their knowledge of weather by learning about concrete things that the wind can and cannot do. I want them to experience different ways the wind works by performing narrative pantomime with the text. I want them to create their own interpretation as they use the scarves to depict the wind. Finally, through active participation in performing things the wind can do, I hope to engage students in a discussion about the content of the story. Because students are actively participating in acting out the story, I expect increased comprehension.

Materials and Setting:
Gilberto and the Wind, by Marie Hall
26 scarves (1 per student + me)
We will use the center of the classroom where we ordinarily sit together for whole-group literature reading.

Introduction (5–10 minutes):
1. Review yesterday's discussion of weather storms, including how storms are a combination of air, heat, and water mixed together.
2. As students describe their various experiences with storms, help probe their developing understanding of wind. What are some things the wind can do? What questions do we have about wind?
3. Today we are going to read a book about a little boy who finds out all kinds of things that the wind can and cannot do.

Procedures (30–35 minutes):
1. Read the book aloud. (The book is about "a tiny boy who finds in the wind a playmate of many moods; one that can sail boats, fly kites, slam gates, and turn umbrellas inside out.") Focus on listening for student understanding of things that the wind can do (move a gate that is unlatched), and can't do (move the gate with Gilberto holding onto the gate), and why the wind can or cannot do certain things.
2. Briefly describe pantomime, including clear directions for expectations. A pantomime is a way to play along with the actions of the story in a *silent* way. You can move around as the wind any way that you wish as long as you do not physically touch anyone else. We will pretend that the scarves are the wind, and move the scarves in different ways. Have students generate examples of the wind moving slowly (floating balloon away) and strongly (slamming gate) and not at all (no wind to fly kite) and practice what each might look like. *Emphasize that pantomime is a silent activity*.
3. Read book aloud again, using lots of expression as cues for different wind movement. Children can dance with scarves to illustrate different ways the wind works.
4. Collect scarves, and direct students back to seats. Each child now has the opportunity to respond to the literature by writing and/or drawing something that he or she has learned about the wind, including the kind of weather that causes this kind of wind. For example, what kind of weather might be happening when the wind slammed the gate? When there wasn't enough breeze to move the kite?

(continued)

Figure 5–2   Sample Lesson Plan by Stanulis.

students know and be able to do? The objectives of the lesson should tell what you, the teacher, want students to accomplish by the end of the instructional time. Objectives that are specific explain how the students can express their mastery of information. Teachers will have a better understanding about the learning that has taken place if the objectives are more precise. With a more specific objective, the teacher will have an accurate understanding of

Closure (5 minutes):
Discuss how they enjoyed being involved in a pantomime of the book content. In what ways did the activity help them learn? What did they learn? How do different things the wind can do link to weather.

Assessment:
Were the students able to listen to directions effectively, control their bodies and physical space, and be creative in their dramatic interpretations? What are some examples of particularly sound connections to aspects of weather? Who was not engaged? Collect student work and assess according to how students could link wind and weather.

Modifications:

Enrichment—Students can write their own story about wind.

Remediation—With individuals, act out certain kinds of wind and discuss links to weather using text pictures.Ω

Reflections:
Some students were hesitant to act out the wind. I need to remember that all learners do not enjoy dramatic activity. I wonder if I could structure the activity in a way that helps those students feel more comfortable? Maybe they could make wind noises, or hold up pictures of different kinds of weather associated with each kind of wind. I think I did an effective job giving detailed directions. Though they did get excited and weren't exactly silent, with enough practice with pantomime, they could learn to control their voices. They did a good job maintaining their own space. Some were incredibly creative in their wind movements. Their drawings illustrated that they made clear connections between the force of the wind and the kind of weather involved. Next time, I would like to make even stronger links between specific weather and the things the wind could and could not do in the story. I think I helped students make the abstract concept of "moving air" concrete through this experience.

Figure 5–2 Sample Lesson Plan by Stanulis. (*continued*)

Content Goals	Goal is to increase knowledge base. *Example*: The students will identify dinosaurs as reptiles.
Attitudinal Objective	Goal is to shape student attitudes about content. *Example*: The students will experience the work of a paleontologist.
Process Objectives	Goal is to engage the students in the process of learning the content. *Example*: The students will discuss and infer reasons that dinosaurs became extinct.

Figure 5–3 General Goals in Unit Planning.
Source: Adapted from Interdisciplinary Instruction: A Practical Guide for Elementary School Teachers, *by Karlyn L. Wood, ©1997. Adapted by permission of Pearson Education, Inc., Upper Saddle River, NJ.*

each child's ability to achieve the goal. Be careful in using such words as *know, understand,* and *show,* in objectives. When used alone, these words convey vagueness. Behaviors associated with learning should be described with specific terminology.

To promote learner responsibility, objectives should ideally be created with students, or at least shared with students. In addition, students should be actively involved in self-evaluation of their progress toward goals. Teachers should not view the goals as "my goals," but rather involve students in goal-setting, monitoring, and evaluating. Teaching for understanding involves students' reflection and evaluation on their own learning goals. According to Joseph McDonald (1992), who developed the planning backwards concept, objectives play a role in planning, but should not lock a teacher into a particular mode of instruction. If a teacher strictly adheres to a particular plan, saying "I have to reach this objective, I have to reach this objective," she is not considering how dynamic classroom life is, and the importance of the role of student ownership in determining the particular direction of a lesson.

Level 1: Knowledge
Objectives indicate that students are able to remember and provide facts.
The student will be able to list four body parts involved in the digestive process.

Level 2: Comprehension
Students are asked to explain, elaborate, summarize, or demonstrate material in their own words that indicates their understanding.
The student will be able to explain the steps of the digestive process.

Level 3: Application
Students use problem-solving techniques to apply the new information to a new situation.
The learner will describe what happens as a hamburger is eaten and digested.

Level 4: Analysis
Students go beyond the literal meanings and are able to draw conclusions on their own, perhaps by making sense of unfamiliar circumstances.
The learner will determine how a cow's digestive system may differ from a human's by examining the cow's digestive organs.

Level 5: Synthesis
Students are able to provide creative responses to open-ended questions that require originality.
The student will create a song, rap, or poem that demonstrates the steps of the digestive process.

Level 6: Evaluation
Students are able to integrate their knowledge and make judgements based on their own personal criteria.
Students will listen to rap songs that demonstrate the steps of the digestive process and evaluate their accuracy.

Figure 5–4 Objectives Categorized by Bloom's Taxonomy.
Source: Adapted from Elementary Classroom Management, 2nd edition, *by C. S. Weinstein and A. J. Mignano, 1997, New York: McGraw Hill; and* Interdisciplinary Instruction: A Practical Guide for Elementary School Teachers, *by Karlyn L. Wood, ©1997. Adapted by permission of Pearson Education, Inc., Upper Saddle River, NJ.*

While thinking about writing objectives, it is helpful to consider Bloom's Taxonomy (Bloom, Englehart, Furst, Hill, & Krathwohl, 1956). As discussed in chapter 8, Bloom outlined six levels of questioning that teachers can use as a guide when planning lesson objectives. Figure 5–4 provides a brief summary of Bloom's Taxonomy, supplemented with possible objectives for a lesson on the digestive system as designed by one group of teachers.

Assessment as an Integral Part of Planning and Instruction

Assessment should be an integral part of planning and instruction. Continual assessment should occur prior to, during, and after instruction to determine the impact of a particular concept, idea, demonstration, or exploration on student learning. Before teaching a particular concept or method, many teachers collect preassessment data. These data are often collected in a K-W-L format. A K-W-L format includes questions such as: What do we **Know** about the rainforest? **What** would we like to learn? What have we **Learned**? Such a format allows students to generate their own questions of interest to pursue. It also provides a basis for helping teachers recognize the prior knowledge of their students. Teachers may have students write or draw about their knowledge of a topic before beginning a unit of study. For example, students might be asked to draw a picture of everything they know about a rainforest, including the climate and kinds of plants and animals that live there. Or, students can complete a paper-and-pencil exercise so teachers can identify the particular areas that need focus.

In addition to helping teachers plan for instruction, preassessment data provide a wonderful mechanism for looking for evidence of growth. After instruction, students may return to their original pictures of the rainforest and add details based on what they have learned, for example. This "pre-" and "post-" method is helpful for documenting specific learning.

While teaching, instructors should be continually assessing. Keep in mind that the skills of self-regulation that promote reflection, including self-questioning, self-directing, self-coping, self-correcting, and self-reinforcing, are means of assessment.

For example, fifth-grade students are discussing the contemporary realistic fiction book, *Mick Harte Was Here* (1996), by Parks, in a literature circle. The teacher is trying to let the students take the lead in the discussion. Although the students are taking the lead in the discussion, the teacher has specific learning goals. She wants to see how the students demonstrate their knowledge of the genre of realistic fiction, how they discuss specific issues of character development, and how they compare this book to other books written by Parks.

Self-questioning: Did I set up the discussion so that students have enough prompts to lead the discussion without much intervention? Will they stay on topic? Will they talk about character, genre, and author's craft?

Self-directing: I need to keep my mouth shut and let the discussion develop. I need to give them a chance! I need to figure out when I should interject comments about the genre, author, and characters.

Self-coping: I need to remember that even when it seems like they are off-topic, a member of the group usually connects ideas together. I can tell more about what they are learning by letting this happen. It is really hard for me to give up control like this.

Self-correcting: Oh, there I go again. I keep trying to move the discussion my way. I need to focus on taking notes about what I hear them discussing. They really are learning a lot.

Self-reinforcing: Wow! When I really sat back and took notes, I realized that they learned a lot. They found a lot of similarities in Park's style in her other books. They really empathized with Mick's sister as she tried to make sense of her brother's death. They did a great job describing her character in ways that showed they understand key issues of the book. And they understand the idea behind realistic fiction—that a contemporary issue is described in a way that relates to issues that we can really confront.

Formative and Summative Assessments

Formative and summative assessments provide students with feedback about their learning. The purpose of all feedback is to increase the students' deep understanding of subject matter knowledge, skills, and development of productive learning habits. Teachers provide feedback so that learners can share in the responsibility for their own learning. If students are not aware of their academic progress, it is difficult for them to share responsibility for their learning and their subsequent growth. Only through this shared knowledge can students redirect their learning.

Formative evaluation is feedback that is intended to help "form," or congeal, understanding (Riner, 2000). It is ongoing and can be thought of as monitoring or reinforcing because it keeps students on task and provides immediate feedback so that students know how they are doing (Lemlech, 1998). Formative assessments provide students with continual feedback, on a daily basis, that guides their progress toward learning goals.

Formative assessment can be achieved by continual teacher monitoring of student's progress to decide whether or not to adapt a lesson plan in action. Many teachers monitor their students simply by circulating around the room, asking questions, and engaging students in conversations about their work. *Reinforcement* is also a part of academic feedback, as it is closely related to a student's achievement. In this case, the teacher may provide feedback and time for correcting work, allowing students to take responsibility to self-correct their work. Students can learn self-questioning to help self-correct and self-reinforce after they have modeled and practiced sufficiently with the teacher.

Throughout this text, we have emphasized the importance of continual feedback, reflection, adaptation, and reinforcement both directed by the teacher and internalized by students. Students and teachers should continually monitor their own learning and identify how they are reaching their learning goals. Teachers should continually assess how their instruction is effectively helping diverse learners be motivated to learn. This means watching for boredom, frustration, defiance, enthusiasm, and ownership. Formative assessments involve data collection and analysis that help teachers realize the different ways that students learn—different "hooks" that motivate different learners and strategies that help improve academic task performance. Formative assessments can be a means for teachers to also analyze their questioning and discussion skills. Think about the kinds of discussions, reports, narratives, and other products students are creating in response to the instructional environment that you create.

Similarly, students can take responsibility for monitoring their academic progress daily. An integral aspect of self-regulation is the ability to self-evaluate and self-reinforce appropriately. Self-regulated learners are able to monitor progress, to know when a goal has been achieved, and to reward themselves appropriately. Likewise, self-regulated learners are able to analyze situations in which they have failed to meet a goal. Such learners are able to figure out what strategies they used initially, what went wrong, and what can be changed next time to complete the task successfully. With productive teacher modeling and sufficient guided practice, students learn ways to analyze whether the goal or the strategies for reaching the goal were inappropriate. This analysis is conducted using a variety of resources that need to be practiced explicitly within the classroom, including discussions with more knowledgeable others, experiences of working through similar goal situations, and new learning (Brown & Palinscar, 1982; Pintrich, 1995; Pressley, 1995; Rohrkemper & Corno, 1988; Shin, 1997).

As self-evaluation becomes a classroom norm, teachers can include a self-evaluation component as part of their daily routine. This assessment could include a variety of questions such as:

- What was something new that I learned today?
- What is one example of a way that I participated in class today?
- Who taught me something today (teacher, classmate, book, video)?
- What confused me today?
- What do I need to work on tomorrow?

The key to involving students in self-evaluation is to use formative assessments explicitly to guide learning. Teachers can collect these assessments and provide quick feedback each day or each week. If students are too young to write, teachers can use the class meeting time at the end of day to discuss one or two of the previous questions with each child.

Formative assessment helps shape the next stages in teaching and learning (Figure 5–5). Teachers rely on formative assessment to drive their planning for subsequent lessons because learning involves building a repertoire of things the students know and can do. We believe that the focus of formative evaluations should be on positive achievements while also determining where more attention needs to be given to increase achievement.

1. What are the purposes of the lesson? What do I hope students will learn?
2. How will I know if the students have learned anything? What kinds of assessment do I have in place? Does my assessment match my purpose/objectives?
3. How am I going to collect evidence that the students have learned? How will the students be involved in assessing their own learning?
4. What specific activities should I use to reach my objectives? How do my activities help to promote self-regulated learning?
5. How can I keep track of students' learning during instruction?

Figure 5–5   Self-Questions to Guide Formative Assessment in Planning.

- Examples of student work including creative and practical writing; experiments; creative work in the arts or music; photos of projects
- Student observation and analyses of what was gained from instruction; what has been understood and not understood
- Surveys of feelings and attitudes about learning
- Individual interest surveys
- Journals kept by students that include personal reflections and evaluations of their own work in the class
- Self evaluations prepared by students
- Journals kept by teachers, reflecting on individual progress
- Teachers' anecdotal records
- Records of individual pupil/teacher conferences
- Formal and informal quizzes, tests, examinations
- Recordings—audiotapes or videotapes of oral readings, reports, recitations

Figure 5–6   Ways to Incorporate Student Work Within Summative Evaluation.
Source: Adapted from Interdisciplinary Instruction: A Practical Guide for Elementary School Teachers, *by Karlyn L. Wood, ©1997. Adapted by permission of Pearson Education, Inc., Upper Saddle River, NJ.*

In contrast, *summative evaluations* are attempts to "sum" the success of learning (Riner, 2000). Such assessments should not occur at the practice stage of learning, like formative evaluations, but rather after the student has been given the opportunity to refine the skills or concepts learned. Summative evaluations provide a summary of students' progress after formative feedback has been provided. Summative evaluations may serve as a progress report to the teacher, the student, and the parent alike. Although summative evaluation instructions do not help teachers monitor instruction in the same interactive way, they do provide a partial picture of a student's level of understanding. Figure 5–6 provides examples of summative evaluations.

After reading this description of summative evaluations, you may be picturing a student sitting at a desk, working on a chapter test. But there are many other ways that teachers can determine mastery of objectives. *Authentic assessments* focus on performances in which the *process* of learning is demonstrated in addition to the *product* of learning, and are discussed in more depth in chapter 9. Authentic assessments can take on almost any form that communicates learning—collections of student-produced, authentic materials selected by the students, or student-performed skits that indicate mastery of the subject. Any assessments that indicate growth can be combined to provide information about learning.

- Were the students motivated by the activities?
- Did the students meet the objectives? If not, why not? How will I re-teach?
- Did they reach the objectives in the ways that I had envisioned? How can I continue to "plan backwards" to learn ways to help students reach learning goals?
- In what ways did I assess student learning? In what ways did students monitor their own learning?
- What things happened unexpectedly?
- What was the best part of the lesson?
- Did the lesson take the amount of time that I had expected it would? If not, why not? Was it due to student questioning, discussing, too much teacher talk, unclear explanations?
- Were my transitions smooth?
- Did the materials work for this lesson?

Figure 5–7   Self-Questions to Consider in Reflections.

Reflection and Modifications

Reflecting on your planning has several benefits and is integral to effective teaching:

1. It helps you know how to re-teach the lesson when needed.
2. It better prepares you for future teaching of the same material.
3. It better prepares you for future teaching of different material to prevent the same mishaps from occurring.

Reflection can be as simple as asking yourself about the kinds of things that went well, and what you would change about the instruction and learner response (Figure 5–7). Reflective teachers often write notes on their lesson plans so they can make revisions the next time they teach the lesson. You should think about planning as a cyclical process, each time refining more and more so that the learners receive maximum benefits.

Remember, you cannot plan for everything, but experience and reflection on experience can help better prepare you for future teaching. (In fact, John Dewey, a famous educator, claimed that an episode only becomes an experience when the participant reflects on that episode.) Modifications should also be discussed in your reflections. What kinds of things will you need to change for certain learners? All students will not benefit from the same instruction. Think about extending your instruction to meet the needs of lower-achieving students, as well as higher-achieving students. What kinds of modifications will be needed for other types of learners, such as ESOL students or students with learning or behavioral disabilities? Try to consider all of your special needs students and plan for their instruction. Following are some ways to enrich and remediate your lessons:

Enrich:

- Carry the lesson further by adding personal responses
- Conduct further research on a topic
- Arrange for peer tutors for lower-achieving students
- Make connections to other academic areas

Remediate:

- Use more concrete ways to explain the same material
- Reduce the number of responses needed (every other math problem)
- Work with students individually or provide a peer tutor
- Design alternate expectations that are realistic and still challenging for the child

Creating Curriculum

Teachers feel varying levels of efficacy when it comes to planning and teaching teacher-made curriculum. Teachers may feel little power to stray from traditional textbooks in school districts and context-specific school administrations where the curriculum on the daily and unit levels are controlled, and where assessments are textbook driven and not tailored to specific learners. Beginning teachers, especially, feel the weight of curricular decisions, as they are trying to fit into the school culture, learn about the developmental needs of their particular students, and find out what these students need to know by the end of each grading period.

Based on research from national organizations and research centers, Hyde, Zemelman, and Daniels (1993) synthesized best practice in the disciplines of reading, writing, mathematics, science, and social studies. Based on this research, they argue that curriculum should be child-centered, experiential, reflective, authentic, holistic, social, collaborative, democratic, cognitive, developmental, constructivist, psycholinguistic, and challenging. A classroom that emphasizes integration of curriculum to more naturally follow the life of a child is one that is filled with wonder, exploration, and reflection. Such practice is in direct contrast to a traditional curriculum, in which students spend time filling in worksheets, textbooks are considered primary sources of knowledge, teachers stress rote memorization as evidence of learning, and administrators rely on standardized tests as indicators of achievement.

LEARNING OUT LOUD 5–2

Collect some examples of worksheets that you see used in elementary and middle schools. Ask yourself, "How can I turn this worksheet into an active learning experience for students?" Perhaps you can think of ways to use the information provided on the worksheet, in an interactive way. For example, instead of practicing sequencing by numbering the order of a set of pictures, you could cut apart the pictures, have students place them in the correct order, and then write a few sentences about what is happening in each picture. Examine your collection of worksheets and decide which skills would be better reinforced with alternate activities.

Scope and Sequence

As you continue to plan lessons and units of study, you must consider a broader framework. To effectively reach goals and objectives within a school year and prepare your students to be successful in the next grade, you need to develop a general scope and sequence of the year's curriculum. This may sound overwhelming to you now, but it is important that you begin to examine the different ways that schools create and rely on scope and sequence, or curriculum mapping charts, to guide progress toward goals.

According to Hicks (1999), a first-grade teacher at Barrow Elementary School in Athens, Georgia, there are several benefits in creating school-based curriculum maps. The first benefit is instructional—a curriculum map provides a skeletal structure to guide teachers as they plan objectives, avoid repetition, identify gaps, consider areas for integration, match their objectives with national standards, and consider ways to integrate technology into the curriculum. A curriculum map provides a way to communicate with fellow teachers, parents, and students. Hicks participated in school-wide professional development in curriculum mapping and found benefits, both for herself and for her students. She found that by talking with peers to develop maps, she no longer feels isolated in curriculum decision making. In addition, she found the process a stimulating opportunity for personal reflection, for collaboration, and for providing a mechanism for teachers to build on students' previous school experiences as they share maps across grade levels. To learn more about curriculum mapping, Hicks and other teachers in the school used Jacob's (1997) book *Mapping the Big Picture*, published by ASCD, as a resource.

Integrating Connections Across Content Areas

Students receive many benefits from making connections across content areas as they link previously learned material with new concepts. As students draw upon prior knowledge, they gain a holistic picture of the material to be learned. We often try to segment learning artificially by subject areas, yet our everyday experiences in the world are not separated naturally by subject areas. The next section discusses ways to integrate content by theme, curriculum integration, and integrating fine arts and technology into the curriculum. Many teachers are finding overwhelming benefits for student learning by involving students in curriculum integration.

Developing an Organizing Center for Curriculum Integration.   An organizing center helps focus integrated subject instruction. The goal of this method of instruction is to make connections wherever possible by helping students to transfer knowledge. The thematic unit is a framework for organizing learning around a central concept or goal; for example, the concept of the environment or the Civil War, rather than a subject such as science or history (Ross, 1998). Instruction in all subjects depends upon the concept of study so that all information is linked by one unifying theme. This unit of study continues for several weeks, each day exploring new areas that work together to create a comprehensive unit of study.

An integrated curriculum approach can benefit students in many ways by providing authentic learning experiences as they apply their knowledge to many situations. Additionally, this learning takes many forms. The thematic approach engages students in a cyclical learning process including formulating problems, forming concepts, applying, evaluating, reflecting, and modifying their knowledge. During this process, students are encouraged to gain insights, construct meaning, and apply new knowledge. All of these aspects work together to promote self-regulation, higher-order thinking, and the ability to transfer concepts across subject areas.

There are many ways to determine what concepts will serve as themes of study. They can be teacher determined or student initiated. Themes may grow naturally out of class discussions and interests. Oftentimes, themes emerge from questions and interests that develop during a previous unit (Ross, 1998). This inspires students' natural curiosity and demonstrates a successful theme—students are enticed to keep learning more and more about an area of study. No matter how the topic is decided, the subject has to be interesting to students and relevant to their lives. Equally important, the topic has to relate closely to the curriculum guide(s) or standard(s) expectations. Even well-planned and well-executed themes will fail if these criteria are not met.

Considering Possibilities for Curriculum Integration.   Curriculum integration (CI) is a specific way to promote the thematic approach to learning (Figure 5–8). Jim Beane, the leading contemporary advocate of this approach, states that, "Curriculum integration begins with the idea that the sources of curriculum ought to be problems, issues, and concerns posed by life itself" (1995, p. 616).

The primary goal of curriculum integration is to improve student learning and increase student achievement. Student learning can be maximized when learning is active and

- Curriculum integration is organized around problems and issues that are of personal and social significance in the real world. No longer are separate subjects the focus of the curriculum. Thus, preplanned units do not dictate the learning, but rather units of study are unveiled as the relevant information is established. Traditional subject matter will be interwoven, but not in a preconceived fashion.
- Learning experiences in relation to the themes are planned so as to integrate pertinent knowledge in the context of that theme. Themes are established from student interests, but also must demonstrate socially significant topics.
- Knowledge is developed and used to address the theme currently under study rather than to prepare for some later test or grade level. The unit of study encompasses study of all subjects. Teachers and students collaboratively plan the curriculum and how it will be covered. The teacher takes on a leadership role to assist in decision making and to make sure the experiences are educational, but this does not mean that the teacher manipulates student decisions to fit a preconceived notion about what a unit will cover or how it will be taught.
- Emphasis is placed on substantive projects and other activities that involve real application of knowledge, thus increasing the possibility for young people to integrate curriculum experiences into their schemes of meaning and to experience the democratic process of problem solving. The democratic classroom is imperative to curriculum integration. It goes well beyond merely voting with the majority ruling, but instead, each person has the right to object to decisions made in the classroom. The class must reach a resolution to the conflict before moving forward. The establishment of a true classroom community is paramount in this effort.

Figure 5–8 Features of Curriculum Integration.
Source: Adapted from Curriculum Integration: Twenty Questions — With Answers, *by G. Nesin and J. Lounsbury, 1999, Atlanta: Georgia Middle School Association. Adapted with permission of Georgia Middle School Association.*

meaningful. With curriculum integration, basic information is still acquired, but the knowledge is far more extensive and, generally, is more easily retained. Curriculum integration relies upon intrinsic motivation, and because students collaborate with the teacher in designing units of study, they have a personal stake in the unit. Such ownership of the curriculum increases student achievement and builds positive attitudes toward school. Most importantly, these opportunities for choice are the centerpiece of self-regulated learning.

The benefits of curriculum integration extend well beyond the elementary and middle school years. Students involved in this setting will likely be prepared for citizenship in a democratic society. Additionally, they will have had opportunities to engage in collaborative problem solving and in considering diverse viewpoints. Finally, these students will be accustomed to taking responsible action as a result of understanding some problem or context. These factors will truly influence their citizenship positively and, of course, their responsibility and independence, as well as their attitudes, knowledge, and skills.

Educational researchers who have studied curriculum integration (Beane, 1995, 1997; Nesin & Lounsbury, 1999; Pate, Homestead, & McGinnis, 1997) recommend the following ways to increase learner responsibility and ownership through curriculum integration:

1. Students come up with their own management plan/classroom policies and procedures. Students are used to entering classrooms with predetermined rules and consequences. However, having students be responsible for creating an effective learning environment will assist them in reflecting on not only the rules, but the justifications of those rules.

2. Students are encouraged to participate in group processing in which they make decisions and hold class meetings to revise decisions that have been made. Teachers should help students explore the nature of a democracy as a way of working with others. Team-building exercises can assist in the development of a collaborative and caring community.

3. Students develop a grading policy in which they have the responsibility for deciding such things as how work will be graded and how late work will be handled. Students help

to set the objectives and assume responsibility for monitoring and assessing their learning. Authentic assessment allows for multiple variations in evaluations. Students may submit checklists, notes, projects, or research as assessment pieces. These materials offer much more information than a single score or letter grade. Report cards may be accompanied by an assessment in the form of a student narrative.

Remember to plan backwards, considering the kinds of assessments that match the kind of learning you want to encourage.

Integrating Fine Arts in Instruction.   Unfortunately, teachers often neglect to include fine arts as a substantive part of classroom instruction. Yet, when the arts are integrated into the curriculum, many students are increasingly motivated and engaged. As educators, we realize that students shine in different ways. Some students who typically do not perform well in response to traditional teaching strategies may meet with success when the arts become an integral part of learning. As you plan lessons and units, we hope that you will facilitate and create opportunities for creative expression. Schirrmacher (1998), in the book *Art and Creative Development for Young Children*, provides suggestions for teachers to integrate fine arts into the curriculum. We see no reason why these suggestions should be reserved for young children. In fact, we see them as excellent suggestions for *all* learners.

1. *Celebrate creativity.*   Help students identify with famous, creative people. Teachers or students can read books about famous inventors and creators and discuss their accomplishments. Students can discuss their own inventions and creations as well.

2. *Value students' creativity.*   Allow students freedom in acting and thinking differently. Realize that creative thought is an important part of child development. Discuss this importance with parents, students, and administrators. Advocate for creativity in school and speak out against budget cuts that attempt to reduce or eliminate the arts in school.

3. *Be a creative partner.*   Let students determine their own creative paths. Engage in imaginary play with them without imposing your own ideas that can stifle their creative thought.

4. *Provide time and space for creative expression.*   Students need to have plenty of space to spread out and manipulate materials. Creative activities should not be rushed; adequate time should be allotted. Teachers who facilitate creativity also need to show a tolerance for clutter, noise, and movement.

5. *Provide materials that are conducive to creativity.*   Allow students to use materials in nontraditional ways. Students may want to use building blocks or other learning materials from one center to produce musical rhythms in another center or context. Providing props can extend students' creativity. Teachers should make efforts to provide manipulatives that can serve more than one function. Play-dough, water, sand blocks, and building pieces are examples of equipment that facilitate creativity in young children. Other age-appropriate materials could be substituted for older learners.

6. *Provide a psychological climate conducive to creativity.*   Students should feel free to express themselves without fear of criticism, rejection, or fear of failure to perform or conform. Providing students opportunities to make decisions, interact with one another, and make independent choices will create a climate of self-regulation, respect, trust, and empowerment.

7. *Weave creativity and creative expression throughout your curriculum.*   Creativity should be a natural part of a child's day and should not be isolated as a separate component of the schedule. Think about ways to integrate creative activities with all subjects, using both left-brain and right-brain activities.

LEARNING OUT LOUD 5–3

Creativity isn't just for children! What have *you* done lately to foster your own creativity? Set aside a creative time for yourself once a week for a month. During this time, do something that you enjoy but have neglected lately. Maybe you can paint pottery, write poetry, design photo albums, or play music. Whatever it is, have fun! Reflect at the end of the month about how you felt after engaging in this creativity, and then note the possible benefits that you derived from the experience.

Teachers who integrate the arts into the curriculum help students learn content in a deeper, more personal way. Such activities connect left-brain activities with right-brain activities, and thus engage learners of both types. There are many avenues to explore with the inclusion of fine arts in the curriculum. Discipline-based arts education (DBAE) suggests using music, drama, and visual arts as springboards for subject integration (Dobbs, 1992).

You may find it most beneficial to begin slowly and build as your teaching experience grows. Following are examples of ways to integrate fine arts with subject areas:

Music

- Play music as children arrive in morning.
- Listen to music associated with countries or time periods of study.
- Have students respond to musical selections.
- Use music as a basis for patterns that facilitate mathematical and reading growth.

Drama

- Have students act out stories.
- Have students interpret historical events through dramatic play.
- Have students dramatize concepts, such as photosynthesis, without words.

Visual Arts

- Develop writing skills by having students respond to pieces of artwork—make up stories about what is happening in the picture.
- Look for mathematical concepts in art, particularly geometric shapes: right angles, arcs, and so forth.
- Have students respond through drawing or visual representation to different concepts.
- Conduct artist studies by having children research an artist's life and study works of art, comparing and contrasting different pieces.

Using Computers in Curriculum Integration.   Technology has quickly become an important part of the elementary school classroom. With so many changes and the influx of new technology, it can be challenging to keep up and to know how to integrate technology effectively in the classroom. Teachers who have a basic knowledge of computers can enrich their classroom instruction. Roblyer and Edwards (2000) offer suggestions to integrate computers into content-area instruction.

Language Arts.   Language arts teachers can have children compose stories as part of the publishing step of the writing process. Instructing children on proper keyboarding techniques may be appropriate for this activity. Of course, teachers should consider the age of the child and the amount of typing that will be required. In addition to word processing, there are many instructional software packages that build and support literacy skills. Many games emphasize reading skills, grammar usage, spelling, and punctuation. The goal of these games often is to make learning by the computer more enticing than traditional methods. One of the most popular packages is the Accelerated Reader (AR) program by Advantage Learning Systems. With this program, students take quizzes on materials they have read and the computer keeps track of their scores and provides a report to the teacher.

The Internet can be a powerful resource for communication with people across the nation and around the world. Students are often motivated to write well when they realize their audience is authentic and their purposes are real. Roblyer and Edwards (2000) suggest the following ways to incorporate the World Wide Web into the language arts classroom:

- E-mail or chats to gather information from experts
- Virtual tours of students' own local history, art, or science museum
- Models for conducting information searches and analyzing and using the results
- Collaborating to develop a survey to gather data on the characteristics of participating students
- Writing a poem or essay as a "verbal postcard" to tell others about some aspect of the local community, and then sending this information through e-mail or chat rooms.
- Sending questions to students' favorite authors; many now have Web sites.

Many of these ideas will translate to other subject areas as well.

Science.   The Internet can be invaluable in the science classroom. Students can search the Internet for information that is constantly changing in the field. In addition, the Internet provides current information in a way that textbooks cannot—the Internet is continuously updated. Through the use of the Internet, students are able to visit government, university, and professional organization sites that can assist them in their research. Roblyer and Edwards (2000) suggest the following ways to incorporate the Web into the science classroom:

- Middle school students use the Internet to conduct research, collect clip art, graphics, and sound effects on dinosaurs. They then use the resources to develop a hypermedia presentation.
- Students use a web survey to help identify environmental problems that need to be addressed.
- Student teams develop and implement a science-based public service campaign via the school's Web site. (p. 256)

Web sites that are helpful for the science curriculum include:

- National Science Teachers Association, at *http://www.nsta.org*. This site includes resources and current issues and is considered one of the largest science teacher organizations.
- Eisenhower National Clearinghouse (ENC), at *http://www.enc.org/*. This site includes lesson plans for teachers and activities for students.

Mathematics.   A variety of computer software is available for math instruction. Drill-and-practice packages and programs that emphasize higher-order thinking skills can be included in the curriculum. Additionally, the Internet offers programs that simulate trading in a mock stock market and using mathematics in real-world situations in occupations such as medicine, engineering, and law enforcement.

Spreadsheets can also be useful in the mathematics curriculum. They can help children ask "what if" questions and allow them to try possibilities in a relatively painless way. Spreadsheets can also allow students to search for patterns and generalize concepts. The following mathematics Web sites can assist students and teachers:

- National Council of Teachers of Mathematics at *http://www.nctm.org/ index.htm*. This site includes many resources on how to implement math standards.
- PBS Mathline at *http://www.pbs.org/learn/mathline/index.html*. This site discusses math content and assessment issues. A monthly feature is included with teaching tips, math challenges, and assessment ideas.

Social Studies.   Many computer software packages are available for inclusion in the social studies curriculum. Many of these include simulations that reenact historical events or involve children in decision-making opportunities that result in complex consequences. Additionally, maps and global positioning systems (GPSs) are impacting schools. GPSs are instruments that pinpoint locations and map coordinates. Such technology may become imperative for social studies curricula in the future.

Spreadsheets and database software are equally as important, as they can help retrieve and synthesize information. For example, students can use this technology to gather current and historical data to predict future trends. Roblyer and Edwards (2000) suggest having students plot population growth and then use this knowledge to consider the social, political, and economic consequences.

The Internet has considerable implications for the social studies curriculum as well. Students are able to contact people all across the world and bring textbook learning to a whole new level. Sorting through all of the available possibilities and resources can be overwhelming, but Roblyer and Edwards (2000) suggest the following Web sites as a starting point:

- National Council for Social Studies at *http://www.ncss.org/*. This comprehensive site includes a guide to resources as well as professional development activities for teachers.
- Smithsonian Institution at *http://www.si.edu*. This site provides on-line publications, photographs, and museum tours.
- Current Events CNN Interactive at *http://www.cnn.com*. This up-to-date site features world-wide events.
- The White House at *http://www.whitehouse.gov*. This site is a link to the President of the United States. (p. 273)

Planning for Home School Connections

The job of an educator extends well beyond instructing students in the classroom, and you will soon find you have many responsibilities that extend to your students' families. Knowing these families and communicating effectively with them can impact students' achievement and their feelings of efficacy in learning. You may find yourself working with families of all sorts. No longer is the traditional, dual-parent family the norm. Today's children come from many types of families: single-parent homes, foster families, grandparent or extended family-headed households, gay or lesbian parents, blended families due to remarriages, and families that do not speak English as their first language. As future teachers, you need to be aware of a child's specific family situation and foster communication between school and home settings in a way that embraces the family setting and helps all participants work together toward helping the student learn. The Teaching Tolerance Project exemplifies how this can be done in the text *Starting Small* (1997):

1. View linguistic and cultural diversity as strengths (e.g., bilingualism is an asset).
2. Use books and other resources that reflect all kinds of families.
3. Display pictures that children draw of their families, or have each child make a page in a class book titled "Our Families."
4. Discuss feelings and experiences children choose to share about what makes their family special.
5. Avoid family-related activities that potentially exclude some children (e.g., holding a Mother's Tea, making Father's Day cards, creating "family trees").
6. Observe a "Someone Special Day" and have children make gifts and invite significant others of their choice to school for breakfast, a play, or other event. (pp. 27–28)

LEARNING OUT LOUD 5–4

Read five literature books for children or adolescents that reflect different kinds of families you can include in your classroom.

Understanding the Community and the School.   It is essential that you become familiar with the community where you are teaching. As part of our teacher preparation program, some instructors require students to drive around the community in groups. Students follow the bus route to see the various places where the students live, to see the distance of the route, and to see the kinds of resources that are available to the students. Our teachers also interview community members, parents, and students to learn more about the school setting. Lemlech (1998) suggests considering the following questions when getting acquainted with the community:

1. Who lives in the community?
2. What is the residential pattern (apartments, single homes)?
3. How do the natural and manmade environments contribute to or detract from the community?
4. What businesses appear to flourish in the community? What businesses appear to flounder?
5. Are there social services within the community available to assist residents (hospitals, clinics, police, fire, legal aid)?
6. Do recreational facilities exist within the community (for children, adults)?
7. Are distinctive cultural characteristics apparent (specialty shops, restaurants, cultural sites, unique patterns, or environmental characteristics)?
8. Are there businesses, places of interest, or sites for field trips?
9. Are resource people available in the community to assist in the classroom?
10. What kinds of work opportunities exist in the community?
11. What special problems are apparent in the community?
12. If there are businesses in the community, does any particular type predominate?
13. What special interests are obvious in the community? Do these interests relate to cultural priorities?
14. How might your own interests and talents assist the community? (p. 97)

Kindergarten News
Mrs. Klein and Mrs. Hodge

Nutrition Unit. Thank you for your great response in sending in labels for our nutrition unit. We learned so much by examining labels for fat and sugar content. We graphed cereal boxes according to how many grams of sugar they contained, and some were quite surprising! We also learned what makes a balanced meal, and discussed the food pyramid that helps us in making good food choices. Additionally, we spent time thinking about where certain foods come from, and now have a better understanding of how we get fruits, vegetables, and grains. We used nutritional and junk foods as a way to sharpen our classification skills. Ask your child to share some nutrition knowledge with you as you grocery shop! Next week we will begin our unit on dental hygiene. Help your child start thinking about healthy habits for our teeth and gums.

Field Trip. Don't forget, we will be taking our field trip to the zoo on Thursday, March 27. The cost is $7.00 for adults and $4.50 for chaperones. We look forward to a great trip as we prepare for our unit on animals.

Teacher Workday. There will be no school on Friday, March 28, as it is a scheduled Teacher Workday.

Figure 5–9   Home School Connection Weekly Newsletter.

Answering these questions may provide you with adequate information to get to know the community surrounding the school.

Initiating a Strong Home-School Connection Plan.   Most parents sincerely want the best academic environment and wish for success for their children. It is important for you to keep open communication with your students' parents or guardians so that learning can be reinforced and continued at home. There are many ways that teachers can initiate this contact with families. One of the most efficient ways to maintain clear communication and expectations for parent involvement is to send home a weekly communication of some sort that informs parents of classroom events. Parents can then be aware of the content and curriculum their child is involved in and learn how they can help their child at home. Figure 5–9 shows an example of a kindergarten newsletter.

In addition to general newsletters, individual children may have special academic or behavioral needs that can be addressed in personalized notes that are sent home. Phone calls or e-mail can also serve as communication devices when parents have the necessary equipment.

Conferences.   Family conferences are another great way to involve families in school activities. Such an experience allows parents the opportunity to see their child's work and talk to the teacher about their child's specific strengths and weaknesses. Both teachers and parents or guardians may initiate a conference. Typically, conferences are held to inform family members of a student's progress, as well as to solve problems or address concerns related to school performance. It is important to set goals for the conference so that the meeting will stay focused on ways to help the child. As facilitator, you should take the lead in helping family members also be a part of goal formulation at the onset of a conference. Such shared responsibility will help both parties feel like they have input and are concerned about the child. Conferences can be conducted at school or other locations. Keep in mind the transportation and child-care needs of the families with whom you want to talk. Conferences should be scheduled at a convenient time and place for all parties. (For a description of student-led conferences as a form of authentic assessment, see chapter 9.) Once a time and place are agreed upon, teachers who initiate conferences must prepare for the meeting by gathering materials that will assist in the conversation and think about key points that need to be addressed. Following are suggestions for ways to prepare for the conference.

Conference Tips.

Before the conference:
- Set up chairs somewhere outside of your door for parents to wait if there is a series of conferences.
- Display class work or photos of the class to occupy parents while they wait.
- Prepare some sort of materials (puzzles, crayons, books, etc.) for small children to play with during the conference so the parents can give their full attention.
- Have documentation of the student's papers, projects, and assessments ready to show parents. Keep a folder accessible so you can easily refer to it.
- Provide pens and paper for parents to use during the conference in case they want to write anything down.
- Arrange for someone (counselor, administrator) to be present if you think the conversation could become heated.
- Arrange for a translator if one is needed to assist in communication.

During the conference:
- Greet the parents in a friendly way and show them where to sit.
- Sit on the same side of the table and at the same or lower level than the parent to eliminate power issues. Talking to someone who is sitting behind a desk can be intimidating.
- Provide soft lighting and a general warm atmosphere.
- Be sure to use the sandwich approach: Begin with something positive: say something negative when you need to address it, and end with something positive.
- Use eye contact frequently.
- Back up what you are saying with written documentation (e.g., children's work) or concrete verbal examples of what you mean.
- Keep notes during the conference about what you discussed so you can refer to them the next time you meet.
- Review the key points of your discussion at the end of the conference.
- Decide together (teacher-parent and possibly student) what actions need to be carried out at home and at school.
- Make an appointment to follow up at a specified time. This can be by phone or in person. Provide your contact information—telephone number or business card.
- Try to end on a positive note.
- Show the parent to the exit at the conclusion of the conference.

After the conference:
- Inform any other teachers or administrators about what was decided or discussed in the conference.
- Send thank you notes to parents for attending if you feel it would help build rapport.
- Make sure to follow up at the agreed-upon time.

In addition to these suggestions, there are several "do's" and "don'ts" that are important to remember when conducting conferences. Adhering to these suggestions will ease the situation and make conferences productive and enjoyable. Figure 5–10 lists some of the many resources available for teachers who wish to learn more about conducting conferences.

Some teachers choose to offer suggestions of ways that families can become involved in the learning process. Providing a calendar of activities may be helpful for families that want to be involved in such situations. Figure 5–11 shows an example of one kindergarten teacher's ideas for student activities for the month of April.

Fuller, M. L., & Olsen, G. (1998). *Home school relations: Working successfully with parents and families*. Boston: Allyn & Bacon.

St. Pierre, R. & Layzer, J. (1999). Using home visits for multiple purposes: The comprehensive child development program. *The Future of Children, 9,* 134–152.

Henderson, A. T., Marburger, C. L., & Ooms, T. (1986). *Beyond the bake sale*. Columbia, MD: National Committee for Citizens in Education.

Kroth, R. L. (1985). *Communication with parents of exceptional children*. Denver, CO: Love Publishing.

Weiss, H. B. (1993). Home visits: Necessary but not sufficient. *The Future of Children, 3* (3), 1–16.

Figure 5–10   References for Teacher-Parent Interactions.

Kindergarten Homework Ideas
Miss Pearson

Sunday	Monday	Tuesday	Wednesday	Thursday	Friday	Saturday
		1 Name 2 kinds of pollution.	**2** Pick up 10 pieces of trash in your neighborhood.	**3** Subtract: 4−3=___ 5−3=___ 8−6=___ 4−1=___ 10−6=___ 11−5=___	**4** Write a letter to a relative.	**5** Help to recycle something at your house.
6 Make a list of what you want to do for VACATION!!!	**7** Stay up late and sleep late, too!!	**8** Do calendar time for Mom or Dad.	**9** Figure out how many more days of vacation you have left.	**10** Read a book to a stuffed animal.	**11** Go to the library and find a book about spring.	**12** Play in the water as your grass and flowers get a drink!
13	**14** Write a postcard to an out-of-town friend.	**15**	**16** Find a place on the map where you would like to camp.	**17** Tell someone all about your trip to Elacheel!	**18** Measure how many steps it is from your bedroom to the kitchen.	**19**
20	**21** Enjoy a day off of school!	**22**	**23** List three things you need to take when you camp.	**24** What should you do for a burn? A cut? A broken bone?	**25** Come to the Spring Carnival!	**26** Tell 5 animals you might see if camping in the Georgia mountains. Georgia coast?
27 Do an extra chore at home without having to be asked!	**28** Draw a picture of an insect. How many body parts? How many legs?	**29** Don't forget your homework!	**30**			

Return with 17 completed by April 29.

Figure 5–11   Kindergarten Homework Ideas.

LEARNING OUT LOUD 5–5

Interview several parents/guardians about their experiences with teacher conferences. What kinds of things are important to them? What did certain teachers do to make them feel more comfortable? Why were certain conferences positive, while others were not? How did the conference impact the student's performance? What advice can they give to beginning teachers?

Understanding Service Learning as Part of the Community Curriculum

There are numerous ways for teachers to become involved in their community. Teachers often talk about the positive rapport that is established just by attending their students' sporting events or other outside activities. Such involvement communicates to parents and students a real sense of caring. However, there are other ways to become immersed in the community. Service learning projects can offer great benefits to the community as well as to the students.

Wade (1995) writes, "If the true mission of our profession is active citizenship, we must help our students learn the value of engaging in long-term efforts to revitalize our democratic society and the skills to respond compassionately to those whose daily needs cannot wait for societal transformation" (p. 122). Service learning is one such way for teachers to engage their students in real-world community involvement. The term itself grew out of the work by Sigmon and Ramsey at the Southern Regional Education Board (Giles & Eyler, 1994). Community service learning (CSL), by definition, involves the connection of worthwhile service to one's school or community atmosphere with scholarly learning and organized reflection on the experience of providing the service (Wade, 1995). In this context, the community becomes a learning laboratory (Lena, 1995). With service learning, students become "learners as doers" (Schukar, 1997, p. 177) and address significant social issues and plan direct action. Learning is authentic, purposeful, self-regulated, and extends well beyond the classroom. Additionally, learning is not bounded by traditional curriculum subject boundaries. Students develop their research, critical-thinking skills, and interpersonal skills through both traditional and nontraditional means by relying on social, ethical, and environmental contexts. This development of students' own authentic learning is at the heart of optimal self-regulated learning.

Lena (1995) says of service learning: it "…blurs the line between content and method in a most productive way, for it transcends each" (p. 109). Within community service learning, students study significant issues by generating their own questions (self-questioning) and then seek to find the answers (self-directing). Often, this service means helping those who are visibly in need and usually those outside of the students' economic, social, or cultural norm (Jones, Maloy, & Steen, 1996). Examples of service learning include activities in which students gather oral histories from senior citizens or create a bird sanctuary as part of an environmental study in science and math (Wade, 1995).

Students can also provide services to the elderly, tutoring for at-risk children, or participate in urban clean-ups. The key component to service learning is that it moves beyond mere community service and makes the vital link to instruction (Sanders, 2000). For example, instead of merely collecting canned food for a food drive, students at one inner-city school in Tuscon applied a service learning approach. They educated their peers about food and hunger issues in the world from a global perspective and then turned to the community for a closer example of hunger. They developed a videotape that explained the function of the local food bank and showed interviews they had conducted with food bank employees, workers, and recipients (Schukar, 1997).

Their design and implementation of a hunger awareness campaign show how learning was integrated throughout the service. The additional components of reflection and preparation distinguish service learning from traditional community service. Community service learning, however, is not only valuable to those receiving services, but to those who provide assistance as well. Service learning has been shown to provide many benefits for students. Adolescents often view the experience as a way to connect "school learning" to real-world issues that are apparent in their lives. With service learning, activities that previously seemed purposeless or boring require students to think critically and make connections between formal curriculum and real life (Jones, Maloy, & Steen, 1996). Opportunities for student choice among worthwhile learning options create the environment necessary for self-regulated learning to thrive.

In fact, more than 80% of schools with service learning programs report that grade point averages of most participating students improve. One study in Springfield, Massachusetts found that students' dropout rate decreased from 12% to 1% when they participated in service learning (Sanders, 2000). Experiential learning allows students to engage in new roles—for example, by serving as a tutor, a caregiver, or a mentor. These new roles bring about additional responsibilities, often contributing positively to students' self identities and feelings of responsibility and autonomy, as well as the higher levels of democratic interdependence.

Students who participate in service learning show increased self-esteem, self-efficacy, and motivation. These benefits, as well as a greater interest in school and greater academic achievement and responsibility, have been noted in the literature (Conrad & Hedin, 1991; Greco, 1992; Harrison, 1986). Teachers who have engaged in service learning also report personal benefits and a commitment to community involvement in their teaching (Wade, 1993). Because service learning often focuses on working with populations unlike the students, these experiences may assist students in breaking down traditional stereotypes. They begin to recognize similarities, as well as differences, that exist between themselves and others (Jones, Maloy, & Steen, 1996). Discussions and reflections about such experiences with adults may help students "reconstruct new frameworks for understanding the larger world and one's self-identity within that world" (Jones, Maloy, & Steen, 1996, p. 38). Programs should foster relationships that build ties across geographic, occupational, and age confines. Involvement in such relationships leads students to become more aware of the independence and dependency, and the cooperation and choices that exist among social organizations, as well as their own place within these social forces (Jones, Maloy, & Steen, 1996). Strengthened student-teacher relationships often result as well. Many teachers who employ service learning report having more positive feelings about their students. They also see their own roles as teachers as having greater importance (Schukar, 1997).

Student reflection and teacher assessment to assure high-quality academic learning are important components of community service learning. Personal testimonies are often used as evidence for the academic effectiveness of the approach. Additionally, journals, discussion, and essays assist students in reflecting on their experiences. These processes challenge students to extend beyond their traditional comfort zones by allowing them to engage in their own thinking and critical reflection, and in developing their own sense of voice. In so doing, they become more capable learners and leaders, both individually and as community citizens. Research indicates that involvement with service learning is even more likely to lead students to become informed voters later in life (Sanders, 2000).

While service learning (sometimes referred to as *academic community learning*) does seem to produce many positive results for all parties, it is not without controversy. Some parents are against service learning because they believe it is unconstitutional to force their child to participate in volunteerism, or they simply do not see the educational value that service learning provides their child (Wade, 1995). Likewise, some school districts have been reluctant to participate in service learning activities because of liability and safety concerns with students leaving the school and going out into the community. Thus, service has been seen as an "add-on" component of the curriculum, and not an essential part of it. Some school districts reject service learning by claiming that it is too difficult or expensive (Wade, 1995). Teachers should be aware that these challenges exist so they will be better prepared to justify the use of service learning as a way to foster curriculum integration.

Summary

This chapter explored various aspects of effective planning. Throughout the chapter, we have provided concrete examples to help you learn more about developing strong lesson plans that consider the "planning backwards" framework, and include attention to local, state, and national content standards. An integral part of planning also involves a shared understanding among students and teachers about goals and objectives. As you plan and teach each lesson, you should continually find ways to assess student learning through formative and summative methods.

To promote active citizenship and responsibility for learning, teachers should consider curriculum integration and community service learning models. The primary goal of curriculum integration is to improve student learning and increase student achievement through shared ownership for learning. As you consider integrating these models within your classrooms, remember to increase student motivation by weaving the fine arts and technology into instruction.

Understanding Instructional Communication in the Classroom

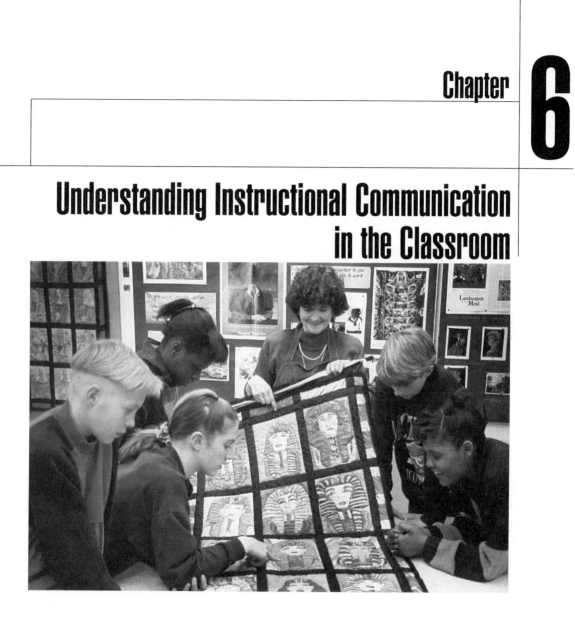

Self-Questions

Knowledge: Offer three guidelines for developing the ability to be an empathetic listener.

Comprehension: Explain Ellen Markman's comprehension monitoring research with elementary school children. What implications does this research have for classroom teachers?

Application: Use the discussion play strategy to create your own play. Integrate several effective and ineffective discussion behaviors within this play.

Analysis: Compare and contrast two teacher Web sites using the criteria adapted from Roblyer and Edwards (2000).

Synthesis: Develop an effective way to integrate spreadsheets into an existing lesson plan. Describe how your spreadsheet helps students learn skills such as organization and problem solving to improve task performance.

Evaluation: Critique the merits of integrating explicit teaching of listening, questioning, and discussion skills to improve oral communication in the classroom.

Introduction

A teacher who plays an active role in creating a classroom environment that is productive, motivational, respectful, and caring is taking important steps to bolster students' desire to be risk-takers and responsible learners. Earlier in the text, we described features of the verbal and nonverbal environments of the classroom and instructional strategies that promote self-regulated learning. Building upon this knowledge, this chapter focuses directly on instructional communication skills that teachers should model and practice with students. We discuss specific aspects of listening such as comprehension monitoring and the importance of listening in creating relationships. We discuss ways for teachers and students to formulate meaningful questions that foster inquiry. Next, we describe elements of effective classroom discussions that encourage multiple voices in teaching and learning along with consideration for a teacher's role in planning for active discussions. Finally, we explore how technology can enhance communication in the classroom. The chapter reinforces the themes of teacher responsiveness, student engagement, and internalization to further develop the concept of the teacher as a reflective practitioner.

Listening

Listening is a skill that is often taken for granted. Many of us believe that we are effective listeners, not realizing that we need to devote time to practicing and developing this critical skill. Many primary-grade teachers reinforce "be a good listener" as a classroom norm, yet take it for granted that students develop good listening habits on their own. According to Steil (1980), in *Your Personal Listening Profile*, listening is the communication skill most used each day. During a typical day, we commonly spend 45% of our time listening, 30% speaking, 16% reading, and 9% writing. We learn to listen before we speak. We use listening more than the other communication skills of speaking, reading, and writing, yet we are taught the least about how to be effective listeners.

Researchers have shown that listening is one of the top skills vital for success in personal and professional relationships (Cooper & Simonds, 1999; Wolvin & Coakley, 1991). Undoubtedly, to work effectively with students, teachers need to model good listening skills such as empathy and perception checking, and ways to block distractors. Such skills provide students opportunities to maximize productive, interpersonal relationships that meet their socioemotional needs. Effective listening skills also provide teachers with critical information about their students' academic progress. Teachers must listen carefully to students' developing understandings of content knowledge. Consistent with the goal of developing reflective, self-regulating learners, it is your responsibility as a teacher to also help students become aware of, practice, and monitor their own listening skills. Improved interpersonal relationships and academic success through active attention to effective listening strategy use are the goals.

Understanding the Role of Empathy in Effective Listening

Teachers and students alike can model, practice, and cue several strategies to become more productive listeners. An important component of developing effective interpersonal relationships is practicing being an empathetic listener. Empathy is an individual's ability to take the perspective of another, trying to understand his viewpoint as accurately as possible in a given situation. Such a skill is critical in helping students respect each other and establish positive peer relationships. Empathetic individuals make others feel valued. The same holds true for teachers—learners who feel safe and valued will be more ready to focus on reaching high levels of academic success. Teachers who demonstrate caring have students who will likely feel cared for—an important component for students to be ready for learning.

In order for a classroom of students to thrive, it is vital that students feel that their teacher displays genuine caring for them as discussed in chapter 4. This form of caring should not be equated with merely taking care of the students—that philosophy contradicts our aim of developing self-regulated learners. In order for self-responsibility to flourish as a norm, a teacher must demonstrate genuine care for individual and collective students' motivation, achievements, and needs. In other words, independence grows out of a firm base of having had dependency needs well-supported. Counterintuitively, independent learners were first dependent, and that dependence was supported by a loving, caring teacher who nudged her students gently toward responsibility. As Kottler and Zehm (2000) write, teachers "continue this pervasive caring by providing all their students with the appropriate amount of support, structure, and expectations they need to be self-directed, responsible learners" (p. 66). When a teacher models such caring, she continually reinforces to students that they should also communicate caring and respect for each other. We learn to care for others by the models of caring around us (e.g., from teachers, parents, grandparents).

Cooper and Simonds (1999) in *Communication for the Classroom Teacher*, describe two components necessary for empathetic listening: (1) predicting accurately and (2) communicating empathy. Their framework provides an excellent example of explicit strategy instruction in listening.

Predicting Accurately.   As you listen carefully to your student and try to take her perspective, try as much as possible to accurately predict her motivation. Be as perceptive as possible about who this student is—her basic feelings, behaviors, and values. It is crucial that you try to remove your own biases so that you can listen effectively. Indeed, you may not agree with the student's perspective, but your goal is to help her feel understood and appreciated, rather than judged. Your goal should be to understand the student's point of view without letting your own point of view color the way in which you listen.

Two strategies, paraphrasing and perception checking, can help students and teachers become more effective listeners. *Paraphrasing* is a strategy used to help the listener and speaker check for accuracy of ideas. This strategy is like "interpretation" in the active listening stage of Gordon's Language of Acceptance. When you paraphrase an idea, you restate both the content and feeling components of a message. For instance, a student may come up to you and say, "I really tried to finish my project. But every night my mom has me cook dinner and put my brothers to bed, and then when I finally get a chance to sit down to do homework, I'm exhausted. Since my mom works at night, I have to be the one who gets up in the middle of the night if one of the twins wakes up. I don't know how much more of this I can take!" Your response to this disclosure could be crucial to the student's academic and emotional success. If you simply respond, "I don't want to hear any more excuses about why your homework isn't done. It's your responsibility to complete assignments

According to Cooper and Simonds (1999, p. 62), there are six guidelines for developing the ability to communicate empathy.

1. Be willing to become involved with the student—be available and accessible.
2. Communicate positive regard for the student—show genuine respect and caring, regardless of behavior.
3. Communicate a supportive climate—emphasize understanding, not judging.
4. Listen to the student's nonverbal as well as verbal communication—be in tune to facial expressions, gestures, posture, eye contact, etc.
5. Accurately reflect and clarify feelings—try to respond to the content of the student's message, not your own values and beliefs.
6. Be genuine and congruent—communicate in a way that accurately reflects your thoughts and feelings, not misleading students to think you are genuine in your empathy and desire to help them.

Figure 6–1   Communicating Empathy.
Source: From Communication for the Classroom Teacher, 6th edition, *by Pamela J. Cooper and Cheri Simonds. ©1999. Reprinted with permission of Allyn & Bacon.*

on time," then you haven't been an active, empathetic listener. If you paraphrase the message first, it shows that you care and are listening actively. Paraphrasing is a skill that is different than simply parroting a response back to the speaker. It involves a synthesis of both the content and feeling of the message. Consider this response: "It sounds like you are really overwhelmed, and you don't have your own time to do things for yourself, like working on your school projects."

To check the accuracy of this paraphrase, you should also employ the strategy of *perception checking*. Perception checking, like paraphrasing, involves checking the accuracy of the message that you believe you heard. Furthermore, perception checking involves information about the speaker that you have noticed over time and includes a question to the speaker for confirmation or elaboration. For example, the teacher could continue, "I noticed that you have been late turning in the last three projects. I have been wondering if there was something going on in your life that was affecting your work. I'm really glad that you came to talk to me. Is this the reason your other assignments have been late? How can we work on this together?"

Communicating Empathy.   Active listening that is empathetic communicates that you care about your students' worries, frustrations, boredom, or sadness (Figure 6–1). To help a troubled student truly feel that you welcome open communication, you could use a question as a "door opener" to invite the student to discuss her concerns (Wolfgang, Bennett, & Irvin, 1999). Examples of door openers include: "Would you like to tell me more? What else happened? Why did this make you sad?" (See chapter 4 for additional discussion of door openers.)

Communication that is "door opening" must contain complementary verbal and nonverbal components. If you ask a student, "Would you like to tell me more?" while looking at your watch or thumbing through a stack of papers, he probably will not believe that you value his feelings. Nonverbal attentiveness complemented by repeated door-opener probes can help young children maintain focus and feel the necessary encouragement to learn to discuss their feelings, as illustrated in the following example:

> *Teacher:*   *What happened on the playground?* (eye level with child, open gestures)
>
> *Ethan:*   *I was playing with Scott, and when Barrett came by, Scott just left me in the middle of our game and went to play with Barrett. He's stupid.*

Teacher:	*Then what happened?* (soft voice, encouraging eye contact)
Ethan:	*I was really mad, so I ran up and bit Scott really hard on his arm. It's not fair.*
Teacher:	*Would you like to tell me more?* (neutral expression, display caring)
Ethan:	*I don't wanna. They don't want to play with me anyhow.*
Teacher:	*What would you like to happen?*
Ethan:	*I'd like to be able to play with them. They should play with other people, too.*

Instead of only reprimanding Ethan for hurting another child, the teacher used active listening skills to get to the root of what was troubling him. By first getting Ethan's perspective, the teacher displayed genuine concern for his point of view and helped him understand the motivation for his physical aggression. After being able to talk through his motives, Ethan may be more able to think about alternate ways to resolve a problem in the future. In addition, the teacher was then able to talk to the entire class about welcoming all classmates to play on the playground, adapting Paley's (1992) norm of "You can't say you can't play."

LEARNING OUT LOUD 6–1

Carry a notebook around with you for 2 days. Monitor one school day and one day during the weekend. Each hour, jot down the amount of time you spend listening and speaking in that hour.

School day	Weekend
10:00 a.m.	10:00 a.m.
12:00 p.m.	12:00 p.m.
2:00 p.m.	2:00 p.m.
6:00 p.m.	6:00 p.m.
9:00 p.m.	9:00 p.m.

Recognizing Barriers to Effective Listening

To be an effective listener, you should examine your own biases and really pay attention to how you listen. Did you begin to rehearse a response midway through a student's question? Did you tune out a student's explanation because you could not block another student's distraction? Were you so sure that you knew what a student was going to say that you cut her off? Did she respond in a way that *you* wanted rather than saying what she wanted to say? We are all guilty of ineffective listening in some circumstances. Unless we bring our listening habits to an explicit level of awareness, we may never realize the impact of our listening "blocks" on student motivation and learning (Figure 6–2). Effective listening necessitates a stance of openness to multiple perspectives, to differing learning and emotional styles, and to cultural differences.

Helping Students Learn Listening Comprehension Skills

Markman (1977, 1978, 1979, 1981) provided groundbreaking research in the area of metacognitive research for comprehension. Her work is referred to as *comprehension monitoring*. Specifically, she examined elementary school students' ability to monitor their own listening comprehension as directions for a game and a magic trick were read aloud to them.

If you want to listen so you really hear what others say, make sure you're not a:

- *Mind reader.* You'll hear little or nothing as you think, "What is this person really thinking or feeling?"
- *Rehearser.* Your mental tryouts for "Here's what I'll say next" tune out the speaker.
- *Filterer.* Some call this selective listening—hearing only what you want to hear.
- *Dreamer.* Drifting off during a face-to-face conversation can lead to an embarrassing "What did you say?" or "Could you repeat that?"
- *Identifier.* If you refer everything you hear to your experience, you probably didn't really hear what was said.
- *Comparer.* When you get side-tracked assessing the messenger, you're sure to miss the message.
- *Derailer.* Changing the subject too quickly tells others you're not interested in anything they have to say.
- *Sparrer.* You hear what's said but quickly belittle it or discount it. That puts you in the same class as the derailer.
- *Placater.* Agreeing with everything you hear just to be nice or to avoid conflict does not mean you're a good listener.

Figure 6–2   Road Blocks to Effective Listening.
Source: Adapted from Messages: The Communication Skills Book, by *McKay, M., Davis, M., & Fanning, P., 1983, Oakland, CA: New Harbinger Press. Adapted with permission of the publisher.*

As Markman (1978) wrote, "One must be sensitive to the level of one's comprehension to know what to reread, when to ask questions, what additional information is needed, etc." (pp. 30–31). As teachers, we need to understand that listening comprehension is a skill that develops slowly and needs consistent modeling, practicing, and cueing. For example, in Markman's 1977 study, she found that when first and third graders were given instructions for playing a game with the omission of a critical step, only 1 out of the 12 first graders recognized the omission before the game was played. This rate of comprehension was compared to that of third graders, wherein 10 out of the 12 students commented on the omission before playing. Markman concluded that the first graders were hearing the directions without mentally processing as they listened, while the third graders seemed to play the game mentally as a way of evaluating the information.

In Markman's comprehension monitoring studies, she found that first graders are often unaware that they do not understand oral directions. Many teachers can identify with the frustration of giving a set of directions, asking for questions, and having students agree that they understand when in reality they do not. Then, when the teacher asks the students to complete the task independently, many students are unable to do so. It is important for teachers, especially those in the primary grades, to provide guided practice and monitor student understanding before releasing responsibility to the students. Markman contends that students in the primary grades often do not realize that they do not understand information, so it is pointless to simply ask these children if they understand.

In keeping with fostering self-regulated learning, students can learn to ask themselves questions that can help improve their listening comprehension skills. For example, in an adaptation of Markman's (1977/1979) study in which she provided incomplete directions to a game, Manning (1991) created the "Can we play?" self-questioning strategy. Within this strategy, a teacher instructs the students to ask themselves three questions: (1) "Does this make sense to me?" (2) "Is there anything missing?" and (3) "What else do I need to know?" The teacher writes these questions on the board or on poster board to display the information as a stimulus or cue. Then, the teacher gives sets of complete and incomplete directions. Students are provided an opportunity to play the game (such as a version of academic Jeopardy or Bingo, or preferably a game that the teacher creates) when they can supply the missing directions. When the students are provided the incomplete directions, they are asked, "Can we play? Why or why not?" Students are then coached to ask the three self-questions to help them.

LEARNING OUT LOUD 6–2

Monitor your own listening and find which "roadblocks" you ordinarily employ. Also note the situation in which you put up this roadblock to effective listening. For example:

Situation: Person telling you why she is unhappy at work

Notes: I kept interrupting and telling my own problems because they seemed so much like hers. I think I kept identifying with her so much that I focused on my own issues instead of really listening to her problems.

Situation: _____

Notes: _____

Situation: _____

Notes: _____

Questioning

Questions can open or close conversations, encourage or discourage multiple points of view, and demonstrate concern or lack of interest. Because of the power of questioning in promoting active participation in learning, questions are one of the most influential communication strategies in teaching (Dillon, 1990).

As a teacher, you need to carefully think through the kinds of questions that you ask to promote learning and inquiry, along with the purpose of the questions. Historically, typical student-teacher interactions have followed the pattern of the teacher asking a question, a student responding, and the teacher reacting to the student's answer (Cazden, 1988). Within the model of learning promoted within this text, learners should take on a much more active and interactive role. Consider the kind of environment you hope to create in your classroom as you structure your questions—questions that encourage and demonstrate interest in individual ideas are more likely to invite further discussion. As you artfully plan the kinds of questions that challenge students to wonder, help your students see that you are modeling ways to ask questions. Students can then actively practice asking each other different kinds of questions. They can learn to become effective "question askers" with explicit modeling and scaffolding.

Effective teachers are aware of and explicitly work to develop effective questioning skills. According to Danielson (1996), who has developed the Framework for Professional Practice for the Educational Testing Service (ETS), effective questioning is an important element of excellent teaching. In her book *Enhancing Professional Practice: A Framework for Teaching (1996)*, Danielson describes teachers who have not learned effective questioning and discussion skills as tending to "pose primarily rapid-fire, short-answer, low-level questions to their students, using the questions as a vehicle for students to demonstrate their knowledge." Although we believe such questioning has a place in practice, students cannot develop their own questioning skills if they are not challenged by different kinds of questions. In contrast, Danielson describes a teacher who effectively uses questions and discussion to engage students in meaningful learning as one who uses questioning "to engage students in an exploration of content" and "to enable students to reflect on their understanding and consider new possibilities." Danielson further states that such questions "rarely require a simple yes/no response and may have many possible correct answers" (p. 92). Finally, Danielson writes that the hallmark of an effective questioner is that the students learn to pose their own questions: "The formulation of questions requires that students engage in analytical thinking and motivates them more than questions the teacher presents" (p. 93). Danielson's work is used across the nation to evaluate the performance of beginning teachers. Within this research-based framework, questioning and discussion techniques are fostered with the goal of helping students develop as self-regulated learners who practice and internalize questioning strategies.

Very young children are the best question-askers, as they naturally wonder about the world around them. Randi Stanulis recently flew on an airplane with her 4-year-old son. People sitting near them chuckled at Scott's curiosity as he asked, "How can the airplane fly at night?" "How can the pilot see where he's going?" "How come it's not raining when we get above the cloud?" "Why can't we touch a cloud?" "Why don't planes bump into each other in the sky?" Scott asked each of these questions with enthusiasm and natural curiosity, and he required an explanation that affirmed that his questions were important. Worn out after 2 hours of constant questions, Randi finally replied, "The 'why' machine has been turned off for the night!" Weary of answering so many questions, Randi stifled his wondering. Although it becomes exhausting and requires a lot of effort, cognitive thought, and creativity, it is more commonplace for parents and teachers to "turn their why machine off" rather than encourage questioning.

Children who learn that their questions are valued can also learn ways to channel their enthusiasm toward answering their own questions through exploration, observation, problem solving, research, and speculation. If you model risk-taking as a teacher, students will be more likely to ask questions freely and take risks to discover their own answers and articulate their developing theories. For example, when Randi asked Scott why *he* thought it wasn't raining when they got above the clouds, his first response was, "I don't know." Then when Randi asked, "Where does rain come from?", Scott thought carefully and said, "Rain comes from clouds and so you have to be *under* a cloud to get wet." As Jarolimek, Foster, and Kellough (2001) write in, *Teaching and Learning in the Elementary School*, "Wonderment + inquisitiveness + curiosity + the enjoyment of problem solving = a sense of efficacy as a thinker. Young children express wonderment, and this should never be stifled" (p. 285). This sense of wonderment needs to be encouraged in children of all ages, and even adults.

The kinds of questions encouraged in discussions play an integral role in the quality of discussion and learning that ensue. For example, Commeyras and Sumner (1996) studied ways to shift responsibility for question asking and discussion monitoring to students in Sumner's second-grade classroom in a culturally diverse setting. Through their work together, teachers and students learned about questions that students want to discuss in the context of reading literature together. Sumner became interested in studying the ways that she could foster questioning in discussions after analyzing her own practice. She found that she structured discussions in the typical "teacher-talk" format—the teacher asks a question, the student recites an answer. Within the study, Commeyras, a university researcher, worked closely with Sumner in her classroom to help students learn to think of questions they would like to bring up for discussion as they listened to a story. Student feedback included comments such as, "I think we pay more attention to the story when we get to make up the questions," "I like writing down questions because you can get ideas," and "I think we're asking more questions because you can't learn unless you ask questions" (Commeyras & Sumner, 1998, p. 137).

As Sumner continually worked to shift responsibility for questioning and discussing to the students, she also reinforced key norms of the classroom. For example, Sumner believes that one way to make the classroom a safe place to take risks is to instill a norm of "no put-downs." Sumner reinforces this norm by talking about particular aspects of discussion with the children:

Sumner: *I heard a put-down which I was surprised to hear. This put-down was not so much the words but the tone of voice used. Carl, how did it make you feel when others acted like your answer was silly?*

Carl: *Bad.*

Sumner: *Carl was making a very good point and it was put down, which meant he never said another word. He wasn't going to chance another put-down.* (Commeyras & Sumner, 1996, p. 3)

As you consciously work to invite questions and model questioning, you need to consider different purposes for asking questions and different kinds of questions to ask. Students should learn to answer questions and should also learn ways to find their own answers. Once students internalize skills involved in both effective questioning and effective problem solving to find answers, they can apply this process to new situations.

Questions require various levels of thinking, depending on purpose, planning, and promoting of critical inquiry. Figure 6–3 shows a chart developed by Cooper and Simonds (1999) that illustrates how questions can be asked according to different levels of Bloom's Taxonomy.

A question that is asked at a higher level of Bloom's Taxonomy is not always a more worthwhile question. Although we hear the tune "ask higher-order questions to get higher-order answers," there is nothing wrong with asking for factual information or getting a sense of students' basic comprehension. The question of higher or lower order is less relevant than the question of purpose. What is it that you want students to learn, discover, and demonstrate by responding to certain questions? If the question matches the purpose and is age-appropriate for the student audience, the question is effective. For example, students in early and middle grades often learn newspaper writing skills of "who, what, where, when, and how" to help them recall, restate, describe, summarize, and report ideas. It is important for students to develop these skills before they work with higher-level questions. Such higher-level questions require students to apply knowledge to a new context, analyze information, and so forth. (Refer to the QAR strategy described in chapter 8 for an explicit example of how to foster higher-order questioning and thinking skills in a scaffolded manner. Students first learn to find answers to questions that are "right there.")

LEARNING OUT LOUD 6–3

Design a series of questions based on one of the following topics, using Figure 6–3 as a guide. Possible topics include pollution, endangered species, the rainforest, and planet Earth.

Knowledge: _____

Comprehension: _____

Application: _____

Analysis: _____

Synthesis: _____

Evaluation: _____

Level	Key Words	Typical Question Terms
A. **Knowledge**: Questions that require simple recall of previously learned material Example: Name the 50 states.	Remember	1. Name 2. List, tell 3. Define 4. Who? When? What? 5. Yes or no questions: "Was. . .?" "Is. . .?" 6. How many? How much? 7. Describe, label, match, select
B. **Comprehension**: Questions that request students to restate or reorganize material in a literal manner to show that they understand the essential meaning Example: Why does the Midwest region's agriculture look so different from that of the south?	Understand	1. Give an example 2. What is the speaker's most important idea? 3. What will the consequences probably be? 4. What caused this? 5. Compare (What things are the same?) 6. Contrast (What things are different?) 7. Paraphrase, rephrase, translate, summarize, defend
C. **Application**: Questions that require students to use previously learned material to solve problems in new situations Example: Given this list of products, what region of the country do you think manufactured them?	Solve the problem	1. Solve 2. Apply the principle (concept) to. . . 3. Compute, prepare, produce, relate, modify, classify
D. **Analysis**: Questions that require students to break an idea into its component parts for logical analysis. Example: Listen to a political campaign ad. Which statements are presented as fact and which indicate emotional appeals?	Logical order	1. What reasons does the author give for his conclusions? 2. What does the author seem to believe? 3. What words indicate bias or emotion? 4. Does the evidence given support the conclusion? 5. Break down, differentiate, distinguish
E. **Synthesis**: Questions that require students to combine their ideas into a statement, plan, product, and so forth, that is new for them Example: You are running for governor of your state. Write a speech that addresses the needs of your state.	Create	1. Develop a model 2. Combine those parts 3. Write a speech 4. Create, combine, design, diagram, propose, write
F. **Evaluation**: Questions that require students to judge something based on some criteria Example: Read three of the speeches mentioned above written by classmates. Which one most accurately depicts the needs of your state?	Judge	1. Evaluate that idea in terms of _____ 2. For what reasons, do you favor _____ 3. Appraise, criticize, justify, _____

Figure 6–3 Determining the Purpose of Questions: Questioning According to the Levels of Bloom's Taxonomy. *Source: From* Communication for the Classroom Teacher, 6th edition, *by Pamela J. Cooper and Cheri Simonds.* ©1999. Adapted with permission of Allyn & Bacon. (Examples in each section have been changed.)

Creating Productive Discussions That Share Responsibility for Learning

Classroom discussions are an integral part of discourse that promotes active learning, shared development of meaning, and application of self-regulating behaviors like self-monitoring and self-coping. As you develop your lesson plans for teaching, we urge you to consider the role of the teacher in fostering productive discussions that include carefully planned questions. Researchers have found that teacher talk oftentimes dominates discussions. Most classroom discussions take on the pattern of the teacher as the leader who decides who may speak, how turn taking is established, and the topics discussed (Cazden, 1998; Wiencek, 1996). In contrast, free-flowing discussions enable participants themselves to practice and regulate their own development of skills such as turn taking, developing a topic, and evaluating multiple points of view.

To aid teachers in creating productive discussions, researchers developed a framework called the *conversational discussion group* (CDG), which defines the teacher's role of facilitator of a discussion (O'Flahavan & Stein, 1992; Wiencek, 1996; Wiencek & O'Flahavan, 1994).

The Conversational Discussion Group (CDG) Framework

The CDG framework was established for use with literature discussion groups, but could easily be adapted for discussion in any content area. Within this framework, teachers focus on helping students develop both interactive and interpretive strengths. *Interactive abilities* include the strategies that people within a group develop that guide the flow of talk, such as deciding that only one person can speak at a time, that everyone in the group gets an opportunity to speak, or that everyone's opinion is valued (O'Flahavan, Stein, Wiencek, & Marks, 1992). *Interpretive abilities* include strategies that students develop to help them evaluate the topic and reach new understandings. For example, within the context of literature discussions, students might talk about character development and actions. Within social studies, students might evaluate cause-and-effect of events. Within mathematics, students might evaluate the concepts and processes used to reach certain operational conclusions.

The CDG involves three phases: (1) the introduction and review, (2) the discussion, and (3) the debriefing. In the *introduction/review* phase, the teacher meets with the discussion group and coaches the students as they develop and review strategies for interaction and interpretation. These are recorded on a chart that remains as a visual cue throughout discussions. In the *discussion* phase, the teacher either leaves the group to have its own discussion or provides a careful perspective as a participant. If the teacher remains in the group, she should limit her talk and assume the roles of observer and coach during the discussion. The teacher need not fade completely from the group, as her presence may well be needed to help students explore a point more fully or examine points from alternative perspectives. She may also add new information that can help the conversation move forward. The emphasis lies in how the teacher performs these roles, and whether she truly supports students as they develop their own discussion strategies and skills. In the *debriefing* phase, the teacher takes the lead in reviewing aspects of the discussion, focuses students on their own goals for discussion, and questions them about different interpretation and interactional skills that were practiced. Students must practice and debrief these new skills to learn new strategies. This phase provides an opportunity for honest reflection and continued learning. Students continue to add items to their discussion chart as they learn, practice, and reflect.

First-Grade Goals

I want my students to:
- Respond to a story by drawing a picture and writing a sentence about the picture
- Share their response in a group
- Talk about the things they liked in the story and the things they disliked
- Learn literary terms such as *character, setting,* and *problem*

Fifth-Grade Goals

I want my students to:
- Participate actively in free-flowing discussions in which they are participants of equal status
- Expand their repertoire of strategies for interpreting literature and utilize them during discussion when appropriate
- Respect the thoughts and interpretations of their peers and teachers
- Develop social abilities that enable them to fully participate
- Become active readers who are thoughtful and reflective about what they read

---

Figure 6–4   Developmentally Appropriate Goals for Interaction and Interpretation.
Source: From "Planning, Initiating, and Sustaining Literature Discussion Groups: The Teacher's Role," by J. Wiencek, 1996, in L. Gambrell & J. Almasi (Eds.), Lively Discussions *(pp. 208–223). Newark, DE: International Reading Association. Reprinted by permission.*

The Teacher's Role in Discussions

The teacher's role in a discussion involves deliberate planning and monitoring. Just as you will plan and evaluate other aspects of instruction, you must also plan the goals of the discussion, the topics you will discuss, group formation, and decisions about your role as a teacher. Teachers often build in time for discussion without exploring why the discussion will benefit the participants. By designing specific goals, you can assess your students' progress in developing discussion skills. Figure 6–4 shows the goals created by Joyce Wiencek for first and fifth graders as they participate in literature groups.

We have observed many teachers as they provide opportunities for discussions. Consistent with a constructivist view of learning, university faculty typically promote the integration of discussion into lesson plans. Discussions are meant to foster active learning, provide opportunities for multiple perspectives, and help students view each other and themselves as teachers and learners. However, teachers are provided with little support in taking on the role of facilitator during discussions. What will your role be during a specific discussion? Different kinds of discussions warrant different kinds of roles. In some cases, especially at the beginning of the school year when you are practicing discussion skills, you will take a more directive role—helping to move the discussion forward, assuming the "role of the mentor, probing the students about how they are thinking rather than what they are thinking" (Walker, 1996, p. 288). Within this model, the teacher "phases in" and "phases out" (Walker, 1996), demonstrating effective ways to move discussions forward and talking aloud about the discussion process. The teacher can then "phase out" as appropriate to let the students take the lead in practicing the discussion behaviors.

Self-monitoring is crucial during discussions. As a teacher, you need to continually monitor how much you are talking, and whether you are truly willing to relinquish some control to let the discussion flow. With younger children, it may be necessary for you to talk more as these students learn about how to carry on a discussion among themselves without adult leadership. After sufficient practice, even young students can internalize effective discussion behaviors such as, "I agree because" and "I disagree because" as ways to build on a peer's explanation.

LEARNING OUT LOUD 6–4

Observe a school or university instructor during a discussion. What kind of role does the teacher play in promoting student awareness and practice of effective discussion skills? Does the teacher play a dominant role in moving the discussion forward or do peers take the lead? Evaluate the effectiveness of the discussion including (a) the role of the teacher, (b) teacher modeling and cueing of effective discussion strategies, (c) effective and ineffective discussion behaviors practiced by students, and (d) student awareness of ineffective and effective discussion behaviors.

Assessing Discussions

Students as well as teachers need to understand productive discussion behavior. To assess students' effectiveness as a participant in discussion, teachers should first model effective discussion behaviors. One strategy for helping students learn about and assess discussion behavior is called the *discussion play* (Matazano, 1996).

The discussion play provides a creative and attention-getting way to model effective discussion strategies. By using this strategy, students can practice effective discussion skills and learn to evaluate effective discussions. In the discussion play strategy, students are involved in generating discussion guidelines and in evaluating the quality of discussions. Discussion behaviors include what was said (verbal communication) and what was done (nonverbal communication). Matanzo (1996) provides examples of discussion behaviors to consider in assessment of effective discussions (see Figure 6–5).

A discussion play can center around any topic or theme. Matanzo primarily used the discussion play as a method for learning to talk about literature. However, this strategy can be used across content areas. For example, students can use discussions to explore and extend their knowledge about science topics. Consider the following example: A third-grade class is studying about the roles of predator and prey in the food chain. Together, the class has

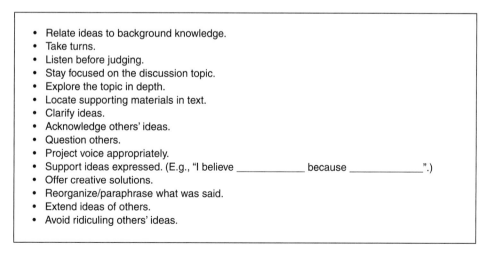

- Relate ideas to background knowledge.
- Take turns.
- Listen before judging.
- Stay focused on the discussion topic.
- Explore the topic in depth.
- Locate supporting materials in text.
- Clarify ideas.
- Acknowledge others' ideas.
- Question others.
- Project voice appropriately.
- Support ideas expressed. (E.g., "I believe _____ because _____".)
- Offer creative solutions.
- Reorganize/paraphrase what was said.
- Extend ideas of others.
- Avoid ridiculing others' ideas.

Figure 6–5   Ideas for Discussion Behaviors.
Source: From "Discussion: Assessing What Was Said and What Was Done," by J. Matanzo, 1996, in L. Gambrell and J. Almasi (Eds.), Lively Discussions *(pp. 250–264). Newark, DE: International Reading Association. Reprinted by permission.*

read about food chains, has seen a video, and is now listening to a song about predator and prey written by Blanchard (1998), a Montessori teacher who specializes in music and sensory experiences for children.

Predator and Prey Discussion

Stay Close to Me
by
Pam Blanchard*

An old gazelle got sick.
No longer was he quick.
And he couldn't help but lag behind the herd.
Well, a cheetah was downwind,
and he struck and took the breath from him.
The cheetah ate his meal while the herd ran away.

Stay close to me, my little one.
For there's danger if you go out there alone.
In the middle of the herd
We'll surround you and you'll be
So much safer if you're close to me.

A pack of hyenas smelled the blood of the gazelle
And they searched until they found the cheetah eating very well.
So they fought and they bit and they chased the cheetah far from it.
The cheetah could only watch while the pack ate his prey.

Stay close to me, my little one.
For there's danger if you go out there alone.
In the middle of the herd
We'll surround you and you'll be
So much safer if you're close to me.

Discussion Play

Teacher: *Who was the predator and who was the prey in this song?*

Kareem: *The cheetah came in and attacked the gazelle and killed it, so he was the hunter.*

Jason: *But then a whole bunch of hyenas came in and took the food away from the cheetah, so weren't they the hunter, too?*

Nicole: *Yeah, those hyenas were a lot tougher than the. . . .*

Melissa: *No, they weren't tougher, there were just more of them, and they. . . .*

Rudy: *. . .cool, they just jumped in there, bit and everything . . . just like sharks.*

Stan: *Yeah, but sharks have much bigger teeth. That would be so cool, in the ocean and everything. I was at the beach once, and this one kid yelled "shark" and everyone ran out of the water. We were all scared.*

Natalie: *Mrs. Stanulis wants us to talk about this song, not about your trip to the ocean. I think BOTH the cheetah and the pack of hyenas are predators, and the cheetah is the prey.*

*Blanchard, P. (1998). Music Makes Me Happy.

Jason:	*That can't be right. That's stupid.*
Tom:	*And it's not fair that a whole pack of hyenas went in and took the food from one cheetah.*
Melissa:	*I think Natalie is right. I think if there was only one hyena, he would not have fought with the cheetah, but because there was a pack of them, they could take on the cheetah.*
Teacher:	*Why do you think the gazelle was prey, even though he was in a herd (or with a bunch of other gazelles)?*
Jason:	*Cuz he was old and slower than the rest. He couldn't be close to the rest of them, so it was easy for the cheetah to get him.*
Kareem:	*That's probably why the song keeps saying "Stay close to me." If you're close, you might not get hurt.*
Rudy:	*Yeah, like my mom always says, "Stay close to me" when I'm in crowded places. Like the other day I was at the mall and I wanted to see the train ride and I went away from my mom, and she came after me hollering that I was in big trouble. I saw the coolest candy, too, at the Yummy Shop. It was pink and. . . .*
Natalie:	*Ugh! We're supposed to be talking about the song! I think you are safer with a lot of people or a lot of animals around. Like it says in our science book, there is "protection in numbers."*
Teacher:	*What else have you read about parents taking care of baby animals and protecting them?*
Jason:	*That the better parents are the ones who can help the babies find food and keep them safe in the pack. Then the babies have more of a chance to live.*

After listening to the song, the teacher has the students act out the discussion play. The students use their own class-generated list of discussion behaviors as a guide to see which behaviors are being enacted and which behaviors need improvement. Once the play has been acted out, the class participates in a discussion about the discussion play. Students identify characters in the play who exhibited positive discussion behaviors, such as Natalie, who helped the group stay focused on the discussion topic, and Melissa, who acknowledged and extended Natalie's ideas. In contrast, students identify ineffective discussion behaviors such as Stan's and Rudy's tendency to wander from the discussion topic, Jason's ridicule of another's ideas, and Jason's, Nicole's, Melissa's, and Rudy's act of cutting off each other's ideas without taking turns.

LEARNING OUT LOUD 6–5

List some discussion behaviors that you want to help students learn. Alongside this list, recall some inappropriate behaviors you have observed during discussions. Create your own activity for helping students learn about and assess effective discussion behaviors. This activity can be a play, a simulated television interview, a commercial, or any other creative activity that will engage learners.

Next, in whole group or a small group (depending on age level and ability), students generate their own discussion play. Similarly, they will include both effective and ineffective discussion behaviors. By modeling and practicing effective discussion behaviors, students will learn more concretely about the kinds of behaviors that help assess whether they have been productive discussion participants.

Using the Computer as a Tool for Improving Speaking and Listening Skills

Technology can greatly enhance teaching and learning in an interactive classroom. Students can use technology to research, create, edit, and enhance artistic talents. Through increased knowledge of technology, students can gain expertise in research and presentational skills that can improve oral communication in the classroom.

One reason to incorporate technology into the classroom is to increase student motivation to learn. As we have discussed throughout the text, students who are motivated are more likely to pay attention and be eager to complete a task on their own. The creation of Web-based, digital, and hypermedia products can increase student attention, expose students to diverse learning styles, and help students practice self-control and self-responsibility. Learners can become actively engaged in productive work when they are involved in technology activities—such involvement fosters creativity, self-expression, and self-efficacy (Roblyer & Edwards, 2000).

To use technology effectively in the classroom, teachers need to identify clear objectives for its use and thoughtfully integrate technology experiences as a natural part of student learning (Figure 6–6). Similar to the ways in which you will plan to teach any lesson, you should use technology as a means to assess a particular outcome. Programs should not be used only because they are "cute" or because they provide a way for teachers to be released from instructional activities.

The teacher's role in supporting the use of technology is pivotal to the success of developing an environment that is enhanced by the use of multiple media. If a teacher promotes discussing, problem solving, questioning, and listening, then technology can provide a natural extension that builds upon these communication skills. For example, if students are problem solving as they learn about why certain sounds create an echo, they can investigate soundwaves and vibrations on the Internet, they can create a Web site, or they can create a Power Point presentation. Each of these activities promotes self-regulated learning as students direct their inquiries through exploration and synthesis.

Using Computers as Tools to Foster Student Learning

As with any other instructional method, teachers need to be effective models and coaches to help students become effective technology users. Students must be provided with adequate hands-on time to practice developing expertise with computers, and not merely be passive class members as a teacher demonstrates use of different programs. Technology is compatible with constructivist theories of learning. For example, Davydov (1995) wrote that Vygotsky's work contributed to constructivist educators' belief that learning should correspond to individual development and that methods should be tailored to individual needs, not uniform across all students. According to Roblyer and Edwards (2000), constructivist teachers facilitate student learning that is focused on solving real-life, practical problems. Students can work individually or in small groups with technology as they focus on projects that seek to find solutions to problems rather than learning isolated skills. As students set their own goals, teachers act as active guides who need to have expertise in multiple forms of technology tools in order to spur individual learning.

Once students become proficient technology users, computers can help students direct their own learning. Three basic computer applications can be particularly useful for teachers and students who may have limited time to learn about various computer programs: (1) the Internet, (2) databases, and (3) presentation programs.

Step 1: Needs assessment—Deciding instructional problems that have technology solutions

_____ Topics that seem especially difficult for students to learn because concepts involved are abstract or foreign to students' experience; students have trouble visualizing meaning and relevance

_____ Activities involved in learning present logistical hurdles for students (handwriting, calculations, data collection) which interfere with acquiring higher-level skills

_____ Learning requires extensive individual, teacher-corrected practice, leaving limited time for individual help

_____ Students find topics uninteresting/tedious; motivation and transfer are constant problems

_____ Teacher-led activities are needed, but teacher and/or materials are not available

_____ Students resist preparing and making paper-based reports and presentations of their work

_____ Students resist working collaboratively on a research and/or development project, and a teacher wants a format that will motivate them to work and present products together

_____ To do a research project, students need information and expertise not available locally

_____ Students need practice in skills that will make them technologically competitive as students and workers: technology literacy, information literacy, and visual literacy

Step 2: Planning instruction—Designing appropriate integration strategies

_____ Will the instruction be single-subject or interdisciplinary?

_____ Should activities be individual, paired, small group, large group, whole class, or a combination of these?

_____ What instructional activities need to come before the introduction of the technology resource?

_____ What instructional activities need to follow the introduction of the technology resource?

_____ How will you assess students' learning progress and products: criteria, checklists, rubrics?

Step 3: Logistics—Preparing the classroom environment; arranging resources

_____ How many computers will be needed? Will the teacher need to schedule time in a lab or media center? Or will the classroom computers be adequate?

_____ If demonstrations and learning stations can be used, will projection devices or large screen monitors be needed?

_____ What other equipment, software, media, and other resources will be needed (printers, printer paper, software/probeware, videodiscs/CDS)?

_____ Over what time period and for how long will technology resources be needed?

Step 4: Preparing yourself and students to use resources

_____ Become familiar with troubleshooting procedures specific to the piece of hardware or software package being used. (Equipment and software manuals often list such procedures.)

_____ Test run an equipment setup before students arrive. (Even if the setup was working the day before, check it once again before class.)

_____ Back up your own files and train students to back up theirs.

_____ Have the original program disks/discs handy to re-install them, if necessary.

_____ Allow students time to get used to materials before beginning a graded activity.

_____ Demonstrate the skills students will need to use both for the equipment and for the specific software for the lesson.

_____ Encourage students to use the help sections in the software manuals.

Step 5: Try it! Evaluating and revising integration strategies

_____ Consider alternative ways to set up equipment to make things easier.

_____ Solicit feedback from students about how to improve activities.

How do you know when you've integrated technology well? (based on Milone's 1989 points)

_____ An outside observer sees the technology activity as a seamless part of the lesson.

_____ The reason for using the technology is obvious to you, the students, and others.

_____ The students are focusing on learning, not the technology.

_____ You can describe how technology is helping a particular student.

(continued)

Figure 6–6 Determining Technology Needs in the Classroom.
Source: From Integrating Educational Technology Into Teaching, _(p. 41–42), by M. D. Roblyer and J. Edwards, © 2000. Reprinted by permission of Pearson Education, Inc., Upper Saddle River, NJ._

_____ You would have difficulty accomplishing lesson objectives if the technology wasn't there.
_____ You can explain easily and concisely what the technology is supposed to contribute.
_____ All students are participating in the use of the technology and benefiting from it.

How do you know when you haven't integrated technology well? (based on Milone's 1989 points)
_____ You consistently see the technology as more trouble than it's worth.
_____ You have trouble justifying cost and preparation time in terms of benefits to your students.
_____ Students spend more time trying to make the technology work than learning the topic.
_____ The problem you were trying to address is still there.

Figure 6–6   Determining Technology Needs in the Classroom. (*continued*)

Figure 6–7 illustrates how teachers at an elementary (K–5) school, Barnett Shoals, brainstormed ways to integrate technology across the curriculum areas of language arts, mathematics, social studies, and science. As you can see, there are many creative ways to apply technology to benefit your students' self-regulated learning.

The Internet

Teachers can set up their own Web sites and establish their own home pages. Home pages can include several links that provide information about the teacher for parents and students to view at the beginning of the school year. Links can also explain and/or display classroom projects. Homework and general class assignments can also be posted on the home page.

It is not difficult to create a Web site. Not only can Web sites provide useful information to parents and students, but creating one can familiarize you with this tool so that you can encourage your own pupils to create a home page. Bitter and Pierson (1999) provide suggestions for developing and maintaining a quality Web site:

1. *Check your site.*   Proofread your information yourself and ask a colleague to provide an extra check. Be sure all links work properly, including an easy return to the home page. Ask for a second opinion about the layout and color scheme of your Web site.

2. *Update your site.*   Make sure that your information remains timely as class projects, homework assignments, and announcements change. Parents and students are more likely to stay in touch if they know that the information is updated regularly. Check your links regularly, adding and deleting as necessary.

3. *Improve your site.*   Additions, surprises, and changes keep a fresh and appealing draw that entices readers to come back to read your Web site regularly. Add features to your Web site as you learn more computer applications.

LEARNING OUT LOUD 6–6

Create your own Web site to become familiar with developing links and moving within a Web site. Be sure to attend to Bitter and Pierson's (1999) criteria for developing and maintaining a quality Web site.

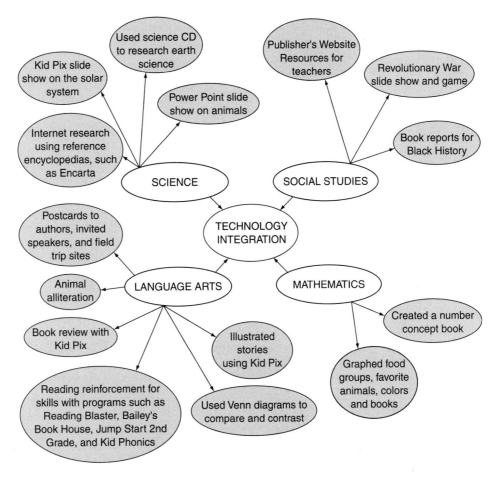

Figure 6–7   Web Integration of Technology.
Source: Reprinted with permission from Barnett Shoals Elementary School teachers, 2000, Athens, GA.

In addition to creating your own Web site, there are several other ways to use the Internet to enhance student learning. Electronic mail (e-mail) can be used to practice letter writing with students in other schools, states, or countries. A public bulletin board can help connect students across sites who are interested in a common topic. Information searches allow students to access libraries and databases of information to extend their knowledge on a particular topic. Chat rooms are available for students to communicate immediately with someone in another location about an academic topic of interest. As you and your students explore various sites, it is important to talk about evaluation of effective sites and appropriate use of sites. For example, teachers and students can apply the following criteria adapted from Roblyer and Edwards (2000):

- Is the teaching strategy appropriate for these students?
- Does the presentation on the screen contain information that misleads or confuses students?
- Is the text written at a desirable level of ease and difficulty for these students?
- Are there any abusive, inappropriate, or insulting comments in the program?
- Do the graphics fulfill important purposes (motivation, information). Are they distracting to learners?

Using Databases and Spreadsheets

Students and teachers can learn to use databases and spreadsheets to organize information. For example, information can be sorted, ranked, calculated, and stored by using databases such as Microsoft® Excel, Filemaker® Pro or ClarisWorks®. Many teachers use databases to organize student records, including attendance and grades. Such files can also include narrative, anecdotal records that track student progress. We know teachers who carry small notebooks around the class with them each day, or who jot notes on post-its and then transfer these notes to a more permanent database at a later time. Because assessment drives instruction and instruction influences assessment, you are encouraged to think of multiple ways to collect, organize, and store as much specific information about learner progress as possible.

Students can learn ways to use databases as a way to strengthen organizational skills and learn about formats to store information electronically. Databases can easily be created around a particular topic, such as dinosaurs, including information such as facts gained from multiple sources, questionnaires developed to learn more information, and information sheets designed from a compilation of the data generated. Such databases can be seen as electronic file cabinets (Heinich, Molenda, Russell & Smaldino, 1999) that help students

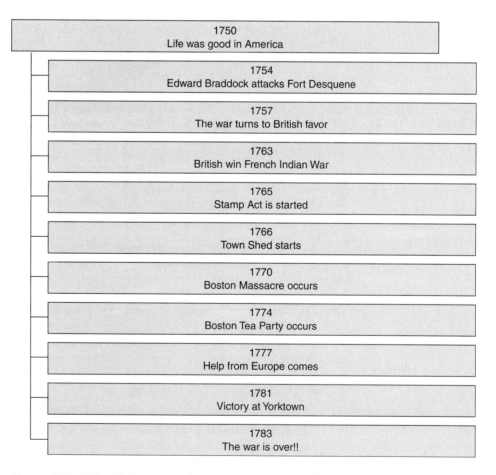

Figure 6–8   Using Technology to Construct a Timeline.
Source: Reprinted with permission from Barnett Shoals Elementary School teachers, 2000, Athens, GA.

engage in higher-level thinking as they select and analyze data to include in a report. Students can practice using spreadsheets in a variety of ways; for example, timelines, charts, and graphs, which help students problem solve (see Figure 6–8).

To foster responsibility for their own learning, students can learn ways to use spreadsheets to keep track of their grades. Such a task can help students practice goal setting, goal monitoring, and goal performance.

Using Hypermedia to Enhance Presentation of Material

Hypermedia involves the use of computer software that connects some combination of text, graphics, video, and audio in a format that is easy for users to move through and has multisensory appeal. The use of hypermedia promotes independent learning as students naturally learn to experiment, create, and interact with several media to create their product. As students explore ways to use hypermedia, they can adapt their creation according to their learning style strengths.

A primary purpose of hypermedia is to help people move freely within an information set. In Heinich, Molenda, Russell, and Smaldino's (1999) text, *Instructional Media and Technologies for Learning*, the authors compare the collection of links in hypermedia to the use of a stack of cards. Each card contains a piece of information, and additional cards contain extensions of the original information, or related information. Programs are typically designed so that the computer screen can display one card, or link, at a time. Hypermedia users can browse through the information by finding cards that are of interest, create additional links that connect information learned on individual cards, or create their own information with connections among text, graphics, video, and audio.

Word Processing

Perhaps the most common use of computers in the classroom is to help students develop word processing skills. Computers provide a motivational forum for students to learn typing, designing, formatting, proofreading, and basic computer functioning skills.

Students can use the computer to apply a combination of several skills, including letter writing, synthesizing research, editing, and publishing. Figure 6–9 shows how one student, Caitlin, integrated several skills to create a "postcard" on the computer.

Summary

This chapter discussed important elements of instructional communication that affect teaching and learning in the classroom. Through analysis of your own listening, questioning, and discussion skills, you will be better positioned to model, practice, and cue effective communication strategies in the classroom. Students who see and hear explicit modeling and are guided to practice effective communication skills will be more likely to learn to monitor and reinforce these skills in daily life.

As technology becomes an increasingly dominant part of the world around us, teachers and students need to be open to learning new ways to use technology to motivate, reach out, and expand knowledge and resources. Technology can be an effective tool to increase student responsibility if used carefully in daily planning.

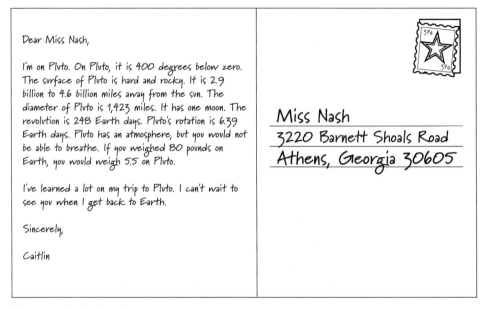

Dear Miss Nash,

I'm on Pluto. On Pluto, it is 400 degrees below zero. The surface of Pluto is hard and rocky. It is 2.9 billion to 4.6 billion miles away from the sun. The diameter of Pluto is 1,423 miles. It has one moon. The revolution is 248 Earth days. Pluto's rotation is 6.39 Earth days. Pluto has an atmosphere, but you would not be able to breathe. If you weighed 80 pounds on Earth, you would weigh 5.5 on Pluto.

I've learned a lot on my trip to Pluto. I can't wait to see you when I get back to Earth.

Sincerely,

Caitlin

Miss Nash
3220 Barnett Shoals Road
Athens, Georgia 30605

Figure 6–9   Postcard.
Source: Reprinted with permission from Barnett Shoals Elementary School teachers, 2001, Athens, GA.

Instructional communication is a domain of classroom teaching easily overlooked—it involves skills that we take for granted each day. But as teachers who want to foster self-regulated learning, we urge you to become aware and help your students become aware of ways they can improve their listening, questioning, and discussing skills in the classroom.

Fostering Student Responsibility: Classroom Applications

Self-Questions

Knowledge: Give an example of a self-regulated learning strategy you might use in your classroom.

Comprehension: Define the work habits outlined in the "Boa Buddy" project.

Application: Identify one school work habit that you developed successfully and one you did not when you were a K–8 student. Write about your experiences and how you dealt with task success and failure.

Analysis: Provide a detailed analysis of Haley's homework problems in teacher Jill Sullivan's project. How would you explain this analysis to your future principal and to the student's parents?

Synthesis: Consider any two of the teacher projects. Take components from each and develop a new, unique strategy for teaching self-regulated learning in your classroom.

Evaluation: Which teacher project seems the most important to you? Why? Describe the elements that make this project so critical to schooling today.

Introduction

Chapter 7 provides examples of ways in which K–8 classroom teachers have integrated metacognition, self-regulated learning, and self-talk strategies in their classrooms. The teacher projects offered in this chapter were used as intervention strategies to assist K–8 students with concentration problems, homework troubles, weak organizational and study skills, and poor motivation for school tasks. These are not the typical "discipline" problems alluded to in chapter 4. However, today's students face these challenges every day. Although these problems are pervasive in classrooms, few teachers provide explicit strategy instruction in the area of developing self-regulated learners.

The classroom prevention and intervention projects created by K–8 teachers who were students of Manning include:

Teacher Project: Rhonda Horton (first-grade teacher), Boa Buddy—Teaching Concentration Through Story (Manning & Payne, 1996)

Teacher Project: Tami McCoy (third-grade teacher), Road to Organization—Teaching Organization Through "Racing" Goals and Goal Monitoring

Teacher Project: Jill Sullivan (fourth-grade teacher), Haley's Homework Troubles—Building Connections Between Home and School

Teacher Project: Julie Bridges (fifth-grade teacher), From Teacher Reflection to Student Responsibility—Creating an Environment for Self-Talk

Teacher Project: Gina Towler (eighth-grade teacher), Taking the "Re" out of Research—Linking Self-Regulated Learning With Research

TEACHER PROJECT: RHONDA HORTON (FIRST-GRADE TEACHER)

Boa Buddy—Teaching Concentration Through Story

I'm my Boa's Buddy.
I'm happy all the time,
But that's because of my Boa.
He helps me walk the line.

I used to have a hard time.
I was never on the ball.
If I was suppose to stand up,
Well, that's just when I would fall.

My mind would not stay focused.
I never was on task.
When all the work was handed in,
Mind would always be last.

Talking, walkers, and the intercom.
Always broke my train of thought.
Completed work, a beautiful "A",
Or even a smile, I couldn't have bought.

Let me give you several examples,
So you'll understand.
Then you can see why,
I needed a helping hand.

One day we went to the library,
To hear a story read.
It was a wonderful story,
But other thoughts filled my head.

The librarian started to read,
There's An Alligator Under My Bed,
And then I noticed the pictures,
And my thoughts to other things lead.

I began to think of my room,
And how I'd forgotten to pick up my toys.
Now, Mom would be upset with me.
and I knew when I got home,
I definitely hear lots of noise.

I hated it when Mom was mad,
Especially with me.
But sometimes I forget things.
I wish that she could see.

Then suddenly the librarian asked,
If I'd enjoyed the book.
But all that I could give her,
Was a long, blank look.

"Oh, no, I've missed the story."
And it seemed to be so good.
How did he get rid of the alligator?
I wish I'd listened. I know I should.

Now I'll have to check the book out.
And read it for myself.
I hope the words aren't too hard,
and I won't have to ask for help.

I wish I could learn to think better.
I've already goofed once today.
I really blew it in math this morning.
I didn't hear my teacher say,

"You have only 10 more minutes,
To finish your math test.
If I had only concentrated,
I could have done my best.

I did the first three problems,
With the greatest of ease,
But my mind began to drift,
And the rest was not a breeze.

(continued)

The answer to the third problem,
Was the number 21.
Hey, that's my baseball number.
Baseball is such fun!

Last night we had a game,
And I hit the ball so hard.
My dad was so proud of me,
He went home and made my own
baseball card.

Maybe one day I'll be famous,
And you'll buy my card in gum.
And the money I'll be making,
Will come in large sums.

Suddenly the intercom scared me.
I almost jumped out of my seat.
Then I remembered by math test.
Oh no, another defeat.

Ten minutes left to finish,
And lots of problems to do.
I'm sure when I get this test back,
I'm going to feel real blue.

I must learn to keep my mind on things,
And not get so behind.
'Cause catching up is impossible.
It's like always being last in line.

And don't let me forget to tell you,
About my lunchroom tale.
I was so hungry that day,
I could have eaten a whale.

I went through the lunch line,
Got my tray and finally sat down.
Yum-m Chocolate Chip Cookies.
That's my favorite treat in town.

Cookies remind me of Grandma.
She makes them when I go to her house.
We stir and mix and bake,
And eat lots of Chocolate Toll House.

And then we go outside and swing,
On the great big tire.
It hangs from a tree limb,
And I kick hard to go higher.

I remember when Grandma took me,
On a mountain trip.
We picked apples from the orchard,
And drank apple cider.
I wouldn't share a sip.

I remember all those Indians,
Making dolls and stringing beads.
They chanted around the campfire,
And danced to the beat.

All at once I was in a whirlwind,
Of children everywhere,
Headed to the window,
Empty trays aflare.

Oh no, I hadn't eaten
Not even one little bite.
And I am really starving,
My stomach growls are a fright.

I stuffed in my mouth quickly,
A chocolate cookie of course.
But a cookie won't quite cut it,
When you're as hungry as a horse.

These daydreams cause me problems.
I'm always having it tough.
I've got to fix this problem,
Or my life is going to be rough.

All this failure makes me feel awful.
I don't like myself.
And then one day my Boa said,
"I think that I can help!"

I used to have the same problems,
Just as you say you do.
I seldom finished my math test either,
and I often feel real blue.

I went many a day without eating lunch.
I always daydreamed instead.
My body got so skinny,
You'd think I'd never been fed.

I missed many good stories,
as I stared off into space.
The other boas loved the story,
But my concentration was always too late.

I decided I had to do something.
I was tired of the daydreaming flu.
I made myself a Boa Buddy,
And you can make one too.

My Boa Buddy sits on my desk,
And he never says a word.
But he reminds me all the time to keep working,
But his voice outloud's never heard.

He whispers in my head.
"Keep working, I can do it."
Don't turn my thoughts to baseball,
And in math I'll make a hit.

Watch those pictures in the story.
I don't want to miss the end.
Make my ears listen closely.
Books can be good friends.

And at lunch, don't go on a diet.
My health is important too.
I can count the bits I've eaten,
and chew and chew and chew.

The secret to all this is thinking,
And talking in my head.
Buddy Boa will remind me,
Through all things how to be lead.

Three are three things to remember,
When Buddy Boa gives me the cue.
STOP, LOOK, and LISTEN.
That's all I have to do.

Each time I look at Buddy,
That's a cue to STOP my thoughts.
Am I doing what I ought to?
Or did I just get caught.

I'll LOOK at my work closely,
And get back to concentrating.
I'm going to stay on task this time.
No more procrastinating.

And then I'm going to LISTEN,
To the good things I say in my mind.
I can do it! It won't take long.
I won't get behind.

And since I've learned to STOP, LOOK, and LISTEN.
I've learned that lifts gets better.
I've had to pat myself on the back.
'Cause in school, I'm a real go-getter!

Pretty soon I'll find I won't need Buddy Boa,
But I wouldn't dare give him away.
Buddy Boa loves me,
And with me he wants to stay."

So let's all listen to Boa's advice,
And learn it all by heart.
And soon we'll all discover,
All along we were really smart.

Source: Rhonda Horton's teacher project first appeared in Self-Talk for Teachers and Students, *by B. H. Manning and B. Payne, © 1996 by Allyn & Bacon. Reprinted by permission.*

TEACHER PROJECT: TAMI MCCOY (THIRD-GRADE TEACHER)

On the Road to Organization—Teaching Organization Through 'Racing' Goals and Goal Monitoring

The inspiration for this project came as a result of the organizational difficulty my third grade students had during this school year. I've always been very organized, yet I have failed to relay this skill to my students. I find it is a necessary skill if I want my students to become self-regulated learners. Thus, I have worked to create a system of organization that will help my students to accomplish this goal.

Corno portrays self-regulated learners as, "enactive, facilitators of their own learning that sustain self-motivation, self-starters, and students who seem to make learning easier for themselves" (Manning & Payne, 1996, p. 16). Through this project, I am hoping to attain these attributes within my students. If I can teach my students when and how to apply organizational strategies, their self-esteem about school work habits and a development of lifelong organizational habits can occur.

I feel the first step in becoming an independent learner is organization. The strategies and activities I have proposed for this project comprise this concept. I have chosen a racing theme to communicate and motivate the teaching of this skill to 25 second-grade students whom I will be teaching next school year. I will begin the school year with these activities, in hopes of creating a pattern of self-responsibility.

I will begin this concept by initiating prior knowledge and finding out what the children know about races/race cars. I want them to realize that when there is a race, it takes everybody being organized, working together, practicing and trying their best, to win. I will then talk with the children about each of the components of a race: the race car, race track, checkered flag, training, pit crew, and a racing log. I will explain that throughout the year we will be looking at each of these components and applying our own organizational skills in our classroom to that of a race.

Next, I will show the children pieces of a puzzle. The pieces of the puzzle represent what it is like to be disorganized. The pieces are all scattered and are not in any organized fashion, so a picture cannot be envisioned. As a class, we will put the picture together and talk through the steps we used in organizing the pieces to form a complete picture. I would offer more examples of organization through stories and timelines of our lives. Through using all of these examples, I hope to express to the children the necessity of organization in our home as well as our school lives.

The organizing strategies I hope to implement within my classroom take the following forms:

1. Help students learn to keep a clean desk.
2. Provide students with a racing log that will contain the necessary materials they will need on a daily basis.
3. Show students how to use an assignment sheet and how to cross tasks off when completed.

4. Encourage careful monitoring by myself as well as parents.
5. Implement a consistent reward program.
6. Develop student awareness of schedules.
7. Practice and provide the use of behavior and organizational self-evaluation sheets.

The following pages within this unit represent the types of strategies and implementation ideas I intend to use with my second grade students. Each of the pages is described in detail as to the process that will take place in putting my organization unit together. Have fun reading them and I look forward to the comments and suggestions you have for me in making this project a success.

ORGANIZATION NOTEBOOK

When the children first arrive at the beginning of the school year I will explain to them that we will be using an organization notebook, which we will call our "Racing Logs." I will define the term-4 organization, again after doing the previous activities. They should begin to have the concept of why organization is important in learning.

Before the preparation of our notebooks, I will divide the class into cooperative groups, which I call "Pit Crews." I will ask the groups to think about how a well-organized notebook could help them be better organized for school. The "pit crews" will be asked to brainstorm ideas of things that a well-organized notebook might contain.

The groups will come together for a whole-class discussion about this topic. With guidance, we should come up with the following list:

- title page
- table of contents
- racing checklist (a reminder of daily tasks)
- racing goals and self-evaluation checklist (goals they want to accomplish and a checklist to self-monitor their organizational performance)
- racing schedule (class daily schedule)
- daily assignment sheet (a place to write our homework)
- monthly assignment sheet (long-term assignments or important dates)
- school-year calendar (calendar of what will be happening throughout our school year)
- desk organization picture (to remind us how to organize our desks)
- homework study area picture (a picture of a place we can study at home without letting distractions prevent us from doing our best)

This may not be all the children will come up with, but it's a start to a well-organized school year.

(continued)

MY RACING LOG

Name: _____

Address: _____

_____

Phone Number: _____

School Name: _____

Room #: _____

In case of emergency call: _____

TABLE OF CONTENTS

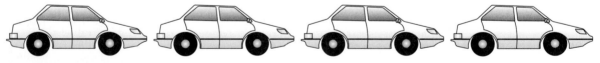

RACING CHECKLIST

Before I go to school:

- Do I have all the books I need for school today?
- Do I have my homework?
- Do I have my lunch/lunch money?

While I'm at school:

- Have I written down all my assignments on my assignment sheet?
- Have I written down the dates of any upcoming tests on my assignment sheet?

Before I go home:

- Do I have all the books I need tonight?
- Do I have my racing log and assignment sheet?
- Do I have all the materials I'll need to complete my assignments?
- Do I need to bring anything else home tonight?

RACING GOALS

Through class discussions, activities, and projects, students can become more aware of both short- and long-term goals and in turn learn about what motivates them to work hard to achieve certain goals.

I will begin this lesson by reading to the children the story *The Little Engine That Could*. We will discuss the type of goal the little engine had while trying to get up the big hill. The discussion will continue with what a personal goal is and how people achieve their goals.

Next, I will model the types of goals, both short- and long-term that I hold for myself. I will express to the children why these goals are important to me and how I would go about attaining them. After modeling for the class, I will again bring up our theme of racing and talk about the types of goals associated with racing. When they have a general understanding of this concept, I will have the children help set up short- and long-term goals for our class. These goals will be written on the board and a discussion will follow with how we will go about achieving these goals. These goals will be left on the board for daily viewing and modifications will be made to them when needed. Our next activity will begin with writing long-term goals. I will ask several questions of the kids, giving them examples of types of goals that they may have. Examples of questions might include: 1. Where will I live when I grow up? 2. What job will I have?

I will ask them to come up with at least three long-term goals that they feel are important to them. A discussion of short-term goals will follow. These will be weekly goals which will be located on each student's self-evaluation sheet for the week. Because my students are only in second grade, I will limit the number of goals to one or two per week. At the end of each week, they will have a chance to evaluate themselves on their goal performance and write new goals for the following week. Please refer to goal and self-evaluation sheets that will be included in the logs.

(continued)

MY SELF-EVALUATION SHEET

1. I tried my best.

2. I kept my desk clean and orderly, with books stacked in a pyramid style.

3. I kept a list of assignments for the week.

4. I kept a work folder.

5. I worked to achieve my goals.

6. I was an active listener.

7. I asked questions.

8. Did I reach my goals?

9. How did I reach my goals?

Goals for the week: ___ / ___ / ___

Goals	How will I accomplish these?
1.	1.
2.	2.

SELF-EVALUATION

Three flags are shown after each item. They are represented as follows:

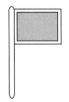

I did not fulfill this statement.   I could have done better.

I did a great job!

I have tried to maintain the racing theme throughout the entire unit. These flags are a representation of the flags used in racing. I will also do an assessment to find out if these flags are a good portrayal of the desired outcomes.

Racing Schedule

7:30–8:10	Arrive/Morning Work
8:10–9:30	Reading
9:30–10:30	Language Arts
10:30–11:00	Science
11:00–11:30	Social Studies
11:30–12:15	Specials
12:15–12:30	Recess
12:30–1:00	Lunch
1:00–2:00	Math
2:00–2:30	Math Review
2:30–	Dismissal

Racing Assignment Sheet for the Week of _____

	Monday ____	Tuesday ____	Wednesday ____	Thursday ____	Friday ____
Spelling					
Language Arts					
Math					
Science					
Social Studies					
Other					
Parent/Guardian Initials					

(continued)

DESK ORGANIZATION

One strategy I will attempt to employ is desk organization. I will teach the children to organize their desks in a "pyramid style." This includes putting all large books on the bottom and continuing with smaller books on top. These books will be located on the left side of their desks, leaving room on the right side for paper, folders, and a box of supplies. I will model this style as well as draw a picture on the board for students to follow. Desk checks will be done once a week on random days. This will encourage all children to have their desks organized at all times.

After we have talked about the importance of keeping our desk organized in this fashion, I will have each of them draw a picture of their desks. They will keep this picture in their racing logs as a reminder to them. They may look at this picture as often as needed.

Does my desk look like this?

STUDY AREA

The best place to practice racing is on a racetrack. Where would you study at home that would be most effective? This is the question I will ask the children when implementing this part of the organizational process I have begun. I will show the children the picture of a disorganized family's house. We will use this to talk about distracters in our study environment. The lesson will continue with a discussion of distracters, creating a list of distractions we are faced with when trying to do our homework or study at home. Our discussion will continue with why distracters present us with difficulty in completing the tasks we set out to accomplish. The lesson will continue with the types of places at home we feel would be the best places to do our homework or study. After listing several ideas, we will talk about the two pictures of bedrooms, one clean and organized; the other messy and not organized. We will personalize this lesson by drawing a picture of the best place in our house to do our homework or study. These pictures will then be put into the students' racing logs and signed by the parents. I will have talked with the parents before school began about this process and asked for their help in designating a special place for their children at home that they may call their study area.

Messy and <u>NOT</u> Organized

Clean and Organized

(continued)

CASE STUDY

Patrick never has a pencil. When asked to look through his desk to find something to write with, he is lost in a mess of old paper, lost assignments, pieces of leftover candy, and overdue library books. Patrick's homework is usually late, if it gets completed at all. He is unaware of when tests are given or how to study for them. In short, Patrick lacks purpose and organization.

MORNING ROUTINE

I have come up with a process that will help my students' morning arrival and prepare them to begin the day. I have designed a race car with five routine duties I want the children to do every morning. I do not expect them to physically check off each one when finished, but to do a mental check when the duties have become routine. I have also found another organizational function to this process.

These race cars will be located on each of my student's desk. When they arrive in the morning and have done a mental check of these items, they are then to take their car and place it on the appropriate side of the lunch count chart entitled, "Start Your Engines…"

This process allows me to take attendance and lunch count all at one time. It is an idea that will help me to start my morning a little more easily.

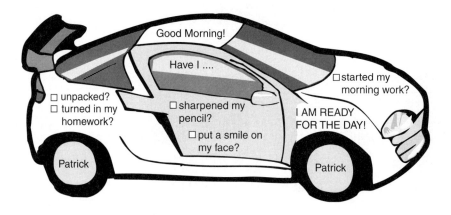

UNDERSTANDING TEXTBOOK ORGANIZATION

Procedure: Divide the class into cooperative groups (called Pit Crews). Tell the groups that their task is to analyze the structure and organization of the textbooks used in the classroom. Assign responsibilities to each group to investigate the organization of their textbooks. After the children become "experts" on their topic, they will teach it to the rest of the class. When they are finished, they will fill out their scavenger hunt sheet.

Sections of the textbook to be studied:

- table of contents
- text itself; units, chapters, etc.
- questions throughout the book; chapter review questions, etc.
- illustrations, photos, maps, charts, diagrams
- new vocabulary; glossary
- atlases
- appendices

Each group should present its report to the class. A group discussion will then take place where the whole group will try to reach a consensus on a one-sentence statement about how each part of the book makes studying easier and more effective.

Evaluation: Students should be able to understand and explain the various parts of their textbook.

BOOK SCAVENGER HUNT

1. What is the title of your book? _____

2. Who is the author? _____

3. What date was the book published? _____

4. What is the title of the first chapter? _____

5. On what page does the fourth chapter begin? _____

6. Read through the chapters in the Table of Contents quickly and write down the name of a chapter that sounds interesting. _____

7. What book part is found at the end of your book? _____

8. Find a chart or graph in your book. Write the page number you found it on. __

9. Do you think this book has some interesting ideas? Yes. No. _____

10. Find four new words and list them below.

_____

_____

_____

_____

REWARD SYSTEM

My reward system is based on a system of "admission tickets" and a series of choices of rewards. There are several instances when a student can receive a ticket. I will use this system for a variety of reasons; a few of these include:

- having a clean desk during a routine desk check
- writing all weekly assignments down in their racing log
- attaining goals
- helping others
- having their racing logs daily for a week
- turning in all homework

When students receive a ticket, they then may put their name on the book and slip it in the checked flag box. Every Monday I will draw three tickets and they will choose a reward from the reward choices.

REWARD IDEAS

- Sit at the teacher's desk.
- Take care of the class pet for the day.
- Have lunch with my favorite friend.
- Have lunch with the principal.

(continued)

- Join another class for recess.
- Have my teacher call my parents to tell them what a good job I've been doing.
- Draw on the chalkboard.
- Be first in line.
- Do only half an assignment.
- Choose any class job for the week.
- Do all the class jobs for the day.
- Invite a visitor to come to school.
- No early morning work.
- Take a class pet home tonight.
- Be a helper in a classroom of younger students.
- Help the custodian.
- Help the secretary.
- Help the librarian.
- Invite a friend to come and have lunch with me.
- Use the teacher's chair.
- Choose a book for the teacher to read to the class.
- Choose someplace in the room to move my desk.
- No homework pass.
- Lunch with the teacher.
- Use the beanbag chair for the day.
- Eat lunch with another class.
- Use the computer.
- Tape a story.
- Extra center time.

WHAT SHOULD I DO WHEN I'M DONE WITH EVERYTHING?

- Check my work for errors. Can I make it better?
- Read a book.
- Write in my journal.
- Write a story.
- Help someone else.
- Clean my desk.
- Work on my homework.
- Ask to help in another class.
- Study for a test.
- Read a book with a friend who is also done with everything.
- Go to the library and check out a book.
- Work on the computer.

Source: Created by Tami McCoy. Used with permission.

TEACHER PROJECT: JILL SULLIVAN (FOURTH-GRADE TEACHER)

Haley's Homework Troubles — Building Connections Between Home and School

"Haley's Homework Troubles" is a project that stems from many years of battling students and homework. Although I have tried many strategies from positive reinforcement to sending students to the principal, nothing seems to "cure" the problem for long. This project has four components: PowerPoint presentation, teacher-directed lessons, classroom practice, and utilizing a checklist. All of these components are derived from Manning's Cognitive Self-Instruction strategies outlined in her book, *Self-Talk for Teachers and Students*.

Homework is an element of education that most students hate. I view homework as a necessary part of a clearly planned curriculum. It serves many functions when it is assigned as a thoughtful part of an instructional plan. It serves as practice of skills, communication with parents, and an opportunity to develop responsible behaviors. I try very hard to assign meaningful work, provide some choice, and vary assignments based on different types of learning styles. Most of the time I find that my thoughtful planning, clear directions, and consistent follow-through are enough to prompt most students to complete their homework each night. However, there are always children who either do not have the support needed at home, or simply do not have the self-guiding skills to get their homework done. This project attempts to address these types of problems.

The first component of the project, the PowerPoint presentation, will be used to introduce the ideas of the seven-step plan to improve homework performance. These steps are presented within the context of a "big book" idea, only the big book is a narrated PowerPoint presentation. This PowerPoint can be used in many ways. It can be used to introduce these ideas to an entire class using a LCD projector, or used on a regular personal computer for individual students who are having difficulty with the steps and need review. If used with an entire class then discussion can be generated before, during, and after the presentation.

(continued)

The teacher-directed lessons will occur after the PowerPoint presentation and will focus on the following topics:

- Memorizing the steps in order
- Teacher modeling of seven steps
- Helping children identify their inner speech and how to utilize it
- Overcoming fears of talking out loud to oneself
- Generating a personalized list of questions for each step if students would like to come up with their own wording
- Understanding that the questions on the checklist should be answered, and what they should do if they answer "no" to a question on the checklist
- Understanding the idea of quality work and what quality work "looks like"
- Helping students understand their own unique needs as learners (i.e., levels of distraction they are comfortable with, their learning styles, etc.)
- Making an "at-home" homework plan that will be signed by parents

Classroom and at-home practice will be an important step. Any time a teacher allows students to practice behaviors in the classroom, she is signaling to the children that the skill is important and expected. I find that allowing time to practice newly introduced skills is the cement that often holds my class together. Practice of the steps will occur in the following ways:

- Practicing the steps at school together and utilizing peer guides if necessary
- Role-playing the seven steps
- Discussing and coming up with solutions to problems with the steps in class meetings
- Seven-Step Journal—children will keep a journal once a week at home about how they used the steps and the outcome of using the steps
- Parent instruction on the journal at open house

The checklist will be the concrete tool that will be the foundation to this plan. Hopefully, the checklist can be used temporarily until the steps and questions are internalized.

MY HOMEWORK HELPER

Step One: I am filling out my agenda book. (At school)

Questions to ask myself:

_____

- Did I write down the assignments exactly like the teacher? _____
- Do I understand all of the directions to all of the assignments? _____

_____

Step Two: I am packing my book bag. (At school)

Questions to ask myself:

_____

- Do I have all my books, papers, and writing utensils I need to do my work? _____
- Do I have any notes that need to go home to my parents? _____

_____

Step Three: I am ready to work at home. (At home)

Questions to ask myself:

_____

- Am I in a quiet area with few distractions? _____
- Do I have all my materials ready? _____
- What order will I do my assignments in?

_____

Step Four: I am completing my homework. (At home)

Questions to ask myself:

- How am I doing? _____
- Am I following directions? _____
- Am I working fast enough? _____
- Am I working too fast? _____
- Am I doing my best? _____

Step Five: I am checking my homework. (At home)

Questions to ask myself:

- Have I completed all the assignments? _____
- Is my work quality work? _____
- Am I proud of this work? _____

Step Six: I feel great! (At home)

What to say to myself:

WAY TO GO!

Step Seven: I am preparing for tomorrow.

Questions to ask myself:

- Are my books, pencils, and work packed neatly in my book bag?
- Is my book bag in a place I can find it easily in the morning?

Reflections:

How do I feel about my homework?
Is this checklist helping me?
What could I do differently tomorrow night?
Other reflections:

By using these components of this project consistently, I hope to create an environment where metacognition flourishes in the classroom and at home. I will strive to incorporate metacognition into others areas and link it to the lessons and experiences the students have using this project. I view this project as a springboard to other places that metacognition can be used in my classroom. It is my hope that eventually parents and students will realize the value and power in this kind of self-guiding activity and will apply it to other facets of life.

(continued)

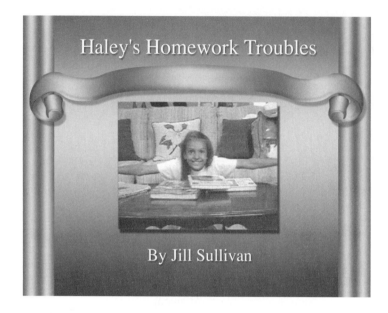

Haley's Homework Troubles

By Jill Sullivan

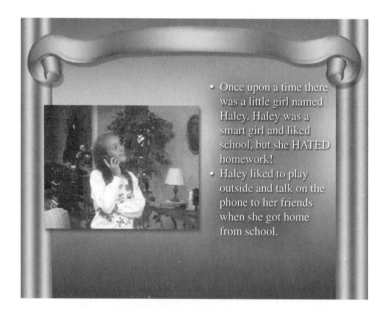

- Once upon a time there was a little girl named Haley. Haley was a smart girl and liked school, but she HATED homework!
- Haley liked to play outside and talk on the phone to her friends when she got home from school.

• Unless her mom or dad yelled at her, she just didn't do her work.

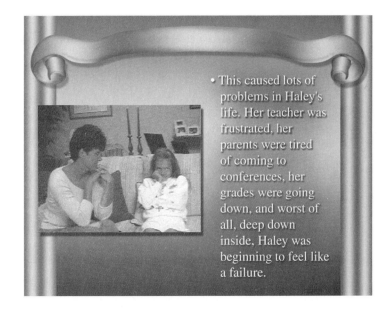

• This caused lots of problems in Haley's life. Her teacher was frustrated, her parents were tired of coming to conferences, her grades were going down, and worst of all, deep down inside, Haley was beginning to feel like a failure.

(continued)

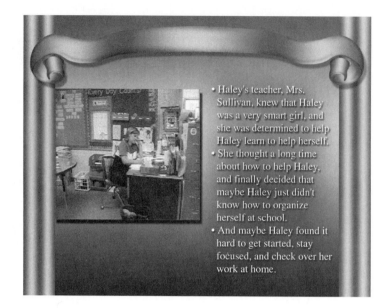

- Haley's teacher, Mrs. Sullivan, knew that Haley was a very smart girl, and she was determined to help Haley learn to help herself.
- She thought a long time about how to help Haley, and finally decided that maybe Haley just didn't know how to organize herself at school.
- And maybe Haley found it hard to get started, stay focused, and check over her work at home.

- Mrs. Sullivan and Haley decided that something had to be done. So they came up with a seven step plan to help Haley with her homework troubles.

Step One: I am filling out my Agenda Book.

- At the end of each day Haley fills out her agenda book then asks herself these questions:
- *Did I write down the assignments exactly like the teacher?*
- *Do I understand all of the directions to all the assignments?*

Step Two: I am packing my book bag.

- Then Haley gets all the materials she will need to complete her homework and places them in her bookbag.
- Then she asks herself these questions:
- *Do I have all my books, papers, and writing utensils I need to do my work?*
- *Do I have any notes that need to go home to my parents?*

(continued)

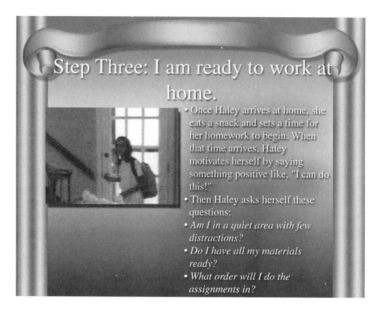

Step Three: I am ready to work at home.

- Once Haley arrives at home, she eats a snack and sets a time for her homework to begin. When that time arrives, Haley motivates herself by saying something positive like, "I can do this!"
- Then Haley asks herself these questions:
- *Am I in a quiet area with few distractions?*
- *Do I have all my materials ready?*
- *What order will I do the assignments in?*

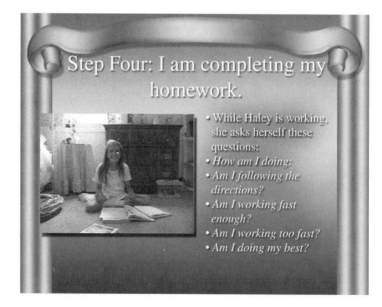

Step Four: I am completing my homework.

- While Haley is working, she asks herself these questions:
- *How am I doing:*
- *Am I following the directions?*
- *Am I working fast enough?*
- *Am I working too fast?*
- *Am I doing my best?*

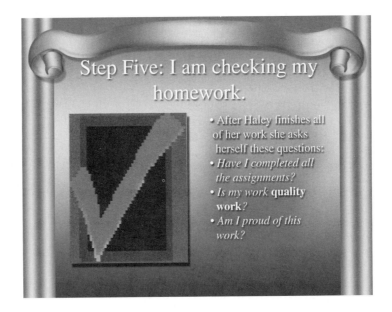

(continued)

Step Seven: I am preparing for tomorrow.

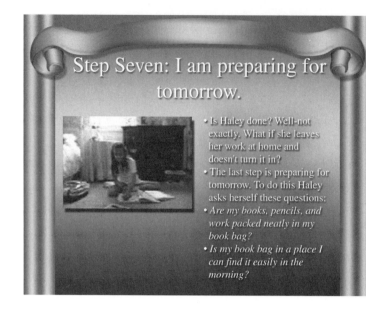

- Is Haley done? Well-not exactly. What if she leaves her work at home and doesn't turn it in?
- The last step is preparing for tomorrow. To do this Haley asks herself these questions:
- *Are my books, pencils, and work packed neatly in my book bag?*
- *Is my book bag in a place I can find it easily in the morning?*

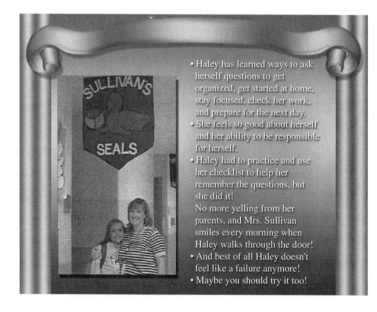

- Haley has learned ways to ask herself questions to get organized, get started at home, stay focused, check her work, and prepare for the next day.
- She feels so good about herself and her ability to be responsible for herself.
- Haley had to practice and use her checklist to help her remember the questions, but she did it! No more yelling from her parents, and Mrs. Sullivan smiles every morning when Haley walks through the door!
- And best of all Haley doesn't feel like a failure anymore!
- Maybe you should try it too!

And that is the end to Haley's
Homework Troubles!

Many thanks to Lauren Evans who appeared as "Haley"
in my story. She is an outstanding student who
demonstrates very effective homeork strategies! Also
to her mom, Julie Evans, and to Maggie Paoletri
Chattahoochee Technology Specialist

Source: Created by Jill Sullivan. Used with permission.

TEACHER PROJECT: JULIE BRIDGES (FIFTH-GRADE TEACHER)

From Teacher Reflection to Student Responsibility—Creating an Environment for Self-talk

INTRODUCTION

My goal with this project was to create checklists to use to gradually change my classroom over to create an environment for cognitive self-talk to be modeled and practiced daily. I wanted to begin immediately and experiment with this current class because this topic is so important and to be prepared to begin at the beginning of the year next year with a plan to be implemented. Both are included under the checklist section. I also went a step further and produced a play with my current students on helpful and unhelpful self talk. The script is included.

To begin I went through the Manning and Payne book, *Self-Talk for Teachers and Students.* I first made a checklist of what the teacher needed to do in her own life to incorporate CSI. When I felt very comfortable using CSI myself, I moved to teaching it to my students. The self-awareness for the teacher was very important in my own life. I have been using self-talk for years, but was truly amazed to reflect on my unhelpful self-talk and my irrational beliefs. This entire course has been so beneficial and life changing. I was truly amazed at what a transformation I have made. I feel the teacher really needs to spend time on this aspect first, and then move to the students.

The next step was to make the classroom checklist (see checklist section). This summer I will make all the necessary items on the checklist to implement the full program. I will also make a master plan of when to implement the different plans. I want it to be a

(continued)

daily implementation with new concepts coming at a steady pace. I want to challenge the children to incorporate CSI into their daily lives as I have, but not to overwhelm them.

After making the checklists I decided upon implementing one of the items—making a videotape of helpful and unhelpful self-talk—and practicing it with first graders. At the beginning of next year we will develop a relationship with Mrs. Chastain's first grade class. My students will write and produce scripts dealing with different aspects of CSI. We will videotape the scripts and show them to the first graders. In this way we will practice the skills ourselves and then model them to the first graders. I chose to pick this portion of the checklist because I have not tried before to videotape the students. I learned a lot by doing this and how to make it better for next year. We found many ways to make the process faster and more efficient. In fact, from the beginning of the tape to the end you can see how much more efficient we became. I learned to divide the kids into groups of actors, scriptwriters, and a video team. In the beginning we tried to do everything as a large group. I also tried to control the situation. I have learned to be more of a director and let them control the activities more.

I began in February, introducing the concept of self-talk to this class. I tried daily to model it and bring it up in discussions daily. Although I was not sure how to directly teach it, I knew it was such an important life lesson that the students needed to be aware of it. I was pleasantly surprised when we were writing the script how much they had incorporated it into their lives.

I was not sure how the presenting would go to the first-grade class. The first grade was very attentive and my fifth-graders were definitely ready. In viewing the videotape, you can see everyone was on task and it was a very productive lesson. The fifth-graders gained a lot by moving from just practicing their own self-talk to modeling it with the first-grade class. I was very pleased with the outcome. Next year, I would begin in September with the first tape being this tape we produced on "Helpful and Unhelpful Self-Talk." I will probably divide them up into teams for the rest. I have outlined what we will do each month. We will do the first one together, and then I will try to let it be student directed as much as possible. The fifth-graders were very familiar with the video camera, so I feel comfortable having them videotape, which really frees up the teacher. The school owns several video cameras; this makes the technical end easier also.

Further lessons will include:

- September: Description of self-talk and changing unhelpful self-talk to helpful self-talk
- October: How to make friends using positive self-talk
- November/December: How to start your day at GACS
- January: Ask, Tell, Try, Check, and Cheer
- February: Homework and bring papers back to school
- March: Self-Talk in Math Class
- April: Self-Talk at PE and Field Day
- May: Self-talk before a big test and incorporating self-talk this summer and into your personal life

Of course, I am open to other topics and probably will let this be student led. I was pleasantly surprised at how excited they are about self-talk and the video camera. I don't want to stand in their way, and many times their ideas far surpass my own.

I am excited about the implementation of my checklists for next year and look forward to implementing them.

SCRIPT FOR FIFTH-GRADE BUDDY PROGRAM

Narrator: Hi! I'm _____ from Mrs. Bridges fifth-grade class. We have been learning that everyone talks in their heads to themselves. Talking to yourself means the words you say out loud or silently to yourself during the day. Sometimes the things we say are helpful, but more often they are unhelpful things. Helpful talking helps build us up and helps us to make good decisions. Unhelpful self-talking tears us down, and we begin to feel bad about ourselves so we can't get things done as well. We have been trying to change our self-talk to be helpful, and it has really helped our schoolwork and how we feel. Let me show you some examples of us at the beginning of the year before we learned how to do this.

Student 1: Rats! I missed another math problem. I never get any problems correct.

Student 2: Nobody likes me. I'll never get any friends at this school.

Student 3: This work problem is just too hard. I just never get these!

Student 4: I'll never get this project completed. I don't have enough time.

Student 5: Why study? I always fail science tests.

Student 6: I can't do this.

We have been learning how to change what we are saying to ourselves and want to show you how to do it, too. To begin to change, first you need to be aware of what you are saying to yourself. Listen as we begin to change our self-talk. We want to be a good friend to ourselves, and not tear ourselves down with unhelpful talk.

Now watch as our friends say their unhelpful things to themselves. Now they are going to change when they realize how what they are saying is hurting themselves.

Student 1: Rats! I missed another math problem. I never get any problems correct.

Wait a minute. Is this being a good friend to myself? I remember that on my last math test I made a 95. I can do this math. I just need to concentrate harder and check over my math.

Student 2: Nobody likes me. I'll never get any friends at this school.

Wait a minute. Is this positive? Jenny likes me and so does Fred. I should try smiling and being friendly to others. I will go stand by Jenny in the lunch line and ask her about her weekend.

Student 3: This work problem is just too hard. I just never get these!

Wait a minute. I will work hard on this first problem and check to see if I did it correctly. If I have any questions, I will ask Stacey.

Student 4: I'll never get this project completed. I don't have enough time.

Wait a minute. I need to first get out a calendar and see how long I have until the project is due. Let's see. I have two weeks. I can plan to work on it an hour each day except for Thursdays when I have soccer. I have enough time to do a good job.

Student 5: Why study? I always fail science tests.

Wait a minute. Is this kind of talk helping me? I can make a good grade if I try hard to concentrate and study. I will write it down in my agenda book and plan to study 30 minutes per night. I can get my mom to make a practice test and write down some important facts on note cards. I have some good ideas already. I know some good steps to get started on studying.

Student 6: I can't do this.

Hold it!!!!! I remember doing this last year. What did my teacher say? That's right. I remember now. Subtract and then add. I will work on this problem and then go ask the teacher if I did it correctly. I can do this if I try.

(continued)

Now we are going to let you practice this skill. We are going to give each of you a sheet with some unhelpful self-talk on it. We are going to read it to you and you are going to change it to be a friend to yourself. Tell us how you would change it and we will write it down for you. We are going to give you a fifth-grade buddy to help each of you. Good luck and remember to think positive and be helpful to yourself.

When you finish we are going to film some of you changing your self-talk so you can be a friend to yourself like we are. Then we are going to show it so all your friends can see how you are changing.

FIRST-GRADE WORKSHEET

1. I write so slowly. I'll never get all this copied from the board.

    Change to: _____

    _____

2. I have been trying to write the letter *F* correctly all morning and it is still written wrong.

    Change to: _____

    _____

3. The people around me always talk. They never let me finish my work. It's their fault I can never get my work done.

    Change to: _____

    _____

4. I will do horrible at Field Day this year. I can't run fast at all.

    Change to: _____

    _____

5. I was terrible in kickball today. I think I am the worst player in the whole first grade.

    Change to: _____

Get back together as a big group and show the first graders on film how they changed their self-talk. I will be filming as they are sharing their answers. I will listen to be sure they have changed it appropriately and then ask them to repeat it and film it to show them.

After showing the film remind them to stop themselves when they begin unhelpful self-talk. Tell them we will be back next month with some more helpful suggestions and we look forward to hearing how their month went.

Begin the above in September about a month after school has begun. This will have given me time to explain, model, and cue my class on self-talk. They will need to understand it and to have begun using it in their own lives. This will begin the practicing step for them. We will have meetings each month on different topics. Each will follow a similar format. We will present a play of the fifth-graders and then let the first-graders watch and then practice the skill. Each month before we begin the new skill we will reinforce the months before. We will also begin a pen pal program once a week, having the fifth-graders write them a note each week telling the first-graders how they have used the skill that week. I thought the first graders would enjoy getting personal mail and this would reinforce the skills.

After we present the first film we will begin working on the next topic. This will give us a month to write, practice, and prepare before we film the next topic. I will have the kids write the scripts, which will reinforce the skills. We have video news that is aired to the entire elementary school each morning. We can broadcast our video over the video news to the entire elementary school or have the films available for checkout in the library for particular grade levels to view. It would be an extra bonus for the other fifth-graders to pick some different topics. We could swap tapes once a month. I think seeing their peers do other topics would really reinforce the skills. Over the summer, I plan to present it to their own fifth-grade teachers to implement this into our curriculum. Also, one teacher in our fifth grade is currently planning to take the self-talk class in the fall which will put two teachers in the grade level and in our school with the training and knowledge to implement this program.*

TEACHER CHECKLIST

1. Be aware of your own self-talk.
2. Categorize your strengths and weaknesses.
3. Share your strengths with someone you trust.
4. Write a strength down weekly and share it.
5. Look at your own rational and irrational beliefs.
6. Begin to unconditionally accept yourself.
7. Check yourself for futurizing.
8. Begin keeping a record of your own self-talk.
9. Check your locus of control. Is it internal or external?
10. Practice sending I-messages to your class.
11. Catch yourself and change unhelpful self-talk to helpful.
12. Identify Drivers, Stoppers, and Confusers in your life.
13. Create an internal buffer of calmness and rational beliefs in your life.
14. Create a helpful self-talk teacher tape. (p. 15)
15. Become an adaptive teacher.
16. Use a self-record checklist.
17. Create a goal story interview. (p. 68)
18. Make personal cue cards.
19. Keep a self-talk diary. (p. 70)
20. Keep a check on your unhelpful self-talk, make a conscious effort to change. Write self-talk in margins of your lesson plans.
21. Evaluate your lesson plans. (p. 97)
22. Set up your classroom to create a self-talk; environment. (p. 99)
23. Are you using reciprocal teaching in your lesson plans? (p. 109)
24. Create lesson plan on Problem Defining, Attention Focusing, Self-Coping, Self-Reinforcing. (p. 119)
25. Be practicing self-talk daily in classroom and in personal life. Be consciously modeling self-talk to students. (p. 118)
26. Are your rules in first person? (p. 199)
27. Create a space in your lesson plans for modeling and practicing. Check it off to be sure it is completed.

This checklist was created by taking the Manning and Payne book, *Self-Talk for Teachers and Students* (1996), and breaking the book down into specific goals to be achieved. The page numbers are for easy reference.

(continued)

*The page numbers listed in the checklists refer to pages in the Manning & Payne 1996 text.

CLASSROOM CHECKLIST

1. Create helpful self-talk cassette tape. Include I-messages. Repeat helpful statements three times, each with a short pause in between statements. End tape with student saying you are a good listener, etc. This will give external validation. Have kids listen to tape at the listening center or out loud. Put background music to tape. (p. 57)
2. Self-record checklist. (p. 68)
3. Goal story interview. (p. 68)
4. Making individual cue cards and cue cards for classroom.
5. Create self-talk diary for students.
6. Make chart for students to fill out. Make graph together. (p. 119)
7. Create videotapes for class to practice their self-talk. Begin with changing unhelpful to helpful self-talk.
8. Play games such as Concentration Zapper and Incomplete Scenarios.
9. Make some cartoons with blank bubbles for students to fill in self-talk. (p. 120)
10. Role-play self-talk with class.
11. Students keep self-talk logs or journals. Students write in first person what they have been saying to themselves. (p. 122)
12. Classify self-talk from journals. (p. 123)
13. CSI Booklet. When to use CSI on cover. (p. 123)
14. Use commercial comics and white out talk. Run off copies for students. Do this as dyads or small groups. Try to find comics with one character per frame. (p. 124)
15. Class makes poster for room. Put class in groups. Titles of posters: Listening, Planning, Working, Checking. Display for cueing purposes. (p. 125)
16. Create language-experience story using real students' names and how students were able to maintain concentration, planning, etc.
17. Incorporate into art activities. Create self-portrait with cartoon bubbles over head. (p. 126)
18. Art activity. Get large sheet of white paper and divide into four equal parts. Have students write Listening, Planning, Working, and Checking. Have students draw themselves with a comic bubble over their heads. Have students write CSI statements to self-question.
19. Role rehearsal. Practice aloud, softly, and then silently. Teacher does specific lessons and reinforces them this way. (p. 126)
20. Change classroom rules to first person. (p. 127)
21. Make individual cue cards for students.
22. Teacher-made cassette tape to practice specific skills you have been teaching. Have checklist on child's desk for on-task or off-task behavior to check to see if student is accomplishing specific skill taught. Have a bell or other sound to signal to student to check behavior. (p. 131)
23. Cue cards up (Ralph Bear or create your own). (p. 136)
24. Use spidey story with spidey puppet or create your own. Show students Ask, Try, Tell, Check, and Cheer. Have them create puppet show for younger kids.
25. Write your own big book together and kids write their own books. Share with younger kids.
26. Checklists for kids. Are they using Ask, Try, Tell, Check, and Cheer skills?
27. Have kids write raps or songs as small groups. Reinforce above skills. Videotape. (p. 165)
28. Teacher developed checklist (p. 168). Distribute to students.
29. Read a book to students. Have them pick out appropriate self-talk.
30. Run off copies of changing unhelpful self-talk to helpful self-talk. Have class discussions and do individually. (p. 195)
31. Write plays with different topics to give to class and younger classes. (p. 207)

Source: Created by Julie Bridges. Used with permission.

TEACHER PROJECT: GINA TOWLER (EIGHTH-GRADE TEACHER)

Take the "Re" Out of Research—Linking Self-Regulated Learning With Research

Research is a fundamental step in student learning. It promotes questioning, interpreting, analyzing, synthesizing, and evaluating, which are all vital steps leading down a path of discovery. Through research, students can make connections between information and reflection. Real discovery enhances understanding. As students begin to develop questions and make connections between new information and prior knowledge, they applaud their search with a "High 5 Hand Jive." The process of the search is just as important as the final project. Students learn ways to monitor their progress and reflect on what they have learned. Through encouraging reflection, students begin to understand how they learn and become successful in guiding their own helpful self-talk.

Excitement and enthusiasm are contagious. A teacher can model her own enthusiasm by asking questions and promoting inquiry with students and their topics. Everyday in the classroom we as teachers provide information. Providing links between old and new information helps create meaning and pattern to learning, which leads to imagination and wonder.

Writing teacher and author Donald Graves states, "The teacher is the chief learner in the classroom." Teachers must learn to discuss their own thinking in order for students to hear the strategy. Teachers must model the search for information for students to see the process. Teachers must provide a safe environment for students to take risks and experience struggle. Teachers must provide opportunities for students to practice self-talk with each other as well as with themselves. As students talk through their search process, they need to respond to their talk on paper by reacting to their thinking. Through talking, responding, and reflecting, students will gain more understanding and confidence in their thinking.

There are many learning strategies that assist and encourage Cognitive Self-Instruction (CSI) (Manning, 1991). In completing research, students need to:

- Take time to think of a topic that is of real interest.
- Build background knowledge.
- Ask questions in every stage of reading (before, during, after).
- Read, reread, retell, and make think links with the material.
- Collect information and decide what is important.
- Write down the information (old and new).
- Reflect on what and how they learned.
- Present the information.

Conferencing with students one-on-one provides an opportunity to model thinking aloud and provide positive reinforcement. Verbal and written cues, such as posters displayed in the room, yellow legal pads, KWF, "high 5's," checklists, and reaction journals, become daily reminders of what is expected in order to achieve success. Posters on the walls model the process of questioning, reflecting, and reacting. Yellow legal pads are reminders to write notes and comments. The KWF chart encourages students to write all that they (K) know about their topic, all they (W) wonder about, and finally what they want to find out (F). "High 5 Hand Jive" announces a job well done. A checklist is placed in their search folder to provide a place for students to write their plan of action for the following day. A reaction journal allows students to react to their own work, create meanings, and draw conclusions about what they have learned.

What is probably the most exciting part of this process is to see students become more self-regulated in their learning. They take ownership of their learning and are eager to share their expertise with others. Teacher and students collaboratively design

(continued)

evaluation rubrics. Students praise each other with verbal and post-it-note praise. In summary, research provides students an opportunity to have an investment in their learning and enjoy the discovery of answers to their natural curiosity.

Take the "Re" out of Research:
Linking Self-Regulated
Learning with Research

Gina Towler
EDMS 8020

May 1, 2000

Research never ends
just abandoned; left
for someone else to
add a piece.

Tell me, I forget
Show me, I remember
Involve me, I understand

Chinese Proverb

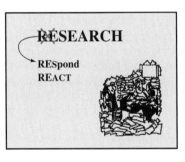

RESEARCH

RESpond
REACT

The search for information

I stands for   Information
                  Involvement
                  Inquiry
                  Interest

In completing research I must take time:

to think
to choose a topic
to build background knowledge
to ask questions
to read and research
to collect information
to write
to reflect
to present findings

Through the **I-Search** process, students set goals and develop strategies to achieve their goals. Throughout the search process, it is important that students monitor their own thinking and reflect in their journals upon strategies they use.

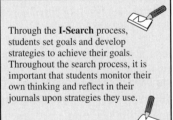

KWF
Pre-Search

What I Know	What I Wonder	What I Want to Find Out

Modeling the ask, tell, try, check, and cheer self-talk, students think aloud:

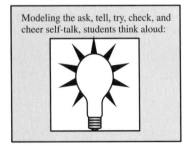

Positive Self-Talk

Man, I'm smart!

Good job Penny. But all you had to do was press "Enter."

Modeling the **ask**, tell, try, check, and cheer self-talk, students think aloud:

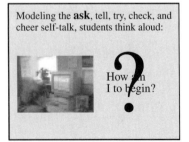

How am I to begin?

Modeling the ask, **tell**, try, check, and cheer self-talk, students think aloud:

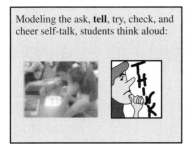

Modeling the ask, tell, **try**, check, and cheer self-talk, students think aloud:

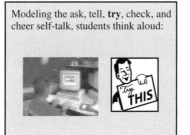

Modeling the ask, tell, try, **check**, and cheer self-talk, students think aloud:

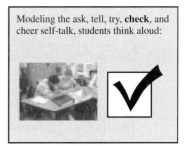

Modeling the ask, tell, try, check, and **cheer** self-talk, students think aloud:

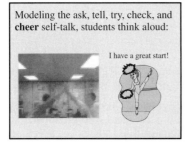

I have a great start!

With the growing quantity and quality of information available, students need to know how to access and use this information.

Students need:
• to learn how to ask the right type of questions
• to know where to access their information
• to draw conclusions
• to know how to evaluate and apply information to other situations
• to learn how to present their information for others to understand

Where can I find information about my topic?

I need to plan a path of discovery.

Internet
Encyclopedia
Newspapers
Interviews

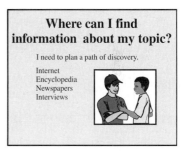

Key Words

The following is a list of key words related to my topic

Word	Page #	Source
Anger	134	dictionary
Rage	88	Elements of Lit
Confidence		

My Research Questions
-Turn key words into questions
-Combine words with
    Who? What ? When? Why? How?
New questions can be written in the "What I Want to Find Out" column.

Remember to ask: WHY is it important to me?
and
HOW am I connected to it?

Fan Fold Research

Reflection

Have students read without taking notes. After reading tell students to write down all the information they have gained through their search. This includes factual information as well as reactions to their material. This promotes ownership of the material.

Double-Entry Log

Information	Reaction

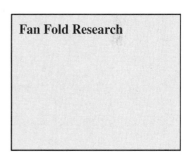 I must always cite my source
Sources

Evaluation Criteria	U	NI	S
I have well thought out research questions.			
I have used my class time efficiently.			
I have taken careful notes.			
I have used my peers and teacher to help me improve and revise my writing.			
I have edited my piece carefully.			
I have submitted all my work in published form.			
I have shown creativity in my work.			
I have written a correct bibliography.			
I have turned my work in on time.			
I have become an expert on my topic.			

Comments: _____

RESEARCH		Reaction	Daily Checklist

RESEARCH

R - Read   I read; a good reader creates a good researcher
E - Excite   I am excited about my subject
S - Seek   I seek answers to my questions
E - Enter   I enter my information and organize
A - Ask   I ask more and more questions
R - Reflect I reflect upon what I have learned
C - Create   I create opportunities to share my information
H - High 5 I deserve a "High 5 Hand Jive" for a job well done!

Reaction
Have student explain what worked and what they could do better

Daily Checklist

Date	Plan of Action

Source: Created by Gina Towler. Used with permission.

Summary

This chapter provides specific examples of ways current K–8 classroom teachers have integrated metacognition, self-regulated learning, and self-talk to foster reflective students who play an active role in taking responsibility for their learning.

The theme of this book, developing reflective practitioners who then foster student responsibility in learning, can be seen through the experiences of these teachers and students. Each of the teachers describes how she internalized her own knowledge of these concepts as a part of reflective practice, and was then able to provide explicit instruction to foster active and responsible student learning. Students and teachers alike can apply metacognition, self-regulated learning, and self-talk to improve performance in schools.

Chapter **8**

Integrating Cognitive Strategy Instruction in the Classroom

Self-Questions

Knowledge: Provide examples of research in the areas of memory, comprehension, problem solving, and school work habits.

Comprehension: Explain the basic premise of verbal rehearsal as a way to improve memory skills.

Application: Show how reciprocal teaching is related to comprehension monitoring.

Analysis: Compare and contrast the teacher-generated examples of Ask-Tell-Try-Check-Cheer with the elements of the strategy as proposed by Manning, Glasner, and Smith.

Synthesis: Develop your own strategy to help students complete an academic task that requires memory, comprehension, problem solving, or school work habits and describe how this strategy complements existing research.

Evaluation: Evaluate the research and strategies presented for memory, comprehension, problem solving, and school work habits and provide a rationale about which strategies could be integrated into your future classroom.

Introduction

This chapter provides additional strategies that focus on metacognition and self-regulated learning. These strategies help teachers promote learner responsibility for academic growth and productive school work habits. Consistent with the theoretical framework promoted throughout this text, the goal of cognitive strategy instruction is to help students understand ways to facilitate their own learning by explicitly modeling, practicing, and cueing (Manning 1988; 1991) a range of instructional strategies to foster self-regulated learning.

Understanding Cognitive Strategy Instruction

Cognitive strategy instruction encourages autonomous learning, as students are introduced to a range of strategies they can learn to accomplish cognitively complex goals (Pressley & Woloshyn, 1995). Cognitive strategy instruction needs to be explicit and consistent, working toward the goal of teaching students to monitor their own learning. As a reflective practitioner, you should model and coach, demonstrating ways for the students to check their progress and learn ways to access strategies when they reach complicated problems across content areas. To reach diverse learners, you will need to present a range of strategies for approaching a specific task, such as pre-reading, during reading, and post-reading. Sadly, most teachers do not spend explicit instructional time modeling and practicing strategies so that students can reach a point where they have internalized a range of strategies to use independently.

The teacher's role during instruction typically involves assigning work, making sure students remain on task, and providing feedback on student progress. However, we agree with Duffy, Roehler, and Mason (1984), who argue that "one of the teacher's primary functions is to provide instruction that leads from other-regulation to self-regulated situations" (p. 301). Duffy, Roehler, and Mason agree that teachers need to present a strategy to students, show students ways to use the strategy, provide scaffolded assistance as students attempt to use the strategy, and provide reinforcement to encourage students' continual growth.

Other researchers, including Moely et al. (1992) have reached similar conclusions. In their study of 69 elementary school teachers, they found that teachers infrequently provided strategy suggestions. They state that "the very limited effort made by most teachers to instruct children in metacognition suggests less than maximally effective cognitive instruction in these elementary school classes" (p. 669). Through our own research and practice, we have found that, in general, classroom teachers do not employ self-regulated learning strategies spontaneously, naturally, and frequently in their daily teaching. They tell us they do not. For successful classroom application of self-regulation to occur daily, teachers need clear examples so they can learn how to blend content knowledge instruction with deliberate attention to self-regulated learning processes as they scaffold students' learning. Just as reflective teachers learn and then modify curriculum and methodology, we believe prospective and in-service teachers must also learn a range of cognitive strategies that embrace self-regulated learning principles and match those strategies with specific students.

Linking Cognitive Strategy Instruction to Self-Regulated Learning

A primary goal of cognitive strategy instruction is to help students learn a range of strategies so they can be their own best teachers. Effective teachers incorporate implicit and explicit instruction and practice of strategies within content-area instruction, guiding students in appropriate strategy use. Through repeated practice and teacher scaffolding, students will begin to internalize strategies, thus encouraging independent learning. For strategy instruction to be most effective, it should be a natural extension of content instruction. Strategy instruction should also be an explicit part of a lesson. For example, a lesson could proceed with the following strategy instruction components: (1) explain the skill of focus (concentration, study skills, main idea); (2) introduce the lesson (include the content and skill portion of the lesson); (3) develop guided practice using the skill; (4) involve the students in a discussion reporting their use of the skill; (5) review and reinforce the skill within the lesson; and (6) continue practice with the skill in other contexts (Richardson & Morgan, 1990). In this way, cognitive strategy instruction facilitates self-regulated learners.

Recently, one of Stanulis's students summarized her understanding of cognitive strategy instruction in the following manner:

> The concept of teaching children to teach themselves seems somewhat complicated. However, once a teacher understands cognitive strategy instruction, the idea is not so abstract. The teacher will realize that this is something that should be practiced in every classroom. Cognitive strategy instruction involves helping students learn how to learn; teachers model many different strategies and the students then use these strategies to become better learners. Some of the strategies that the teacher uses include using self-talk to problem solve, using motivational strategies to monitor progress during problem solving, and adapting the environment in order to enhance learning. The main goal of cognitive strategy instruction is to have the students choose strategies best suited for them. Once they have used a strategy, or a range of strategies, they are able to handle tasks independently, thus becoming self-regulated learners.

—Ashley McRae, Summer 1999

To make cognitive strategy instruction a part of daily classroom life, a cooperative and collaborative investment is needed between students and teachers. Learners must begin to recognize the distinction between cognition and metacognition in order to become self-regulated learners. According to Forrest-Pressley and Waller (1984), cognition refers to the actual processes and strategies used by the learner. Metacognition includes an awareness of one's own cognition and learning strategies to gain control over one's own cognition. We believe teachers must play an active role in helping students become aware of their own metacognitive processes and implicit and explicit strategy use when facing a frustrating or boring task. When educators are actively aware of the thinking processes used by their students, they then tend to be more sensitive about providing instructional practices and curriculum methods that best meet student needs (Carpenter, Fennema, Franke, & Carey, 1996).

Categories of Learning Strategies

According to Weinstein and Mayer (1986), there are eight categories of learning strategies that teachers incorporate into their curriculum. Students can become active learners by identifying categories of learning strategies and encouraging themselves to continue practicing across categories. Following are the eight categories as described by Weinstein and Mayer. We have generated concrete examples of classroom activities associated with each category to provide visualization of actual classroom application of this research.

1. *Rehearsal strategies for basic learning tasks*   (*Memory*)—include repeating names of items in an ordered list and rehearsing basic tasks until they are internalized. Examples: Learning the order of the planets; learning to count by 2s, 5s, and 10s to reach 100; learning phone number; learning life skills such as illustrated in the following song for the primary grades, to the tune of "Farmer in the Dell": "My hands are by my side, I'm standing straight and tall; My eyes are looking straight ahead, I'm ready for the hall."

2. *Rehearsal strategies for complex learning tasks*   (*Memory*)—include copying, underlining, and highlighting to improve memory. Examples: Highlighting or underlining main ideas; copying grammar and mathematical rules; copying passages.

3. *Elaboration strategies for basic learning tasks*   (*Comprehension*)—include forming a mental image to help promote understanding. Examples: Creating a concept map; visualizing a scene described by a poem or song.

4. *Elaboration strategies for complex tasks*   (*Comprehension*)—include paraphrasing, summarizing, or describing how new information connects to existing knowledge. Examples: Relating voting to how elections work; using analogy of class store to economy.

5. *Organizational strategies for basic learning tasks*   (*Problem Solving*)—include grouping or ordering items from a list. Examples: Learning to organize self by following daily schedule in class each day; organizing chronological list of events leading to a war.

6. *Organizational strategies for complex tasks*   (*Problem Solving*)—include outlining or creating a hierarchy. Examples: Venn diagrams; story maps; webbing to show relationships and contrasts.

7. *Comprehension monitoring strategies*   (*Comprehension*)—include checking own comprehension. Examples: Self-questioning to monitor progress; checking predictions; using comprehension strategy such as QAR (question-answer-relationship).

8. *Affective strategies*   (*School Work Habits*)—include school work habits such as being alert and relaxed and ready to learn. Examples: Concentration and focusing strategies; deep breathing and relaxation strategies; singing songs to get ready to work.

LEARNING OUT LOUD 8–1

Think of a classroom activity within a specific grade level for each of the categories of learning. For example, rehearsal strategies for primary, intermediate, and upper grades will vary.

The eight categories of learning strategies can be collapsed into four domains that can serve as an umbrella over classroom learning: *memory, comprehension, problem solving,* and *school work habits* (Manning, 1991).

Memory

Strategies such as mnemonics, verbal rehearsal, rhythmic activities, and elaborative interrogation assist retention and recall of certain information. Important areas of academics that rely heavily on recall include remembering how words are spelled; learning mathematics facts; understanding critical terms in science, social science, health, and physical education; and learning certain sequential steps and techniques to solve problems and perform tasks.

Mnemonics.   *Mnemonics* are extremely effective memory strategies that can enhance student learning. The goal of mnemonics is to find a personally effective mental strategy to aid memory, thus helping students to retrieve varying types of stored information. Mnemonic instruction is used to increase the initial learning and long-term retention of information. Researchers such as Pressley, Woods, and Woloshyn (1992) believe that mnemonic strategies are the most effective instructional strategy to aid students in remembering new vocabulary.

Students need to be active participants in understanding the purpose of mnemonics. If used effectively, students can analyze the information before them, organize this information into groups, relate the information to prior knowledge, and then access cues to retrieve the information they have stored. Teachers often use mnemonic devices, such as learning the order of the planets with the sentence "*M*y *V*ery *E*ducated *M*other *J*ust *S*erved *U*s *N*ine *P*izzas" to remember Mercury, Venus, Earth, Mars, Jupiter, Saturn, Uranus, Neptune, and Pluto; or *HOMES* for remembering the five great lakes: Huron, Ontario, Michigan, Erie, and Superior. Students use such devices to model and practice, with the goal of independent use. If the students are active participants in creating mnemonics together with the teacher or as a class activity, they will more readily be able to create their own mnemonics in independent situations. According to Leal and Rafoth (1991), teachers can follow the following procedures for memory strategy development: (1) *Train (model and practice)*—Provide repetition to increase the chance that students will use the strategy; (2) *Provide feedback*—Emphasize how this strategy will help students memorize difficult information; and (3) *Suggest generalizations*—Model ways that this strategy can be used with other information and encourage student participation in these applications.

Acrostics are another popular type of mnemonic used to help students remember information. Acrostics, the opposite of acronyms, involve creating a set of memory cues alongside a word to reinforce meaning. For example, acrostics that promote productive school work habits can be made from the words *LISTEN* and *NEAT,* as illustrated in Figure 8–1. These acrostics, developed by Heaton and O'Shea (1995), were adapted to incorporate first-person language. The information contained within acrostics must be relatively familiar to students to be meaningful. The acrostic needs to be practiced aloud before the visual cue alone can be effective.

LEARNING OUT LOUD 8–2:

What are some mnemonics you learned as a student? When in your education did you learn these strategies? On what occasions do you create mnemonics to help you learn?

Look at the teacher.
Ignore the student next to me.
Stay in my place.
Try to visualize and understand the story.
Enjoy the story.
Nice job! I am a good listener.

Never hand in messy work.
Every paper should be readable.
Always keep my paper clean.
Try to remember to put my name and date on every paper.

Figure 8–1   Acrostics.
Source: From "Using Mnemonics to Make Mnemonics," by S. Heaton and D. O'Shea, 1995, Teaching Exceptional Children 28(1), pp. 34–36. Used with permission.

Verbal Rehearsal.   Verbal rehearsal is repeating information aloud to oneself with the distinct purpose of recalling the information from memory (Manning, 1991, p. 181). Information that is rehearsed verbally is much more likely to be remembered, as the words are spoken aloud and heard back in one's own ears. The basic premise of verbal rehearsal is that it is much more effective for children to hear information repeated aloud by themselves than to have the information repeated back to them by another. Manning (1991) illustrates this point from an observation of an undergraduate student teaching the ending sound /f/ in a reading lesson to a small group:

> One child was having difficulty hearing the ending sound. The student teacher kept repeating to this child: "What does this word end in? Now listen, "LeaF." The student teacher was exaggerating the /f/ sound on the end. She continued to repeat the word over and over for the child. I kept hoping she would ask the child to repeat the word for himself. To me, it seemed such an obvious thing to try next. Finally in exasperation she said to the child, "Say *leaf.*" The child said, "Leaf. Oh, that ends in a 'f' sound." Children are their own best teachers. They need to create their own metacognitive reality. Verbal rehearsal is a simple, straightforward way to teach children how to remember (recognize and recall) information. (p. 181)

Many teachers frown on students who talk while they are completing work at their seats. Rather than discouraging this behavior, we believe that teachers should encourage students to whisper aloud, whether it be in rehearsal of spelling words, mathematics facts, or vocabulary terms. Once students have sufficient practice in whispering aloud, they can then be encouraged to rehearse the word or fact silently to themselves for extra reinforcement (see Figure 8–2).

Rhythmic Activities.   *Rhythmic activities* are a wonderful way to incorporate music and songs to aid memory. Many researchers believe that music promotes learning and retention of learning for students of diverse backgrounds and ages. Orlando (1993), for example, believes that music can be integrated into the curriculum to aid in retention of academic subjects, as indicated in her study of students who took a mathematics test on money facts. In Orlando's study, the control group did not have music included as part of its teaching. The experimental group learned the money facts in a curriculum strongly rooted in music. The

1. *Choral response.* Have all the students repeat words, terms, facts, etc., together in unison. Ask students wearing tennis shoes to repeat together; students whose last names begin with *R* repeat together, etc.

2. *Singing.* Ask students to sing the information, putting the information to be recalled to the tune of a familiar song (e.g., *"Row, Row, Row Your Boat"*). Divide the class into groups (three or four) and ask each group to put the class directions for hall behavior, etc., to the tune of their favorite song. Groups share their creations with each other.

3. *High/low.* Rehearse the information in a little, squeaky high voice—like a mouse. Then rehearse using the deepest voice possible—like a huge grizzly bear. Repeat vocabulary words the way Papa Bear, Mama Bear, and Baby Bear would probably say them.

4. *Loud/soft.* Rehearse the information (on the playground) at the top of students' lungs, then whisper the information in their softest, but still audible, voices.

5. *Dramatized.* Rehearse information in a father voice, mother voice, teacher voice. Rehearse like a washing machine would say the information, or the vacuum cleaner, or a chipmunk, or well-known rock singer, etc.

Figure 8–2   Variations in Verbal Rehearsal.
Source: From Cognitive Self-Instruction for Classroom Processes, *by B. H. Manning, 1996, Albany: State University of New York Press, p. 185.*

experimental group scored higher, on average, than did the control group on retention of mathematics facts.

Many of us can easily think of songs that we learned during our school years to help us retain information. Songs can help students remember the 50 states, the 50 capitals, and the seven days of the week. Students of all ages refer to the alphabet song when trying to remember the order of letters. Recently, Stanulis was observing in her son's preschool classroom, where they sang songs to learn the life cycle of a butterfly, the order of the planets, and the steps in making a pizza.

Consistent with the premise of verbal rehearsal, music provides students with an opportunity to audibly express their learning as they sing or hum the words of a song. Rap music seems to be particularly effective in gaining and maintaining student interest and memory.

EXAMPLE "MATH RAP"

$\bigcirc + \square = \square$
Gotta know my math sums—
Not me, not me, I won't be a math bum—

Gotta know that 0 plus any fun number
Will be the sum of the "any fun number"
What a hummer! What a hummer!
So 0 + 1 = 1 What fun!
So 0 + 2 = 2 So true!
So 0 + 3 = 3 Now I see!
So 0 + 4 = 4 Not a bore!
So 0 + 5 = 5 I have arrived!

So 0 + 6 = 6 Now I'm fixed!
So 0 + 7 = 7 Math is heaven–LY!
So 0 + 8 = 8 This is truly great!
So 0 + 9 = 9 Got it down–real fine!
So 0 + 10 = 10 Yeah! Yeah!

Gotta know my math sums
Not me, not me, I won't be a math bum.

Rhythmic activities can be especially effective in helping English as a Second Language students become familiar with vocabulary commonly used in the United States. Sonya Sanchez, a classroom teacher who is particularly interested in ESOL, studied rhythmic activities during a course with Stanulis. She is enthusiastic about the use of music in the classroom to aid memory, and wrote in a class paper:

> Because children seem to enjoy the songs, they request to sing them. This results in daily practice and frequent exposure. In some cases, the students will sing these songs on their own, and thus gain even more practice than possible during school hours. These children consider it a challenge to learn all of the lyrics and be able to sing the songs from beginning to end. In many cases, the children will bring tapes of their songs home to practice, or simply sing these songs at home and begin to expose their families at home to the English language through song.

Elaborative Interrogation.   *Elaborative interrogation* is most useful for upper elementary and middle school learners. The gist of this strategy is that students learn to interrogate themselves by posing questions about the material to be learned (Pressley & Woloshyn, 1995). When presented with a fact, the student asks herself, "Is this fact true? Why or why not?" Elaborative interrogation can be used alone or in small groups (Woloshyn, Paiviot, & Pressley, 1994).

Woloshyn et al. (1994) found that elaborative interrogation can be especially effective when students use it to learn scientific facts, primarily because some of the facts conflict with common, prior knowledge. When students have misconceptions about the information, this strategy provides an opportunity for self-exploration (or interrogation). For example, when students in the Woloshyn et al. (1994) study were presented with facts about the solar system, the facts were sometimes accompanied by a signal of a potential misconception. Following are some of the facts the sixth- and seventh-grade students were asked to learn by elaborative interrogation:

1. In space, the sun's heat cannot even roast a potato *(signal: inconsistent with prior knowledge)*.
2. Moon soil is made up of small pieces of rock and glass *(signal: consistent with prior knowledge)*.

When students use elaborative interrogation to investigate facts, they ask and answer the question, "Why is that fact true?" In the Woloshyn et al. (1994) study, which divided the middle school students into control and experimental groups, there was great success. "Regardless of whether the fact was consistent or inconsistent with students' prior knowledge, or whether the fact was presented unembellished or with refutation, students using elaborative interrogation remembered more facts than control students" (Pressley & Woloshyn, 1995, p. 238). This memory strategy resulted in learning gains for these students up to 6 months after the original presentation of the facts.

Comprehension

Comprehension Monitoring.   Throughout this text we have promoted the belief, grounded in theory, that explicit metacognitive instruction is necessary to improve classroom learning. Reading comprehension research supports this premise: a distinguishing characteristic of good readers is the use of metacognitive skills in the reading process (Moore, Moore, Cunningham, & Cunningham, 1998). Extensive research by Moore et al. (1998) found that effective readers, or those who comprehend well, actively use self-questioning and self-monitoring strategies. Students who struggle to comprehend text, on the other hand, do not spontaneously apply metacognitive strategies that could facilitate reading comprehension. Students can be taught these skills and can achieve significant gains in their ability to comprehend text and apply these learned strategies when facing unknown text. Students need to be taught self-monitoring and other metacognitive strategies to improve basic skills. Research on reading comprehension monitoring and listening (Duffy, Roehler, & Mason, 1984) (including the overseeing of one's own understanding during listening and reading school tasks) indicates that the use of self-monitoring strategies reaps profound benefits; however, one serious limitation is that students often forget to use the strategies. Thus, we believe that visual and verbal cues are critical components in aiding comprehension monitoring.

Palincsar and Brown (1984) first introduced the term *comprehension monitoring.* Their work prompted a shift in the role of the teacher to that of a facilitator who scaffolds instruction for students. Teachers help students acquire comprehension monitoring strategies and skills that can support improved comprehension (Rosenshine & Meister, 1994). The two comprehension strategies that we will discuss within this chapter are reciprocal teaching (Palincsar & Brown, 1984) and question-answer-relationship. Both strategies focus on developing metacognitive skills to promote self-monitoring and improve reading comprehension.

Reciprocal Teaching.   Palincsar and Brown (1984) are responsible for introducing a now-famous comprehension monitoring strategy called *reciprocal teaching.* This cognitive strategy encourages students to be active learners and teachers. According to Palincsar and Brown (1984), students "first experience a particular set of cognitive activities in the presence of experts, and only gradually come to perform these functions by themselves" (p. 123). While engaged in reciprocal teaching, students learn specific comprehension strategies they can apply to the reading of a new text. Dialogue between student-teacher or student-expert peer is central to reciprocal teaching.

In their review of the literature on reciprocal teaching, Rosenshine and Meister (1994) provide an excellent summary of how reciprocal teaching works in the classroom. As students begin to read from expository text paragraph by paragraph, the teacher introduces four reading comprehension strategies: (1) generating questions, (2) summarizing, (3) attempting to clarify word meanings or confusing text, and (4) predicting what might appear in the next paragraph. During early instruction in reciprocal teaching, the teacher primarily takes the important role of model—modeling the process of using these strategies within a passage of expository text. Repeated student practice is critical to the success of the strategy as the students apply what they have learned about using these strategies to help them understand the next passage of text. The teacher's role becomes one of support "through specific feedback, additional modeling, coaching, hints, and explanation" (Rosenshine & Meister, 1994, p. 480). The teacher continually adjusts the difficulty of the task as the students are ready to take over more responsibility in using the strategies independently. The dialogue between student and teacher is the center of learning this strategy. In this dialogue, the teacher and students take turns assuming the role of teacher in leading the dialogue about a passage of a text.

To ready students for reciprocal teaching, the teacher can model the following procedures:

1. Invite the students to use titles, illustrations, graphics, or aspects of the layout to predict the nature and content of the text.
2. Ask students to read the text silently with you.
3. Encourage students to clarify confusing parts of the text (words, phrases, ideas) by asking you or other students questions to clarify meanings.
4. Ask students questions about the text.
5. Invite students to explain the meaning of the passage in their own words (summarize).
6. Predict what the next paragraph will be about and ask students if they agree or disagree with the prediction.

Next, the teacher can divide the class into small groups and invite students to elect a leader or "teacher" to assist the group through the various steps of reciprocal teaching. Finally, the teacher needs to provide feedback to students about their questions, summaries, and predictions (Palincsar & Brown, 1984).

Reciprocal Teaching in Action.   Carolyn Carter (1997) describes her experience using reciprocal teaching as an instructional strategy to effect change in an elementary school. In 1992, Carter began working in Highland Park District, Michigan, first as a curriculum director and later as assistant superintendent. This district, located in Detroit, has a population of almost 100% African American students, and was not meeting the minimum standard of student achievement required for special resources. Something had to be done to improve student motivation and achievement.

After extensive research in reading comprehension strategies, Carter and a team of colleagues selected reciprocal teaching as a comprehension strategy to improve reading comprehension district-wide at both the elementary and secondary levels. They specifically selected the program because of its emphasis on self-monitoring of comprehension while reading, therefore helping struggling readers learn to internalize the strategies that excellent readers unconsciously use while reading. Carter and her colleagues believed it was a program that parents also could learn and help reinforce at home, and that students could play an active role in and improve their self-efficacy.

The following describes the implementation of reciprocal teaching within the Highland Park district. Palincsar, co-creator of the reciprocal teaching comprehension strategies, assisted Highland Park in its initial training of staff:

> Using (resource) funds, we established (and later expanded) a team of 10 professional and paraprofessional educators at each school except the high school. At our K–2 school, we deployed two teachers and two paraprofessionals. We called these teams the Academic Response Teams. The teams worked with small groups of students (six to eight) who experienced difficulty in math and reading achievement. The aim was to teach each child how to boost his or her learning through instruction in metacognitive skills. We first focused on mathematics and social studies classes because we felt these two areas were key routes to higher achievement on the MEAP (Michigan Educational Assessment Program). . . . (p. 67).

During the course of the project, students were pulled from their classrooms and were taught reciprocal teaching strategies for 30 minutes, 20 days in a row. Carter (1997) states that the program, begun in 1993, had specific objectives, which included:

- To ensure that students at highest risk received instruction in monitoring and regulating their reading comprehension
- To help teachers realize firsthand the benefits of small-group dialogues as vehicles of comprehension because these matched the new definition of reading exactly
- To encourage a new, basic requirement among teachers: proficiency in using the Reciprocal Teaching technique (p. 67)

The results of this immersion in reciprocal teaching are astounding. For example, the fourth-grade students in the district realized the following gains on the MEAP reading scores (Highland Park began using reciprocal teaching in the 1993–1994 school year):

Percentage of students meeting state standards in reading

1991	1992	1993	1995	1996
8.6%	9.8%	14.4%	28.8%	31.5%

Reciprocal teaching can also be used within a whole classroom to help learners at different levels. For example, a third-grade teacher, Melissa Ward, studied reciprocal teaching during a course with Stanulis. She adapted ideas from the research on reciprocal teaching and created a bookmark as a visual cue to help students remember the strategies involved in reciprocal teaching. After practicing with the students herself, modeling the reciprocal teaching strategy, she intends to take on more of a coaching role in helping the students assume the dialogic roles in reciprocal teaching. This project shows Ward's written exercise, which provides students with practice. Her written hints allow her to fade from prominence in the instruction.

TEACHER PROJECT: MELISSA WARD (THIRD-GRADE TEACHER)

Bookmark/Worksheet—Reciprocal Teaching

Use your *Reciprocal Teaching* bookmark to help you complete this sheet. The answers to these questions may be done in any order as you read, but your group must fill in each section.

Predicting.   Write one or two sentences that predict what the rest of the passage or poem will be about.

Picture in Your Mind.   After you have finished reading, draw a picture of what this passage or poem makes you see in your imagination. You may draw it on this paper or on another sheet of paper that the teacher will give you.

(continued)

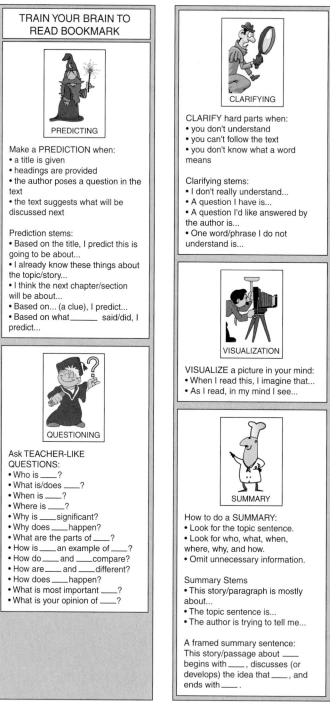

TRAIN YOUR BRAIN TO READ BOOKMARK

PREDICTING

Make a PREDICTION when:
• a title is given
• headings are provided
• the author poses a question in the text
• the text suggests what will be discussed next

Prediction stems:
• Based on the title, I predict this is going to be about...
• I already know these things about the topic/story...
• I think the next chapter/section will be about...
• Based on... (a clue), I predict...
• Based on what _____ said/did, I predict...

QUESTIONING

Ask TEACHER-LIKE QUESTIONS:
• Who is ____?
• What is/does ____?
• When is ____?
• Where is ____?
• Why is ____ significant?
• Why does ____ happen?
• What are the parts of ____?
• How is ____ an example of ____?
• How do ____ and ____ compare?
• How are ____ and ____ different?
• How does ____ happen?
• What is most important ____?
• What is your opinion of ____?

(front)

CLARIFYING

CLARIFY hard parts when:
• you don't understand
• you can't follow the text
• you don't know what a word means

Clarifying stems:
• I don't really understand...
• A question I have is...
• A question I'd like answered by the author is...
• One word/phrase I do not understand is...

VISUALIZATION

VISUALIZE a picture in your mind:
• When I read this, I imagine that...
• As I read, in my mind I see...

SUMMARY

How to do a SUMMARY:
• Look for the topic sentence.
• Look for who, what, when, where, why, and how.
• Omit unnecessary information.

Summary Stems
• This story/paragraph is mostly about...
• The topic sentence is...
• The author is trying to tell me...

A framed summary sentence:
This story/passage about ____ begins with ____, discusses (or develops) the idea that ____, and ends with ____.

(back)

Clarifying.   Write down any words, phrases, or ideas that you do not understand.

Teacher-like Questions.   Pretend that you are the teacher and you are going to give a test about what you have just read. Using the back of your bookmark as a guide, write three "teacher" questions about the passage.

Summarizing.   Write a summary of what you read. Give only the main ideas.

Source: Created by Melissa Ward. Used with permission.

Reciprocal teaching, indeed, has been found to be an effective way to help readers internalize the skills and strategies necessary for effective comprehension. Palincsar and Brown's 1984 work has had far-reaching impact as students in elementary and secondary classrooms continue to learn this strategy that fosters dialogue and independence in learning.

Question-Answer-Relationship.   Questioning is an important part of classroom life, whether a teacher is asking questions to generate discussion, a student is asking a question to clarify, or students are involved in answering questions at the end of a chapter or section of a text. Within the context of developing an active learner, questioning is fostered in classrooms as a way to develop and assess comprehension.

Few studies have explored how children develop the skills to ask questions or ways to illustrate how developing questioning skills are related to comprehension. Raphael (1986) developed the *question-answer-relationship* (QAR) strategy to focus students on learning ways to generate questions as a tool for comprehension monitoring. Raphael believes that when students learn the skills of asking questions and learning where to find answers for questions, these skills provide a vital link for improving comprehension.

The QAR strategy provides a tool for helping students look for answers within reading material. There are four types of QARs that students are taught under two main categories: "In the book" and "In my head" (see Figure 8–3). Like all of the strategies advocated in this text, it is imperative that the teacher provide sufficient modeling, practicing, and cueing (Manning, 1991) of this strategy before learners are ready for independent use.

In the Book

Right There: Students can locate the answer to a question "right there" in the text. This kind of question is easily answered in one or two sentences.

Think and Search: Answers are available in the text, but students need to put together information from throughout the reading to find the answer.

In My Head

The Author and You: This kind of question combines a reader's background knowledge with elements from the text in order to integrate prior knowledge and text information.

On Your Own: The answer for this type of question primarily comes from a reader's background knowledge.

Figure 8–3   Question-Answer-Relationship Strategy.
Source: From "Teaching Children Question-Answering Strategies," by Taffy Raphael, 1982, The Reading Teacher, 36, *pp. 186–191. Used by permission.*

LEARNING OUT LOUD 8–3

Create a visual cue for the question-answer relationship strategy within a grade level of your choosing.

When Raphael and her colleagues helped students learn the QAR strategy (Raphael & Pearson, 1985; Raphael & Wonnacott, 1985), they advocated the following approach:

1. Introduce the QAR strategy by providing definitions and visual cues.

   a. Talk about the types of QARs.
   b. Provide students with a short passage (two to three sentences) to read and questions of each type to answer.
   c. Provide students with answers to the questions and discuss why each is a certain type of QAR.
   d. Provide another short passage with questions and responses, and let the students take the lead in identifying the type of QAR represented.
   e. Provide students another short passage with questions, but let them decide the type of QAR and responses to the questions.
   f. Provide feedback on accuracy of responses and QAR type.

2. Introduce longer passages with more questions.

   a. Facilitate as students identify the QAR type, answer questions, and explain QAR choice.
   b. Provide feedback on accuracy of responses and QAR type.

3. Provide multiple opportunities for practice using QAR across a consistent period of time.

LEARNING OUT LOUD 8–4

Identify the QAR types after reading the following passage:
Mammals are warm-blooded. Mammals have fur or hair. Humans are mammals.

1. What do mammals have? (Right There)
2. What makes humans mammals? (Think and Search)
3. What are some other mammals that share these same characteristics? (Author and You)
4. What else makes mammals unique? (On My Own)

Source: Adapted from Stanulis's graduate students Shannon Davis and Nicole Campbell's 1999 presentation on QAR.

Problem Solving.   Each of us is involved in problem-solving activities on a daily basis. Problem solving is how we work to find a solution that is not always obvious. It is common for people to become frustrated as they work to find a solution to a problem. In anticipation of the frustration that solving a problem may cause, it is important for students to internalize a range of problem-solving methods: self-coping, self-monitoring, and self-reinforcing strategies. Educators suggest some general problem-solving strategies to help their students cope with problem-solving frustrations. For example, students can *look for a pattern* by organizing the data to try and see whether there is a regularity. Some students enjoy *making a drawing* to help organize information and see new relationships that were not first apparent. Other students find that *solving a simpler problem* helps to learn about the processes needed to solve a more complex problem. Hands-on students enjoy using manipulatives or materials to *make a model* that will simulate the problem and help lead toward a solution. Students may also enjoy *acting out the problem* to think through a solution.

Ask, Tell, Try, Check, Cheer.   One effective method that has been researched and adapted for practice among many classroom teachers is the *Ask-Tell-Try-Check-Cheer* self-regulation strategy steps for problem solving (Manning, Glasner, & Smith, 1996). According to Manning, and colleagues, students can learn these steps for talking to themselves while working through a task. As White and Manning (1994) conducted a study with kindergartners to help them learn this strategy, they used puppets, role-play, and puzzle solving to introduce think-aloud strategies. Age-appropriate techniques such as art projects, math problems, and phrases of text can be used to help older students practice this strategy. The purpose of this strategy is to teach students *how* to think aloud, not *what* to think. The strategy helps students follow through and finish tasks accurately and promptly by self-monitoring their progress. Figure 8–4 shows the metacognitive steps of problem-defining (*ask*), self-guiding (*tell*), self-coping (*try*), self-correcting (*check*), and self-reinforcing (*cheer*). Classroom teachers and peers should model this strategy verbally. Sufficient time must be allocated for individual practice so that students can internalize the strategy.

Many classroom teachers have adapted this strategy for use in their classrooms. One very concrete way for students to internalize the self-dialogue steps of the strategy after sufficient modeling and practicing is with visual cues. The following teacher projects

1. *Ask* myself questions about the assignment or how to do the assignment. Another name for *ask* is *problem defining*.

2. *Tell* myself how to proceed with the school task at hand. Another name for *tell* is *self-guiding*.

3. Tell myself to *try* my very best to focus, follow through, and finish my school work even if it is sometimes boring and sometimes too difficult. Another name for *try* is *self-coping*.

4. Next, I tell myself to *check* over my work to make sure I completed everything I was supposed to and to see if I made any errors. Another name for *check* is *self-correcting*.

5. Finally, I *cheer* for myself if I have tried my very best. I note any progress that I have made even if everything is not always 100%. Another name for *cheer* is *self-reinforcing*.

Figure 8–4   Ask-Tell-Try-Check-Cheer Strategy for Problem Solving.
Source: From "Metacognition as an Aspect of Self-Regulated Learning Strategies," by B.H. Manning, S.E. Glasner, and E. Smith, 1996, Roper Review, 18*(30), pp. 217–223.*

show examples of how a first-grade, a fifth-grade, and an eighth-grade teacher have created visual cues to help their students remember the steps of this problem-solving process. Teachers often tape individual copies of these cues on students' desks so they are accessible when students need them for problem solving to complete a task.

TEACHER PROJECT: DOROTHY RICE (FIRST-GRADE TEACHER)

Verbal and Visual Cues for Ask-Tell-Try-Check-Cheer: Completing School Tasks

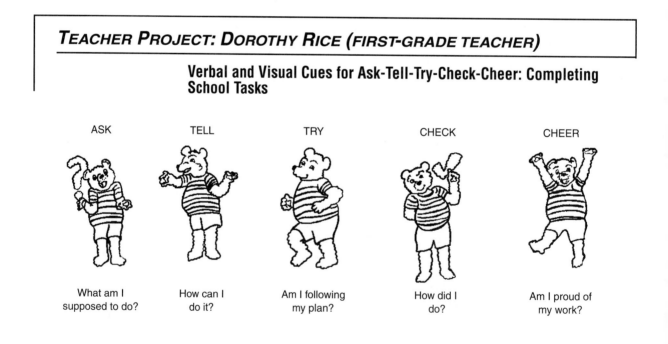

ASK	TELL	TRY	CHECK	CHEER
What am I supposed to do?	How can I do it?	Am I following my plan?	How did I do?	Am I proud of my work?

Source: Developed by first-grade teacher Dorothy Rice, in Self-Talk for Teachers and Students, *by B. H. Manning and B. Payne, © 1996, Allyn & Bacon. Used with permission.*

TEACHER PROJECT: LYNN WILLIAMS (FIFTH-GRADE TEACHER)

Verbal and Visual Cues for Ask-Tell-Try-Check-Cheer: Controlling Anger at School

ASK
• What exactly is the problem?
• Why am I angry?
• How can I calm down?
• How can I solve the problem?

TELL
• What happened is not my fault.
• I need to calm down.
• There is no need to be angry.
• Let's take this issue point by point.

TRY
• I don't understand, but I'm going to try to work this out anyway!
• Hang in there. You can figure this out.
• Just slowly count backwards from 10.
• Look for the positives. Don't assume the worst or jump to conclusions.

CHECK
• I need to check with _____ to see if he or she heard what I might have said.
• I wonder if _____ heard what _____ said?
• I need to check out all the facts before I jump to conclusions.

CHEER
• Hey! I feel better!
• Yeah! I calmed myself down. Now I can deal with the problem with a clear head.
• I feel much calmer now.
• I didn't jump to conclusions; therefore, no one is in any trouble now. Way to go!

Source: Created by Lynn Williams. Used with permission.

TEACHER PROJECT: JUDY POWELL (EIGHTH-GRADE TEACHER)

Verbal and Visual Cues for Ask-Tell-Try-Check-Cheer: Completing Mathematics Tasks

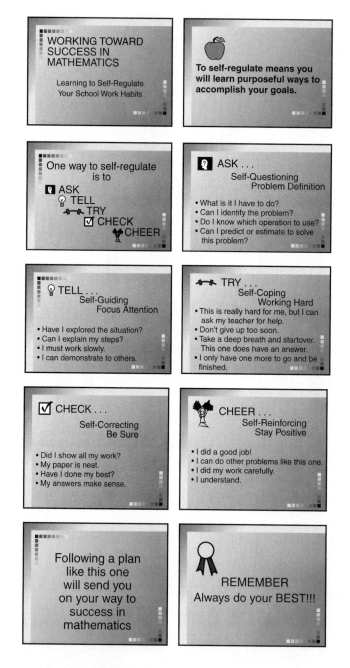

Source: Created by Judy Powell. Used with permission.

Elementary and middle school teachers report that this process has helped students develop a powerful tool for problem solving that transfers to the successful accomplishment of other school tasks such as creating poems, writing stories, computing mathematical problems, doing seatwork, and finishing homework. Figure 8–5 provides three separate examples of Ask-Tell-Try-Check-Cheer self-instructions. The first example describes self-instructions for heading a paper correctly, the second for returning materials to their proper place, and the third for helping organize material.

Problem Solving in the Content Areas.   Problem-solving strategies are necessary in all content areas. Within the areas of science and mathematics, in particular, students need to learn strategies to effectively understand more cognitively complex subject matter. The project that follows illustrates a creative way to involve students in learning about problem solving. Middle school teacher, Kathy Rogers, who took a graduate course from us in 1998, created the following humorous story that helps students learn about the scientific method.

ASK	First, teachers or peers ask questions of themselves to define problems and identify specific needs. Some examples are as follows: 1. What did the teacher say to do first? 2. Where does this go now? 3. Why do I have so many of these?
TELL	Then teachers or peers state to themselves focusing and guiding statements. Some examples are as follows: 1. She said to head my paper with the date, subject, and my name. 2. This goes back on the reading table for others to see. 3. I need to organize these to see what's extra.
TRY	Then teachers or peers reason with themselves that, on the one hand, they are frustrated by difficulty, tedium, complexity, or boredom and, on the other hand, they can cope with their frustration regardless of its type or source. Some examples are as follows: 1. I get really tired of heading my paper the same way all the time but I guess the teacher needs this information to keep herself organized. 2. Sure I'm in a hurry, but if I don't put the book back, others will miss a great book! Come on! 3. This is really hard to do, but I will slow down and take a deep breath. I will take one step at a time.
CHECK	Next, teachers or peers verbally correct themselves as they monitor work in progress or monitor completed work for errors, omissions, or irrelevant material. Some examples are as follows: 1. Did I include everything in the heading: name, date, subject? 2. Did I put the check-out card in the book I returned? 3. I have three categories. Which one is not needed?
CHEER	Finally, teachers or peers verbally reinforce themselves for effort, excellent performance, or an outstanding product or achievement. Some examples are as follows: 1. Yes, good for me. My heading is perfect. 2. The reading book center looks great! I did my part to be a good citizen. I'm proud. 3. I stayed calm until I organized and deleted the extra material! YES!

Figure 8–5   Modeling Think-Aloud for Ask-Tell-Try-Check-Cheer.
Source: From "Metacognition as an Aspect of Self-Regulated Learning Strategies," by B. H. Manning, S.E. Glasner, and E. Smith, 1996, Roper Review, 18*(30), pp. 217–223.*

TEACHER PROJECT: KATHY ROGERS

One day Dragonella was working in her laboratory. She was trying to determine which shampoo worked better: Soapy or Puffy. Just as she put her head under the running water the phone began to ring. With water running down her back, Dragonella answered, "Hello."

"Dragonella, this is Mayor Willybe. We have a serious problem and need your help. The Jefferson River is in trouble! This morning two fishermen called to tell me that the Jefferson River is filled with bubbling purple ooze! Dragonella, our town depends on that river for food and water. Will you please help us?"

Dragonella draped a towel around her shoulders and wiped the phone. "Yes, Mayor Willybe, I'll help. Just let me gather my things, and I'll get started right away."

Dragonella gathered the things she considered necessary for examining the Jefferson River. A magnifying glass, lightweight microscope, test tubes with stoppers, science notebook and pencil were all placed in her giant bag. As she drove to the river she began to wonder if she was up to the job. "What if I can't find the problem and fix it?" Dragonella asked herself. Then she remembered the wise words of her Aunt Bev. "You can do anything Dragonella. Just try."

As Dragonella pulled up to the river's edge she smiled to herself. "I can do this," she thought, "but I'll have to work hard and use all my skills." As she began to collect her things she opened her science notebook. The first step was always to STATE THE PROBLEM. "OK," thought Dragonella, peering into the river. "Let's look at this mess." Dragonella walked along the edge of the river. In order to STATE THE PROBLEM she must ask herself several questions. First, what's the real problem here? Second, do I see anything out of the ordinary? Third, is there a connection between the purple ooze

and anything else? Under the STATE THE PROBLEM Dragonella writes: "Jefferson River has purple ooze flowing through it? Why?"

Next Dragonella began thinking of reasons that could cause purple ooze. In order to complete the next step, FORM A HYPOTHESIS, she must again ask herself several questions: (1) How are the water and the purple ooze flowing? (2) Does the ooze float on top of the water, or is it mixed in with the water? (3) Is there a source that's causing the purple ooze? By using self-questioning, Dragonella felt ready to write the second step down. Under FORM A HYPOTHESIS Dragonella wrote: "The purple ooze is coming from a source up the river that is spilling into the water."

Dragonella knew that she would need to walk farther up the river to investigate for the third step, OBSERVATION and EXPERIMENTATION. She leaned down into the water and touched the ooze. "What? This isn't ooze at all!" exclaimed Dragonella to herself. As she felt the water she marveled over the feel of the purple water. "It doesn't feel different," she told herself. After several minutes of OBSERVATION Dragonella began to EXPERIMENT with the purple water. She scooped up a test tube full and closed it with a stopper.

Then she placed her microscope on the ground and placed a slide of water underneath the lens. As she adjusted the fine tuning knob she noticed the water looked as it always does on the slide. There were small organisms floating around. The only difference was the color. Under step three, OBSERVATION and EXPERIMENTATION, Dragonella wrote: "No ooze, feels like water to touch, slight smell (I think I've smelled it before), has no effect on water when observed under a microscope." Dragonella snapped her notebook shut and took her things to the car.

The next step for Dragonella was to INTERPRET DATA. For this, Dragonella began to recall her observations. As she thought about what she already knew, she talked to herself aloud so that her ideas would come easily. "I know that the purple stuff has no distinct texture, and its physical properties are similar to water. It flows, sloshing back and forth, and acts like water. It has a funny smell, which I think is similar to grapes. It doesn't add anything to water except its color. I can't taste it, but there are fish swimming in the river, and I didn't find any evidence of dead animals. Under close observation with a magnifying glass and a microscope the water looks the same, except it's purple." Dragonella flipped open her science notebook and under INTERPRETING DATA she wrote: "The river has become polluted by some type of a grape spill. The water itself is not harmful."

To tie this problem up Dragonella decided to drive up to the mouth of the river. The beginning of the Jefferson River was located near the industrial park in Hall County. As Dragonella entered Hall County, she noticed signs pointing toward the Welch's Plant. "Ah, hah!" Dragonella exclaimed to herself. "This could be the source of our problem." Dragonella pulled her car up by the plant and began to investigate the metal pipes that hung over the river's mouth. Sure enough, there was a small slit in the side of a pipe, and from it slowly trickled a line of purple grape juice. Dragonella flipped open her notebook and under step five, DRAWING CONCLUSIONS, she wrote: "The purple ooze in the Jefferson River is grape juice that is leaking out of a hole in a metal pipe at the Welch's Plant." Further down on the page, she added another statement: "Call manager at Welch's Plant and buy extra cups."

Two days later the town gathered on Main Street to present Dragonella with an "I Saved the Jefferson River Award." As Major Willybe handed Dragonella the award, which by the way was a giant golden grape, he asked her what led her to solve the problem so quickly. Dragonella just smiled and said, "The scientific method and lots of questions." "Questions?" asked the mayor. "I thought you were alone. Who did you talk to?" Dragonella smiled as she responded, "Why, myself, of course. I'm my best source for solving problems."

Source: Created by Kathy Rogers. Used with permission.

Rogers created this story to make the scientific process come alive for her middle school students. The main character, Dragonella, uses helpful self-talk to work in constructive ways to reach her goal. She successfully solved the inquiry by talking herself step-by-step through the scientific process of stating the problem, forming a hypothesis, observing and experimenting, interpreting the data, and drawing conclusions. Students can be involved in creating their own narratives to solve a particular problem posed in class. Such integration of literacy and scientific content enhances creativity and provides a mechanism for making the process of inquiry come alive for students, connecting them to a character and modeling ways they can help themselves work through a similar problem.

Matz and Leier (1992) also highlight active learner involvement and responsibility through the explicit understanding of strategies for problem solving. They developed a way to integrate mathematics and drama to help students work with word problems. Word problems often pose difficulties for students as they make decisions about what operations to apply to a particular problem when it is posed in a narrative form. In addition, word problems often include multiple steps, adding complexity and, often, confusion (Matz & Leier, 1992).

Matz and Leier combined several methods to create a strategy they call "word-problem playlets." In this strategy, students incorporate the "stop method" (Leutzinger, 1985), wherein students are asked to stop and check procedures as they progress through the problem. To involve the students as active participants in the process, role playing was included. Finally, Matz and Leier believed that by involving students in their own problems, students could learn a lot about solving word problems (Fennell & Ammon, 1985).

These methods were combined as students were encouraged to write and perform their own word problems using a technique the authors called "stage freeze." Each time a computation is needed for the problem, the narrator in the problem shouts "Freeze!" and the actors within the playlet stop as the audience is directed to provide the appropriate computation. Then the action of the playlet resumes as the students incorporate the information supplied by the audience into the playlet.

As with any strategy advocated in this text, it is imperative that proper modeling occurs before students create their own playlets. A teacher could begin by acting out a pre-written playlet together with students. Then, the students could rewrite a typical word problem from their textbook into a class playlet. Finally, small groups could create and perform their own playlets. See Figure 8–6 for two examples of playlets created by elementary school students that appeared in Matz and Leier (1992).

LEARNING OUT LOUD 8–5

In small groups, transform a mathematical word problem into a playlet that you can use as a model for students.

School Work Habits.   School work habits are an important aspect of learning often left unattended. Early in their schooling, most students figure out how classrooms work—they discover that it is important to listen, pay attention, follow directions, focus on a task, and concentrate to reach task completion. The development of these skills oftentimes occurs unconsciously. Corno and Rohrkemper (1988) refer to this set of skills as *classroom literacy*. We refer to this same concept in terms of helping students become active participants in the creation of productive school work habits. In a series of studies conducted by Manning (1990), children who were designated by their teachers as productive workers talked to themselves before, during, and after task performance in ways that were qualitatively dif-

Example 1

Jodi
Erica
Cory
David-Narrator

(TWO) customers, one sales clerk,
and a narrator)

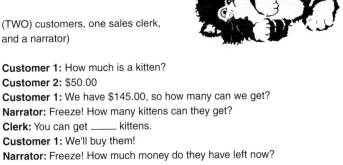

Customer 1: How much is a kitten?
Customer 2: $50.00
Customer 1: We have $145.00, so how many can we get?
Narrator: Freeze! How many kittens can they get?
Clerk: You can get _____ kittens.
Customer 1: We'll buy them!
Narrator: Freeze! How much money do they have left now?
Customer 1: We have $_____ left.
Customer 2: How much is a litter box?
Clerk: $4.00
Customer 1: We'd better get two.
Narrator: Freeze! What is the cost for two litter boxes?
Clerk: That's $_____ for the litter boxes.
Customer 1: Now how much money do we have left?
Narrator: Freeze! How much do they have left after they bought the kittens
    and the litter boxes?
Customer 2: We still have $_____ left.
Customer 1: Well, it's twelve o'clock. We have to go. Bye!

(continued)

Figure 8–6   Student Playlet Examples.

ferent from those of students who were designated by their teachers as less productive
workers during independent school tasks.

The goal of helping students learn to focus, follow through, and finish tasks independently
(Manning, 1990) is one teachers should not leave to chance. Through adult and peer modeling
of productive self-guiding speech-to-self, practicing activities, and cueing or reminders to use
the most facilitative self-guiding speech (Manning, 1988; 1991), we can expect to foster optimal learning in our students. In short, the focusing, following through, and finishing school
work habits Manning (1990) should be supported by the skills of self-regulation (Brown &
DeLoache, 1978): problem defining, self-starting, self-guiding, self-coping, and self-reinforcing.

Teachers need to play an active role in motivating students to understand how they learn
and to share in the responsibility for learning. In a study of at-risk middle school students,
Gert Nesin (2000) interviewed focus groups of students to find out their perceptions of
teacher and student responsibility for learning. One student, Kid, spoke specifically about
motivation as a key factor in his application of productive school work habits: "I think education is all about want. If you want to learn, you can tune them in. If you don't want to be
interrupted, or you don't want to learn it, you can tune them out. It's very simple. And if they
tell you to do something, you can do it, but it doesn't mean you're going to learn from it.
They can't make you learn" (Focus Group Analysis, Team 1, p. 4). This student, typically
labeled a "nonproductive learner," clearly understands how classrooms work, yet does not

Example 2

One customer, one sales clerk, and a narrator—any combination of boys and girls

Setting: A grocery store

Customer: I'm supposed to buy two loaves of bread and a can of beets.

Clerk: How much money do you have?

Customer: Five dollars. How much is bread?

Clerk: Ummmm. It's on sale; three loaves cost two dollars and seventy cents.

Narrator: Freeze! How much will the customer pay for two loaves if three loaves cost two dollars and seventy cents?

Customer: Let's see. Two loaves would be _____ . Okay. How much are beets?

Clerk: *(Smiling)*. Guess!

Customer: How can I guess?

Clerk: I'll give you a hint. A can of beets is fifteen cents more than half the price of one loaf of bread.

Narrator: Freeze! What is the cost of one loaf of bread?

Customer: Okay. Let's see. If three loaves are two dollars and seventy cents, then one loaf is _____. Now I need to know what half of that is.

Narrator: Freeze! What is half the price of one loaf?

Customer: That's _____ . And beets are fifteen cents more than that.

Narrator: Freeze! What is _____ plus fifteen cents?

Customer: So that's _____ for the beets! Now you tell me, what's the total for the bread and the beets!

Clerk: Wait! Let me review. The bread was _____ for two loaves and the beets are _____ .

Narrator: Freeze! What's the total?

Clerk: So that means the total is _____ .

Customer: I should get back some change. I have five dollars; the bread and beets are _____ .

Narrator: Freeze! How much change should the customer receive?

Customer: I should get _____ in change.

Clerk: Great! We have enough to play some video games at the arcade.

Customer: *(as they exit)* No, my mom needs the money for the laundromat.

Figure 8–6   Student Playlet Examples. *(continued)*
Source: These student examples appear in "Word Problems and the Language Connection," by K. Matz and C. Leier, Arithmetic Teacher, *(April), 14–17. Reprinted by permission.*

feel motivated to use effective school work habits. Throughout the transcripts, he seems to bear the weight of responsibility for learning, never mentioning how teachers have helped him gain strategies to learn. He later said: "The Board of Education... They determine what you need to learn... You basically, you have to decide to learn it" (p. 5). But what is the teacher's role in helping students learn how to learn?

The Power to Learn: Helping Students Research Their Own Learning.[*]   Rarely do teachers focus instructional time on helping students actually analyze the school work habits they use that either enhance or distract from their learning. A notable exception is Pearson (Pearson & Santa, 1995), who has created a powerful method that embraces the goals of cognitive strategy instruction by helping students become researchers of their own learning so they can understand the strategies that best help them learn. Pearson has involved middle and high school students in exploring the effects of different strategies such as background knowledge, organization, discussion, and metacognition. The inspiration for the creation of this strategy came from an eighth-grade history teacher who changed the way Pearson thought about learning and teaching:

> I can picture her blue-gray hair piled on top of her head and vivid blue eyes peering through thick bifocals. I can even remember some of the ancient history content that she taught us. Yet what I recall most about her is what she did for me as a student. She taught me how to learn. She took my hand and showed me how to underline, how to take notes, and how to write coherent answers to essay tests. She taught me about the need for self-testing. What power she gave me... I want to give [my students] the power that Mrs. Rolscheim gave me. They deserve to leave my classroom knowing about ways of learning. (p. 462)

With her own students now, Pearson includes the strategies of background knowledge, organization, discussion, and metacognition to help students research their own learning. After using these strategic processes, students write a self-reflection on how the strategies are helping or not helping them learn. For a complete version of the specific activities used by Pearson, see Pearson and Santa's (1995) article titled "Students as Researchers of Their Own Learning," published in the *Journal of Reading*. The following sections highlight some of the approaches Pearson used that bring together many categories of learning discussed within this chapter.

Background Knowledge.   Pearson's first activity to help students research their own learning involved splitting the class in half, and sending half of the class into the hallway. The students who remained in the classroom were asked what they knew about Christopher Columbus (any topic could be substituted here). They engaged in a short discussion about this knowledge. Then the students from the hallway came back into the room. The teacher next read a passage aloud and asked all members of the class to write down what they remembered. (It was not obvious from reading the passage that it was about Christopher Columbus.) Clearly, the students who had participated in the pre-reading activity of activating background knowledge and discussing the topic remembered considerably more information than the students who had been out in the hallway. Then all the students engaged in a discussion of how background knowledge influences their learning.

Organizing Information.   Next, Pearson moved to introduce the habit of organizing information for greater comprehension. She distributed List A to half of the students in her class and List B to the other half of the class:

---

*This section borrows from "Students as Researchers of Their Own Learning," by Jenny Watson Pearson and Carol Minnick Santa, 1995, *Journal of Reading, 38* (6), pp. 462–469. Reprinted by permission of the International Reading Association.

LIST A	LIST B
Washington	California
Elephant	Nevada
March	Oregon
	Washington
Martin Luther King	Christopher Columbus
Oregon	Martin Luther King
August	President Clinton
Squirrel	
California	Elephant
Christopher Columbus	Squirrel
Nevada	Wolverine
President Clinton	August
October	March
Wolverine	October

The students were asked to study their individual list for 1 minute and then write down all the words they could remember without looking at their list. In the discussion that followed, students quickly found out that those who had List B remembered more words. They also noticed that the words in List B were categorized by subject. Interestingly, the students who had List A who had remembered the greatest number of words had created their own organizational system or mnemonic device to remember the words. As students began to realize the benefits of organization, they discussed important skills such as underlining, highlighting, notetaking, and mapping.

From Pearson's description of these skills, the discussion flows naturally to aspects of metacognition, or helping students become more aware of how they learn. By concretely involving them in activities that examine how they learn, the process becomes individualized and meaningful.

Experimenting With Learning Strategies

Teachers realize that there is not time to teach strategies void of content, nor is it advisable. Pearson situated her students' investigation about their own learning in a real learning activity. She had them experiment with five different procedures for learning that would prepare them to read an upcoming novel in class. During each of the procedures, students read an article that provided background information on the topic of the novel, then put aside the article and notes. On a blank sheet of paper, students recorded information they recalled from the article. Students were responsible for scoring their results for each procedure on individual graphs so that they could compare their results across different strategies used.

Strategy One	Pearson asked them to read an article. She provided no background knowledge or pre-reading activity.
Strategy Two	The class brainstormed what students already knew about the topic of the next article. Each student read the article independently.

Strategy Three	The class began by brainstorming existing knowledge about the next topic. Students then skimmed the article and added new ideas to the class-brainstormed list. Independently, they then read the article, highlighting major points and writing study questions from the main points they highlighted.
Strategy Four	The class began by brainstorming existing knowledge about the next topic. Each student independently read the article, highlighting main ideas and then organizing the main ideas into individual concept maps.
Strategy Five	The students skimmed the last article and then read it again, highlighting the main points. Then students had a choice of either writing study questions or designing a concept map. Students then met in small groups to discuss the article and study questions or concept map.

At the end of these five procedures, students were asked to review their work and their reflections across the strategies used. They were asked to write about which kinds of strategies best helped them feel like active, organized, metacognitive learners. The students found that different strategies worked well for different students. This is a key point for teachers to understand as well, as it underscores the importance of modeling, practicing, and cueing a wide range of strategies. With the exception of two students in Pearson's class, all students found that they recalled more information when they applied specific study strategies. The self-analysis was made more powerful by involving the students in graphing their own learning.

Summary

The techniques described in this chapter can be powerful ways to motivate students to identify new strategies for successful learning. Instruction of this kind can be most effective early in the school year so that students, with teacher guidance, can have ample practice throughout the school year to foster internalization of strategy use. Understanding school work habits and the strategies used to memorize, comprehend, and problem solve can increase productive school success as well as self-efficacy for learning.

This chapter provided a research-based examination of cognitive strategy instruction in four domains: memory, comprehension, problem solving, and school work habits (Manning, 1991). Cognitive strategy instruction must be explicit, with teacher modeling, as students are introduced to a variety of ways to monitor and improve their own learning. Building upon the theme of developing reflective teachers, we advocate habits that can develop reflective students as well. Students can improve their task performance when they become aware of their own metacognitive processes and the ways that they approach tasks when they are frustrated, bored, or unsuccessful.

Chapter 9

Valuing Multiple Models of Assessment of Student Learning*

Self-Questions

Knowledge: Describe the three different types of standardized tests.

Comprehension: Summarize the benefits and limitations of standardized tests.

Application: Construct a behavioral-content matrix for a sequence of instruction.

Analysis: Compare and contrast traditional parent-teacher conferences with student-led parent-teacher conferences.

*This chapter was written by Stacey Neuharth-Pritchett of the University of Georgia and Gert Nesin of Shapleigh Middle School in Kittery, Maine.

Synthesis: Propose a lesson and an authentic form of assessment that could be utilized with it.

Evaluation: Evaluate the different types of assessment models presented and formulate some conclusions about which assessment strategy is most consistent with your teaching philosophy.

Introduction

This chapter provides an overview of traditional and authentic assessment approaches and tools. A discussion of standardized testing provides information on the types of testing and their purposes along with the benefits and limitations of assessment strategies. Teacher-made tests are presented to formulate the connections among planning, instruction, and assessment. Journals, portfolios, and digital portfolios are highlighted as forms of authentic assessment that promote student self-evaluation and inclusion of parents in the assessment process. The chapter concludes with a discussion of a recent trend in education—student-led parent-teacher conferences—and the outcomes associated with including multiple stakeholders in assessment.

Developing Self-Regulated Learners: A View of Assessment

Throughout this text, we have presented strategies that foster your development as a self-regulated learner and teacher who engages in self-monitoring and goal setting. Because planning, delivery of instruction, and assessment are so intricately linked, it is helpful to view assessment in both its traditional sense and through the lens of authentic assessment strategies. Authentic assessment approaches pair well with the teaching and learning strategies discussed in this book. Specifically, authentic assessment is a natural part of learning and helps promote learner responsibility to monitor and reinforce progress. These types of strategies structure the learning environment to allow students to shape their learning rather than be shaped by that environment. Assessment tools such as journals, checklists, anecdotal records, and portfolios enable the development of skills for superior teaching and learning.

Understanding the Language of Standardized Testing in the Classroom

One of the most difficult tasks that classroom teachers face is the appropriate assessment of children. Indeed, effective teachers think just as much about their assessment strategies as they do about how they instruct their students. Teachers are constantly making judgments and decisions about their students. "Did John understand how to correctly modify that verb?" "Why doesn't Sally correctly line up her multiplication problem so the decimal point in her answer is accurate?" While teachers draw conclusions about their students each day, it is also important that they critically examine their own instructional practices. Good teachers ask themselves, "Did I really get the main idea of that story across?" "Should I have done this activity in small groups instead of with the whole class?" Therefore, everything we do in the classroom involves assessment.

Assessment is comprised of both evaluation and measurement. *Evaluation* is defined as the decision making about student performance as well as appropriate teaching methods. *Measurement* is this evaluation expressed in quantitative or numeric terms. When we think about John's ability to modify a verb, we can also express his performance as 80% correct, or 8 out of 10 test items correct. This numeric information allows us to describe how well students have performed against a standard. Measurement also enables us to make comparisons among our students. Not all decisions made by teachers about students have to result in a numeric score, however. Teachers might also describe a student's performance with more holistic approaches such as pass/fail or mastery/nonmastery. Whatever the system utilized by the teacher, the resulting assessment serves as an indicator and the best estimate of a student's success in the classroom.

If you reflect back on your own experiences as a student, you could probably cite differing examples of assessments that your teachers utilized. There are two main types of assessment, differentiated by the types of comparisons that are made with the results. Comparisons that are made against a given criterion or standard of performance are called *criterion-referenced assessments*. These assessments measure mastery of a few, but highly specialized, sets of objectives. Criterion-referenced tests are often utilized (a) to determine if students have the prerequisite skills to begin a particular sequence of instruction; (b) for measurement of affective or psychomotor objectives; and (c) when the teacher is working with a group of students with a relatively homogeneous level of ability. If you are a kindergarten teacher and you are interested in a student's ability to recognize the letter *G* in the alphabet, a criterion-referenced assessment is the most appropriate choice. Here, you are concerned about your student's ability to recognize the letter *G* each time the task is presented to him; that is, the student competes against a criterion or standard.

The second type of assessment, *norm-referenced assessment*, provides the teacher with information on how well one student performs in comparison to another student. For the kindergarten teacher who is interested in her student's ability to recognize the letter *G*, not much information is gained from knowing that five students were able to accurately recognize the letter *G* and 12 students were unable to recognize the letter *G*. Norm-referenced assessment is an appropriate strategy when you are measuring general ability over a large sequence of instruction. For example, an entire chapter on land formations in the social studies curriculum would necessitate an examination of the key concepts of the chapter. Although you could assess every objective for which you had planned, you most probably would learn more about your students' abilities by choosing fewer questions that sample the most important points of the lesson. Norm-referenced assessments are helpful in assessing the range of abilities in either a large group of students or of a group of students with a wide range of abilities.

Norm-referenced testing is appropriate for selecting students when only a few openings in a program are available (e.g., entrance into gifted and talented programs or special education programs). As teachers, you will most often encounter norm-referenced testing when you administer yearly standardized tests to your students. Standardized tests are part and parcel of the school experience for children. More than 1 million standardized tests are given per school day in the United States (Woolfolk, 1995). Standardized tests are given under uniform conditions and scored according to uniform procedures. Most of the standardized tests you will encounter are classified into three large domains: achievement, diagnostic, and aptitude.

Achievement tests are designed to measure a student's learning over a specific set of objectives or content. While most tests in schools are administered to large groups of students at one time, achievement tests can also be administered individually. Frequently used achievement tests, such as the *Iowa Tests of Basic Skills* or the *California Achievement Test,* provide many useful pieces of information about a student's performance. One student's score is compared to the scores of a normative group of children across the country who also took the same examination. Most often, these scores are reported as percentiles or normal curve equivalent scores. This reporting format tells the teacher the percentage of students in the norming sample who scored at or below a particular child's score. Take, for example, Margaret, whose percentile score was 83. Her teacher would interpret that 83% of the students who took this particular test scored at or below Margaret's score. These types of tests are useful for making comparisons across large groups of students. There are other types of reporting formats in which scores are also reported. The most common of these is a standard score, which is a score based on the number of standard deviation scores away from the mean or average score. If you have ever had the opportunity to look at a standard printout for a national achievement test, you may have also noticed T-scores, z-scores, CEEB scores, stanine scores, and grade-equivalent scores.

There are some problems with the interpretation of some of these scores—specifically, the stanine and grade-equivalent scores. Not all of the methods for reporting scores are sensitive to the properties of the normal curve—the distance between one score and the next does not take up the same amount of area under the curve. Grade-equivalent scores are the most misinterpreted score by teachers and parents alike. Grade-equivalent scores are derived to represent pupils' achievement in terms of a scale based on grade and month in school.

For example, Jack, a third grader, has a grade-equivalent score of 3.2. This score would be interpreted that Jack is achieving at the level of third grade, second month. However, Maria, Jack's classmate, has a grade-equivalent score of 5.5. Does this mean that Maria, a third grader, is capable of doing fifth-grade, fifth-month work? No. This score means that Maria, a third grader, scored well above the national average on this achievement test when compared to her peer group. Her score was higher that the expected average third grader who took the test at the start of the third grade. You can plainly see how easily this scoring method is misinterpreted. When examining a test score printout, it is best to utilize the normal curve equivalent data when reporting scores to children or parents.

LEARNING OUT LOUD 9–1

Obtain a student's test score printout. Examine the types of scores that are reported and write a summary of what those scores mean. Jot down some ideas about how you would explain a child's scores to his or her parents.

Diagnostic tests are normally used to identify specific learning or behavioral difficulties. Undoubtedly, throughout your teaching career you will be required to make interpretations about the results of diagnostic tests. These tests are usually given to students by a specially trained administrator who also analyzes the students' performance on the tests. Diagnostic tests enable us to identify learning difficulties such as auditory processing problems or the inability to attend to a task. This information is very useful for teachers in modifying their curriculum and in individualizing the products that they request from students.

Aptitude tests measure a child's current achievement and predict how well that child will do in learning unfamiliar material. The SAT (Scholastic Aptitude Test) and the ACT (American College Testing Program) are aptitude tests. IQ tests also fall within this category. Aptitude tests are also utilized to identify children for inclusion in gifted and talented programs. These tests are usually given off-grade level. This means that a first-grader, identified by a teacher as exhibiting signs of giftedness, is given a test for a third-grader. If a first-grade child performs well on such a test, the results provide evidence for placing that child in special classes for gifted and talented instruction.

Even though there are many uses for tests in our classrooms, there are also some growing concerns about the heavy reliance on standardized testing in schools. Decisions that are made from the results of standardized tests impact students and teachers alike. Standardized tests are often required for 4- and 5-year-old children to enter prekindergarten or kindergarten (Shepard & Smith, 1989). Tests are used to qualify children for special placement in magnet schools or gifted and talented programs. Standardized tests are utilized to determine whether children who may have special needs will receive services. These tests are also used to make comparisons among classrooms within a school or community (Guskey, 1994). These days, even real estate agents sell houses by using test scores to promote a community as a successful place for children to learn! Standardized test scores are also tied to local, state, and national spending and financing of education. American test scores are routinely compared to test scores of children from nations around the world. And, yes, test scores of children in your classrooms are also utilized to determine your efficacy as a teacher—and sometimes determine if you should receive a pay increase or even retain your position.

Despite all of the uses of standardized tests, there are limitations to their use. Bias in testing has had some negative impact on specific ethnic and racial groups in the United States. Even issues of economic status have been shown to correlate with students' performance on standardized tests. While many test developers are aware of these issues, the development of culture-free tests has not been very successful (Sattler, 1992). Another negative outcome from the use of standardized tests is "teaching to the test" (Canner et al., 1991). Because of the significant amount of pressure placed on children and teachers regarding their standardized test results, many teachers find themselves devoting more time to objectives they know will be covered on the standardized test and leaving out other curricula that are just as important (Madaus & Kellaghan, 1992; Smith & Rottenburg, 1991). Further, there is a booming market for test preparation materials for yearly standardized testing in public schools. This phenomenon occurs even for kindergarten and the first grade. The most significant impact, however, is the degree to which parents emphasize their child's standardized test results as the major indicator of their child's performance, and de-emphasize the teacher's judgment despite the teacher's 180 days or more of observation and daily assessments of their child (Airasian, 1996).

All teachers should emphasize to parents that a standardized test score is just one indicator of a child's performance. Over the course of one academic year, teachers rely on a tremendous amount of data to assess students—a child's work ethic, persistence, engagement, analysis of mistakes, and processing of information. All of these elements, when combined, give the most accurate picture of a child. Indeed, this view of a teacher's role in the classroom brings us to the topic of teacher-made assessments.

Constructing Teacher-Made Assessments

One of the most critical errors that classroom teachers make involves the connection among planning, instruction, and assessment. So much energy is devoted to the first two tasks that often the last element receives less attention than it should. When an effective teacher plans and implements a sequence of instruction, he should also be thinking about the assessment that he will utilize. Teacher-made assessments have many advantages over the tests that appear at the end of chapters in a curriculum series and the generous number of worksheets that accompany textbooks. Although most of these materials are well-designed, they do not account for the amount of emphasis placed on a given set of objectives in a teacher's instruction. Take, for example, a science unit that focuses on electricity. Perhaps the assessment included in the teacher's manual has three questions that focus on electrical current in a 10-question quiz. What would happen if a fourth-grade class grasped that basic content, but had conversations in class that centered around the use of alternative resources of energy instead of electricity? As you can see, the end-of-chapter test would not really represent what was covered in that class with that group of students. It might be useful to think of the assessments supplied by textbook publishers as useful resources for your assessments.

Teachers use assessments for a number of purposes to summarize their students' progress. It is helpful to think of these in two broad categories: formative and summative assessment.

Formative assessments typically are ungraded tests used before and during instruction to aid in planning and delivery of lessons. Sometimes this formative assessment is referred to as a *pretest*. Data from pretests allow the teacher to get a basic understanding of how much the students already know about a given set of objectives. You can imagine how useful a pretest might be if all of your students already know the elements of the food pyramid. Think of how little they might get out of your unit of instruction if the majority of the content focuses on identifying the levels of the food pyramid. If you know that the students are familiar with the basic facts of the food pyramid, you can move on to more complex objectives associated with that unit of instruction. In this case, you and your students could focus on aspects such as the number of calories associated with each type of food or the unique combinations of food that constitute a balanced diet.

Critical assessment allows the teacher to gather important information that radically changes the focus of instruction. In addition to paper-and-pencil assessment, formative assessments can take many different forms; for example, student drawings of characteristics of animals; "yes" or "no" placards that students hold up in response to questions you pose; written answers to math problems on small chalkboards that students hold up for your review; interactive computer games that monitor students' knowledge about prefixes and suffixes; and a number of other formats. The key to formative assessment is the quick gathering of information to guide your instruction that will ultimately change your overall assessment of a unit of instruction.

This overall evaluation of instruction is called *summative assessment* and is defined as testing that follows instruction that assesses a student's achievement over the entire set of objectives. This information is useful to the teacher as she judges her overall sequence of instruction, as she evaluates each student's mastery of the content, and as she plans for teaching the content in the future. Again, when most people think of the phrase "summative assessment," they think of a paper-and-pencil device. However, these assessments might also be a story, a sequence of drawings, and verbal answers to the teacher's questions, as well as a number of other creative devices. Whether you use formative or summative assessment, you should remember always to anchor your instruction in specific behavioral objectives. It may be helpful to construct a behavior-content matrix so that you know you have covered all of the important elements of a unit and focused on differing levels of thinking skills. Figure 9–1 shows an example of a behavior-content matrix for a second-grade unit of instruction on community helpers.

A behavior-content matrix assists you in identifying the main ideas that you need to address in a sequence of instruction. You can also determine if you are focusing your question on a certain thinking skill, such as knowledge. You can then modify your content or the process by which you teach to accommodate higher levels of thinking from your students. However, the most critical connection to constructing a high-quality assessment is the link between the way you plan and the way you instruct, and their association to how you assess (Popham, 1999).

Behavior / Content	Knowledge Objectives	Comprehension Objectives	Application Analysis Synthesis Evaluation Objectives
Types of community helpers (police, firefighters, librarians, etc)	Define what each community helper does.	If presented a situation, choose from which community helper to seek assistance.	Consider what our community would be like without a community helper (e.g., firefighter).
Training requirements for community helpers	Define the requirements to become a community helper.	Compare and contrast whether other helping professions have the same requirements (e.g., teachers, doctors).	Describe how a person with a physical disability might still work for the police department.
Characteristics of community helpers	Define the characteristics of community helpers.	Given a description of a community helper that has not been discussed, identify the characteristics necessary for the job.	Evaluate whether only men can be firefighters.

Figure 9–1   Behavior-Content Matrix.

LEARNING OUT LOUD 9–2

Construct a behavior-content matrix for a unit of instruction that you are writing. Match your topical areas and objectives to various levels of cognitive processing.

There are a number of traditional ways that you can construct teacher-made assessments. If you reflect back on your own career as a student, you most likely completed routine assessments that we call *objective assessments*. These types of assessments include multiple-choice questions, matching exercises, true/false statements, short-answer or fill-in items, and some essay items. The advantages of objective assessments include:

- quick assessment of basic information
- ease in scoring and reporting the results to students
- getting a large sample of students' understanding over a few topics
- teachers' limited time in constructing other assessments

The major disadvantage of objective assessments is that teachers usually cannot see where a student's thinking went astray or exactly how a student solved a problem if the student is merely choosing from A, B, C, or D. These types of assessments tend to center on knowledge-based items and do not promote higher-level thinking skills. A more complete description of each of these types of objective tests is beyond the scope of this chapter and can be found in many other texts, such as Kellough and Kellough's *Middle School Teaching: A Guide to Methods and Resources* (1999, chapter 11, pp. 396–406). The controversy surrounding these types of assessments has led some educators to examine alternative types of assessment that are student-driven and allow students to display and demonstrate their knowledge. Thus, let's examine authentic assessment in the classroom.

Authentic Assessment in the Classroom

If you think back to your own schooling experience, you probably recall being assessed over many skills and asking yourself the question, "What does this have to do with what I will do in the future?" This type of questioning has promoted educational professionals to look for an alternative to traditional testing formats (Airasian, 2000). This alternative is known as *authentic*, or *performance, assessment*. There are three main reasons for the increased popularity of performance assessments: (1) the push to include this performance assessment as part of formal or statewide assessment programs; (2) the emphasis on higher-level thinking and problem-solving skills; and (3) an alternative for students who often score poorly on traditional assessments to illustrate their competence in alternative ways (Airasian, 2000).

Authentic or performance assessments test a child's skills and abilities as they would be applied in real-life situations (Wiggins, 1992). These types of assessments go beyond the basic knowledge that a student might have, and actually encourage students to construct a product or carry out a performance. Performance assessments can take many forms, such as constructing a poem, writing in a journal, creating a science fair project, making a collage, giving a speech in front of a class, and many other mechanisms wherein students show how to apply the knowledge or skill they have learned. According to Airasian (2000), all performance assessments should:

- Have a clear purpose
- Stipulate what aspects of the performance are to be judged
- Provide an appropriate setting for the performance assessment to be carried out
- Provide information in the form of a score or holistic rating that describes the student's performance

Just as there are a number of ways that students can illustrate their understanding of a concept in authentic assessments, there are also a number of different ways to evaluate performance assessments. Suppose you are teaching a unit on plot development in mystery books and you have a set of objectives you want your students to master. These objectives might include the students' ability to (1) identify the main characters of the story, (2) describe the context in which the story takes place, (3) identify a critical incident in the story where the problem is posed, and (4) identify parts of the text where the author introduces clues to mislead the reader. Using the authentic assessment technique of constructing an *anecdotal record*, you could record a student's comments as he participates in a small discussion group (Figure 9–2).

Student: Susan Gray   Date: 4/13/02

Observer: Mr. Jergens, Teacher

Today, during our small-group class discussion over chapter 8 of the mystery novel, Susan identified some elements of the story where she perceived that the author was introducing some facts that made her think that the shopkeeper was somehow involved in the crime (*Objective #4*). She engaged in a vigorous debate with Jack about her ideas. By the end of the debate, she had convinced her group members of the author's intent and cautioned her peers to look for other inconsistencies as they read the next chapter.

Figure 9–2   Anecdotal Record.

Teachers are constantly observing students on a daily basis. The anecdotal record is an assessment tool that is used to highlight a significant occurrence. Constructing and maintaining an anecdotal record is a very time-consuming process. Yet, such records provide an explicit description of a student's performance in relation to an objective within a context. How does the example shown in Figure 9–2 compare and contrast with a more traditional assessment, such as a multiple-choice item?

Learning Out Loud 9–3

Observe a classroom of students and select one or two students for whom to compose anecdotal records. Critique your anecdotal records for completeness and the objectives that the students have achieved. Highlight the positives and negatives of this type of system.

Classroom objectives might also be assessed with the use of a *checklist*. Imagine that you have just assigned an activity to your fifth-graders that requires them to research a topic and present a 5-minute speech to the rest of the class. A traditional assessment strategy would be quite difficult to implement with this assignment. A checklist is a more appropriate assessment tool to utilize with this real-world assignment. A checklist is a list of the criteria by which a performance should be judged. Completed checklists serve as diagnostic tools and are useful to show to students so they can see where to improve their performance. There are some disadvantages to using checklists, such as forcing a teacher to make an absolute decision about each performance criterion (Airasian, 2000) as well as summarizing all of the information on the checklist to a single score. What elements of the checklist shown in Figure 9–3 do you think are important?

Another assessment tool that is utilized with authentic assessments is a *rating scale*, or *rubric*. Rating scales have an advantage over checklists in that they allow the teacher to rate the student's performance on a continuous scale rather than on a dichotomy (absence or presence of a performance). Rating scales provide a quick and consistent way to document the performance of students. Teachers who devise rating scales should be cautious to limit the number of choices under each item to three to five ratings. When at all possible, the

---

Name: Javier Gonzales   Date: May 2, 2002

1. Thoroughness of research presented

    ☒ Use of current information (last 5 years)
    ☒ Use of at least three different sources (newspaper, personal interview, etc.)
    ☐ Use of transitions between major points
    ☒ Use of one or more visual aids (poster, object, etc.)

2. Physical expression and presentation
    ☒ Speaks clearly
    ☒ Uses emphasis to make a point
    ☒ Speaks loudly
    ☒ Faces and speaks directly to audience

Figure 9–3   Checklist for Speech Presentation.

same rating categories should be utilized with each question. Following is an example of an item on a rating scale:

The student followed all of the safety precautions when beginning the science laboratory experiment.

Strongly Disagree	Disagree	Undecided	Agree	Strongly Disagree
1	2	3	4	5

When you think about the types of instruction you deliver in your classroom and how you should assess your students' progress, it is practical to consider the use of authentic assessments. Now that you understand what an authentic assessment is and how to assess students using them, let us carefully consider three specific authentic assessments: journals, portfolios, and digital portfolios.

Journals.   The use of *journals* in the classroom is an effective means to document students' process of learning. Journals encourage students to write and think critically about what they are learning. There are many different types of journal writing structures that are applicable to all content areas. In a *process journal*, students document the process of learning by logging their activities, observations, and critiques of those observations. Consider a science unit on the phases of the moon. Students could keep a process journal that documents how they made their observations of the moon cycles, a description or drawing of the moon each night, and other observations of how they think the moon cycles impact life on earth.

This type of journal differs from a *response journal*, wherein students compose their thoughts and feelings about something they are studying. For example, a book study of *Roll of Thunder Hear My Cry* (Taylor, 1976) might elicit some strong responses from students that they might not like to share with the entire class. However, writing their responses to a portion of that text would give the teacher powerful insight into the students' depth of understanding of the meaning of the book. In addition, teachers often use this format to write thoughtful responses back to their students and engage in meaningful dialogue about concepts they have mastered.

Journals also serve a purpose when utilized as *dialogue journal*. These journals allow children to express their thoughts on topics about which they have a passion to write. The role of the teacher in this type of journaling process is to sometimes pose questions to which the children respond. There are no right or wrong answers in this type of assessment—it is an ongoing dialogue between the teacher and the student about a topic. There are a number of advantages to using journals as authentic assessments: (1) All children are free to display the knowledge they have learned in a piece of writing that is specific to their understanding. (2) The use of journals is meritorious for some children who may have difficulty with more traditional assessments. (3) Besides gathering information on the topic about which the entry is written, the teacher also gains some very meaningful information about the students' ability to exercise the mechanics of writing as well as the cohesiveness of their presentation. (4) A journal serves as another important source of communication between students and teachers, students and parents, and students and their peers. One major limitation to the use of journals is the extended time necessary in assessing them. Also, there is more subjectivity associated with assigning a holistic grade to a journal. Therefore, journals often serve only as a device to communicate information between teachers and students and are not graded.

> ## LEARNING OUT LOUD 9–4
>
> Document your thoughts as you read your students' journal entries. Highlight some of the unique information you have gathered by reading children's thoughts as expressed in their journals.

Portfolios.   Over the last few years, another type of performance or authentic assessment has become a regular part of classroom assessment. A *portfolio* is a purposeful collection of student work that can be utilized to document students' effort, progress, or achievement in a content area (Arter & Spandel, 1992). A wide variety of examples of work can comprise a portfolio, including pictures, videos, audiotapes, student reflections, individual work (papers, lab reports, etc.), group projects, preliminary drafts of products as well as products in their final form, and many others. However, all portfolios should be (1) purposeful, (2) selective, (3) diverse, (4) ongoing, (5) reflective, and (6) collaborative (Wolfe & Dietz, 1998). Portfolios are not just a random collection of a student's work. They are purposeful in their orientation—information in the portfolio highlights specific objectives, skills, and growth.

For example, a portfolio that focuses on the development of a first grader's writing progress should contain work samples from the beginning to the end of the year and should represent the amount of emphasis that a teacher placed on a given skill. Specifically, if a teacher spent a large amount of time practicing the skill of writing on the lines of the paper and not in the spaces in between, there should be some documentation in the portfolio with both work samples and a note summarizing a child's accomplishment of that goal. If the writing portfolio was one of a fifth-grader, perhaps samples of work would reflect the student's understanding of the construction of a thesis statement and the supporting paragraphs that follow the statement. There may be only two examples or many more, depending on the degree and ease with which the student understood the concept.

Portfolios should also be selective, showing learning across contexts and over time. Most skills in school, although often taught as discrete skills, are applicable to a number of contexts. Consider a mathematics example in which the students are adding two-digit numbers. The standard form of solving such a problem includes such skills as aligning the numbers written on top of one another and showing the regrouping strategies. This skill is also used in science, for example, when children report their research on the number of materials (that would require two-digit addition) that are thrown in the trash instead of being recycled. These two samples taken together give strength to the argument that the child has truly understood the concept and has skills that are transferrable to multiple contexts.

Portfolios should also be reflective. This reflection should be that of the teacher and the student, along with other important stakeholders such as parents. The content of a child's portfolio should be public, with ongoing dialogue between the teacher and the student about the specific skills that the sample represents. Over a year's time, such documented reflection can be very powerful in the child's eyes when reflecting on the sheer amount of content that she has mastered.

The development of a portfolio should also be a collaborative process. Because learning is a social process, much information is gained by asking the child to choose his best work sample. Even more information is gained when teachers and students converse about work samples that should be included that show a need for improvement. Teachers may also consider allowing a child and her parents, or a child and his peers, to choose a representative piece of work for the portfolio (Costa & Kallick, 1993).

While there are many benefits to the use of portfolios in the classroom, there are a number of limitations to their use. The development and assessment of portfolios is a time-consuming process for both children and teachers. Because each individual piece is judged, as well as the summative portfolio, there are multiple layers of analysis that necessitate an increased amount of time and coordination over more traditional assessments. Although teachers tend to be very good judges of their students' performance, some critics argue that there is a level of subjectivity to the assessment of a portfolio that is often reason enough not to employ portfolios in the classroom. In addition, because each student's portfolio is its own unique collection of work samples, it is difficult to make summary statements of the performance of an entire class. Finally, other issues are of concern with regard to portfolios, namely storage of the portfolios, access, and ownership of the portfolio contents (Georgi & Crowe, 1998).

LEARNING OUT LOUD 9–5

Interview teachers who are utilizing portfolio assessment in their classrooms and examine some of the students' work. Write a reflection about how you might utilize this assessment method in your own classroom.

Digital Portfolios.   The popularity of portfolios as authentic assessment tools is as infectious as the use of technology in schools. There are several reasons to consider developing a digital portfolio. For example, a teacher's technology competence can be demonstrated through use of a digital portfolio, a portfolio published on the Internet provides opportunities for feedback via an e-mail link, digital portfolios allow for immediate connections to local and national standards through hypertext links, and digital portfolios provide an opportunity for viewers to watch a lesson and hear teacher-student interactions (Costantino & DeLorenzo, 2002).

Another advantage to the digital portfolio is its transferability and its ability to reach a wider audience (Riel, 1994). In addition, because assessment is a social process, the portfolio is readily accessible and examinable by others, thus increasing the magnitude of its value to the student (Barrett, 1995). Another major positive outcome is that students are excited about using technology to construct their portfolios and learn the necessary software. Portfolios stored on disk are easy to save and, thus, the documentation of a student's development is not destroyed.

While there are some incredible benefits to digitized storage of portfolios, there are some limitations to the process. Among these are cost of software and hardware to store students' work; the need for teacher knowledge about software and hardware to facilitate a digital portfolio; access to technology; and content, privacy, and security issues (Georgi & Crowe, 1998). The research evidence on the efficacy of digital portfolios for elementary and middle grade students is not well accumulated at present, but one study by Tancock and Ford (1996) with college undergraduates found that students generated a more complete picture of their progress and achievement with digital portfolios than that measured by traditional assessments. In addition, students were able to demonstrate a wider array of competencies and took greater responsibility for their learning. The authors of this study also found that students became more skilled at accurate self-evaluation that ultimately also increased their level of responsibility to the subject matter.

Self-Assessment for Students and Teachers.

A growing trend in classrooms is the fostering of *self-assessment strategies* to allow students ownership over their learning and the development of reflective practice (Guyton & Fielstein, 1989; Rothenberg, 1997). Take, for example, a sixth-grade assignment on the influence of various cultural groups on American society. Perhaps you have assigned this topic and given students some choice with regard to how they research, compile, and present their findings. One student in your class, Pamela, decides to construct her presentation on the contributions of the Appalachian people to music. Using a traditional assessment framework, Pamela might write a paper and present a small synopsis of the information to the class. You would assign a summative grade about the breadth and depth of her presentation, a grade ranging from A to F.

Now think about this assignment. Pamela is allowed to assess her own progress. She might decide that she would like to use an interview technique to get some historical perspective on Appalachian music. She decides to interview two musicians about their thoughts and feelings regarding the evolution of music in Appalachia. Pamela decides to videotape her interviews and edit a 10-minute piece that she will share with the rest of the class. As part of her presentation, she will field questions from her classmates. She also poses some questions to her peers about what they learned from her presentation. Following her presentation, she sits with her teachers and critically discusses her presentation and her growth as a student after completing the project. How much more powerful is this approach for Pamela? Do you think that she will be more invested in this material? What is the likelihood that she will remember this information and make connections to it at a later date?

Student-Led Parent-Teacher Conferences.

Student-led parent-teacher conferences are designed to promote students' learning as a central theme in the assessment process (Davies, 1997). All of the individuals who assist student success in school are involved in the process (Kellough & Kellough, 1999), including students, parents, and teachers. The student shares representative samples of his work and describes the goals he has accomplished, what assistance he may need, and the goals on which he would like to work. Parents are connected to the material by asking questions and discussing ways to support learning efforts at home. Teachers are included as facilitators to support the student and provide clarifying information.

There are a number of different formats in which student-led parent-teacher conferences take place. The first is a *two-way conference* in which the student and parents discuss the student's materials and the teacher is available for consultation. This type of model allows for many conferences to take place at the same time within a classroom. The second model, the *three-way conference*, also involves the teacher directly. The conference begins as the parents and the student discuss the work samples, with the teacher joining in as the conference progresses to help the student and parents establish learning goals.

Data indicate that parents and students alike prefer student-led parent-teacher conferences over a more traditional format (Countryman & Schroeder, 1996). However, there are some limitations noted in the research literature, including some perceptions by parents that they need more feedback about their child from the teacher (Shannon, 1997).

Student-Led Conferences in Action: The "Nurse Shark" Team at Shapleigh Middle School

When conducted as part of an ongoing program of student self-evaluation, student-led conferences teach students to be reflective about their learning and progress, including strengths, challenges, and preferences. The conferences also provide a forum for thoughtful discussion among students, parents, and teachers. Perhaps most importantly, they allow young people to recognize the power of embracing personal responsibility for learning. To receive the full benefits of student-led conferences, teachers—in partnership with students and parents—carefully plan the classroom environment, opportunities for student reflection, and the process of the conference itself.

A partner team at Shapleigh Middle School in Kittery, Maine incorporated student-led conferences to promote student self-evaluation and effective and open relationships among students, parents, and teachers. The team, the "Nurse Sharks," consisted of two teachers and approximately 40 students looping from sixth through eighth grade. Curriculum centered around the questions and concerns of students. Teachers and students collaborated on planned activities, incorporation of standards, and ongoing assessment of the process and products of learning. Teachers expected students not only to take the responsibility to do the assigned work, but to find ways to make their own learning personally meaningful. Student-led conferences, therefore, became a natural extension of assessment, reflection, communication of, and responsibility for learning.

Teaching Responsibility, Reflection, and Self-Assessment

To be most effective, teachers, parents, and students must perceive student-led conferences as a process and not an event (Hackmann, Kenworthy, & Nibbelink, 1998). The conference becomes part of continuous self-assessment, goal-setting, and communication primarily by students in conjunction with teachers and parents. Student preparation in thinking about learning and setting goals becomes essential (Davies, Cameron, Politano, & Gregory, 1992). On the Nurse Shark team, students started their loop in the sixth grade with little understanding of their own learning processes and even less understanding of reflective practices. The teachers consciously used discussions and activities to promote self-assessment of learning.

On the first day, students wrote a paper explaining themselves as students: their strengths and challenges, the learning they enjoyed, and the learning they disliked. Teachers conducted daily discussions about activities and the extent to which they promoted learning for individuals and for the group. The teachers immediately incorporated a weekly assessment (see Figure 9–4). For the beginning assessments, students and teachers together discussed the learning activities of the week and the effectiveness of the activities. After the discussion, students then filled out individual assessments. Some students adequately reflected and wrote acceptable answers to the questions on the assessment. Others needed more individual time and assistance from the teacher. None of the students completed the assessment to show a deep understanding of themselves as learners. Teachers designed rubrics so that students appreciated degrees of quality and, specifically, how they could improve.

Classroom environment supported growth in honest self-assessment. Teachers believed that students could intelligently and honestly think and talk about themselves as learners, if taught to do so.

Name _____   Week ___/___/___ to ___/___/___

What I did/learned this week:

_____

_____

_____

Late work I still owe: _____

Upcoming projects, due dates, events: _____

Things I could be working on at home: _____

Accomplishments I am proud of: _____

My goals for the past week: _____

How I did with the past week's goal: _____

My goal for next week: _____

Specific action to reach next week's goal: _____

Student Comments:

Student Signature _____

Teacher Comments:

Teacher Signature _____

Parent Comments:

Parent Signature _____

Figure 9–4   Weekly Self-Assessment.

Teachers encouraged students to take risks with learning, emphasizing learning as the goal. Teachers allowed students to learn at different rates and in different ways, without penalty (especially in grades) for needing more time or falling short along the way. Students were given responsibility to make important decisions about learning and acted on that belief. When students trusted the teachers, they found the confidence to engage in honest self-assessment.

As the year progressed and students became more reflective thinkers, they also took on a larger role in designing self-assessment. They designed daily evaluations for their work (see Figure 9–5) and assisted teachers in designing rubrics and project and presentation evaluations, and in redesigning the weekly assessment. In addition to setting short-term goals on a weekly basis, students set goals for daily work and projects, and for long-term academic and personal growth. This emphasis on self-assessment, and the expectations of growth in the ability to self-assess, set the stage for successful student-led conferences.

Name _____ Co-Evaluator _____ Date _____

This is what I did today:

_____

_____

This is what I learned today:

_____

_____

This is what I did well today:

_____

_____

This is what I will improve next class:

_____

_____

Materials I will need next class:

_____

_____

Objectives Me and Co-E Agreed

Fill out the top completely and thoughtfully ...._____ _____ _____
Stayed on task ...._____ _____ _____
Shared thoughts and ideas ...._____ _____ _____
Brought needed materials ...._____ _____ _____
Worked positively with everyone ...._____ _____ _____
Contributed equally to group's work ...._____ _____ _____
Stayed where I was supposed to be ...._____ _____ _____
Picked up ...._____ _____ _____
Listened to others when they were talking ...._____ _____ _____
Used group voice ...._____ _____ _____

Student Comments:

_____

_____

_____

Teacher Comments:

_____

_____

_____

Figure 9–5 Daily Self-Evaluation.

Preparation for Conferences

Although learning to practice reflective thinking and assessment functioned as the cornerstone for successful student-led conferences, students also prepared in other ways. Most importantly, they prepared portfolios, a common element of student-led conferences (Countryman & Schroeder, 1996; Hackmann, Kenworthy, & Nibbelink, 1998). The Nurse Shark portfolios served the specific purpose of presenting evidence of students' academic, personal, and reflective growth. They started a file the first week of school in which they saved and organized all of their work and self-assessments. They divided their files into math, reading, writing, integrated block, and self-assessment, which also became the divisions for their portfolios.

As the time for student-led conferences approached, students perused their files, searching for evolution of learning processes and products. Teachers prompted them with questions such as, "What skill/knowledge did you find easy to learn and why?" "What skill/knowledge required concentrated effort but you learned it in the end?" "What did you do to be successful?" "How do you take responsibility for learning?" "How has that changed since the beginning of the year?" Students filled their portfolios with evidence to support the answers to these and other questions.

Final student preparations for the conferences included writing an agenda and talking points and repeated practice. All students worked with a common agenda compiled by the teachers. In developing the agenda, the teachers considered student and parent concerns along with their own. Students also added individual agenda items as needed or requested. Students wrote talking points—short, bulleted phrases—based on the prompts written by teachers. The talking points led students logically through their portfolios.

Practice consisted of two phases. In the first phase, one brave student, Mark, volunteered to conduct a mock student-led conference for all of his classmates to observe. One teacher played the role of the teacher and the other teacher played the role of the parent. After the staged conference, the class discussed aspects that went well and others they might change. Students then moved into the second phase of practicing. Teachers assigned groups of three in which students practiced, in turn, each role of a student-led conference: student, parent, and teacher. Each turn required 15 to 30 minutes and students practiced only one conference each day. Some students remained apprehensive about facilitating a conference, but almost all felt adequately prepared for their new role.

In addition to students, parents also need preparation for their children to lead conferences (Countryman & Schroeder, 1996; Hackmann, Kenworthy, & Nibbelink, 1998). During the very first week of school, the Nurse Shark teachers met with parents to explain changes in the way their children would learn. They emphasized the integrated curriculum, but also discussed student-led conferences. Along with weekly student self-assessments, teachers also sent home weekly newsletters that included information about the upcoming student-led conferences. Teachers invited parents to school one evening each month to discuss any concerns or questions about any aspect of their child's education. For the first few months, student-led conferences remained part of the agenda for those meetings. Some parents felt more comfortable talking to teachers about the student-led conferences on an individual basis—through notes, phone calls, and occasional conferences at school. Teachers encouraged all questions and concerns through any avenue. Parents eventually expressed understanding and support of the student-led conferences, although some reserved the right to later meet with only the teachers, if they desired.

Fall Conferences

Student-led conferences can be structured in many ways, according to the situation and needs of involved teachers, parents, and students. Most teachers start with three-way conferences, which involve the student, the parents, and the teacher for the entire time, and schedule only one conference at any given time. Teachers generally schedule the conferences for 15 to 30 minutes (Countrymann & Schroeder, 1996; Hackmann, Kenworthy, & Nibbelink, 1998). The Nurse Sharks scheduled three-way conferences in slots of 30 minutes each. All parents signed up for conferences—all but three with just the prompt of notices sent home with weekly self-assessments and the weekly newsletter. Each teacher scheduled and attended the conferences for his or her homeroom.

Conference time arrived soon after the end of the first quarter. Teachers found that some students facilitated their conferences with little prompting from the teacher or parents. Tyler shared his portfolio with his father, confidently and accurately discussing his strengths, challenges, and growth. He used his talking points as an outline for meaningful reflection and communication. Tyler's father asked questions that required Tyler to further explain, clarify, and reflect on his learning. The teacher mostly observed the half-hour conference, saying very little beyond the welcome at the start of the conference.

A few students needed prompting and encouragement throughout the conference to do more than flip quickly through their portfolios. Justin started by flipping through his portfolio pages quickly, with only a word or two of explanation. Both his teacher and his mother slowed him down by asking for explanations of papers and talking points. The conference lasted about 20 minutes, but required a great deal of involvement by the teacher.

Most students ran their conferences well, but appreciated the support of their teacher. Courtney started her conference a bit nervous, but confident in her preparation. She explained her portfolio and talking points, but looked to her teacher often for encouragement and reinforcement. Courtney's conference took the entire half hour allotted.

Three conferences presented some difficulties, especially for the students involved. John worried that his mother would judge his work harshly and hesitated to say anything she might perceive as negative. His teacher filled in silences with many positive and honest comments. Janie's parents listened to her portfolio presentation without asking a single question or providing one word of encouragement. Her teacher, instead, provided the questions and support. Billie's mother stopped at every talking point to degrade Billie's performance and choices. Her teacher spent a lengthy time convincing both Billie and her mother that Billie possessed some excellent qualities as a learner and as a person. For these three students especially, the teacher's attendance was vital.

Conference Feedback

From the teacher's perspective, the student-led conferences succeeded. Of the 40 students on the team, 38 (95%) brought at least one parent and many brought two parents and/or stepparents. Attendance rates were high even though parents received no incentive other than the promise of their child leading the conference. Students compiled excellent reflective portfolios and discussed their progress intelligently with their parents. They provided overwhelmingly positive feedback about the conferences and their ability to facilitate meaningful communication with their parents. Through the process of the conferences, students set goals for further growth. Teachers turned part of the responsibility for communication over to the students—and the students, for the most part, handled that responsibility very well.

Teachers also asked parents for feedback about the student-led conferences. In addition to informal questions, comments, and discussions about the conferences, teachers also distributed a survey to each family following the conference. Most, but not all, parents responded. The parents of Janie and Billie responded neither formally nor informally. Without exception, however, all comments supported portfolios and student-led conferences.

Tyler's father responded:

> I was impressed with Tyler's confidence in his presentation. I found out later that they had rehearsed and I think that's great! I liked the way the student took a more active role in the conference. It was helpful for me to see the way that Tyler viewed his accomplishments and goals. I'd like to see more of the same.

Justin's mother also responded positively, stating that "Justin was involved in telling me his accomplishments and progress. Follow the same format—it was great." Courtney's mother also provided supportive comments: "Courtney is really seeing that she is doing better as the year goes on. [It was helpful to hear] what Courtney thinks she needs help in and that she is doing better in math." Mark's mother mentioned not only the conferences, but the daily preparation for it:

> I like that the student took charge of his own accomplishments and presented it to us. I liked the three-way communication. The scoring guides and self-assessments were helpful. The fact that my son understood every score he received and how he could improve... I thought the portfolio reflected his work very well.

Spring Conferences

With many signs of success, the Nurse Sharks conducted student-led conferences after the third quarter, with some changes. Teachers provided students and parents with the choice of three-way conferences as in the fall, two-way conferences in which the student conducted most of the conference without the teacher present, and home conferences led by the student. If parents chose home conferences, teachers asked them to fill out a short response sheet to be returned with the student's portfolio. Teachers felt that some students needed support to be successful; teachers strongly recommended school conferences for these students. Students accepted those recommendations. Parents divided themselves about equally among the three options, and 100% of parents participated in conferences.

Again, parents provided positive feedback without exception. One parent, whose child presented her portfolio at home, responded: "Kimi did an excellent job in presenting her portfolio. It took approximately 45 minutes. And she gave us a lot of details about each section. She seems to know exactly what she needs to improve on." Kirk's mother, who also chose a home portfolio conference, wrote: "It gave me a good view of his work. Kirk was well prepared with his portfolio. He knew what he needed to tell me and was able to answer all the questions I had." Feedback from the home conferences read very much like responses from school conferences—a tribute to the students' ability to communicate their learning.

Conclusion

Student-led conferences provided benefits including partnerships among parents, students, and teachers focused on learning; understood and supported learning goals;

increased parent participation; students becoming active learners; and a supportive conference atmosphere (Davies, Cameron, Politano, & Gregory, 1992). To maximize these benefits, however, conferences must become part of a larger process of student responsibility and self-assessment on a daily basis. Students accept responsibility when educators give them the power to think about and control their learning environment through curriculum, activities, and assessment. Participation in important decisions leads to meaningful and lasting student responsibility, reflection, and growth.

LEARNING OUT LOUD 9–6

Role play a student-led conference with your peers. Write a reflection that describes what it was like to take the student's role and discuss your progress with your parents. Critique the role of the teachers utilizing this method and speculate as to whether or not this is a strategy that you will utilize in your classroom.

Summary

The shifts in assessment over the past few years are the beginnings of exciting changes in the educational community. This chapter discussed both the traditional and authentic assessments that play a role in the classroom. Increased participation of multiple stakeholders in the assessment process only seeks to strengthen the links between planning, instruction, and assessment. Teachers, students, and parents all play a critical part in the assessment process. The effective teacher who develops a reflective perspective on assessment will make assessment a meaningful and important part of the schooling process.

References

Airasian, P. W. (1996). *Assessment in the classroom*. New York: McGraw-Hill.

Airasian, P. W. (2000). *Assessment in the classroom: A concise approach* (2nd ed.). New York: McGraw-Hill.

Albert, L. (1989). *A teacher's guide to cooperative discipline: How to manage your classroom and promote self-esteem*. Circle Pines, MN: American Guidance Service.

Alberti, R. E., & Emmons, M. L. (1975). *Stand up, speak out, talk back*. New York: Pocket Books.

Allard, H., & Marshall, J. (1977). *Miss Nelson is missing!* New York: Houghton Mifflin.

Arter, J., & Spandel, V. (1992). Using portfolios of student work in instruction and assessment. *Educational Measurement: Issues & Practice, 11*, 36–44.

Bandura, A. (1986). *Social foundations of thought and action: A social cognitive theory*. Englewood Cliffs, NJ: Prentice-Hall.

Barrett, H. (1995). *Technology support for alternative assessment: Handouts for presentations* [On-line]. Available http://transition.alaska.edu/www/portfolios/TechPort1.html.

Bash, M., & Camp, B. (1975). *Think aloud program: Group manual*. Unpublished manuscript. University of Colorado Medical School.

Beane, J. A. (1995). Curriculum integration and the disciplines of knowledge. *Phi Delta Kappan, 76*(8), 616–622.

Berliner, D. C. (1987). Simple views of effective teaching and a simple theory of classroom instruction. In D. C. Berliner & B. V. Rosenshine (Eds.), *Talks to teachers* (pp. 93–110). New York: Random House.

Berne, E. (1964). *Games people play: The psychology of human relations*. New York: Grove Press.

Bitter, G. G., & Pierson, M. E. (1999). *Using technology in the classroom* (4th ed.). Boston: Allyn & Bacon.

Blanchard, P. (1998). Music makes me happy. Commerce, GA: Sold-Out Studios.

Bloom, B., Englehart, M., Furst, E., Hill, W., & Krathwohl, D. (1956). *Taxonomy of educational objectives: Cognitive domain*. New York: Longman.

Boostrom, R. (1991). The nature and functions of classroom rules. *Curriculum Inquiry, 21*(2), 193–213.

Brophy, J. E., & Evertson, C. M. (1976). *Learning from teaching: A developmental perspective*. Boston: Allyn & Bacon.

Brophy, J., & McCaslin, M. (1992). Teachers' reports of how they perceive and cope with problem students. *The Elementary Journal, 93*(1), 3–68.

Brown, A. L., & DeLoache, J. S. (1978). Skills, plans, and self-regulation. In R. S. Siegler (Ed.), *Children's thinking: What develops?* (pp. 3–36). Hillsdale, NJ: Erlbaum.

Brown, A. L., & Palincsar, A. S. (1982). Inducing strategic learning from text by means of informed, self-control training. *Topics in Learning and Learning Disabilities, 2*, 1–17.

Burgoon, J., Buller, D., & Woodall, W. (1989). *Nonverbal communication: The unspoken dialogue.* New York: Harper & Row.

Burns, D. D. (1980). *Feeling good: The new mood therapy.* New York: William Morrow and Company, Inc.

Butler, P. E. (1992). *Talking to yourself: Learning the language of self-affirmation.* San Francisco: Harper & Row.

Canfield, J., & Wells, H. C. (1976). *100 ways to enhanced self-concept in the classroom: A handbook for teachers and parents.* Englewood Cliffs, N.J.: Prentice Hall.

Canner, J., Fisher, T., Fremer, J., Haladyna, T., Hall, J., Mehrens, W., Perlman, C., Roeber, E., & Sandifer, P. (1991, April). *Regaining trust: Enhancing the credibility of school testing programs.* A report from the National Council on Measurement in Education Task Force. Mimeo.

Canter, L., & Canter, M. (1976). *Assertive discipline: A take-charge approach for today's educator.* Santa Monica, CA: Canter and Associates, Inc.

Canter, L., & Canter, M. (1992). *Assertive discipline: Positive management for today's classroom.* Santa Monica, CA: Lee Canter & Associates.

Canter, L., & Canter, M. (1993). *Succeeding with difficult students: New strategies for reaching your most challenging students.* Santa Monica, CA: Lee Canter & Associates.

Carpenter, T. P., Fennema, F., Franke, M. L., & Carey, D. A. (1996). Cognitively guided instruction: A knowledge base for reform in primary mathematics instruction. *The Elementary School Journal, 97*, 3–20.

Carter, C. (1997, March). Why reciprocal teaching? *Educational Leadership, 54* (6), 64–68.

Carter, K. (1994). Preservice teachers' well remembered events and the acquisition of event-structured knowledge. *Journal of Curriculum Studies, 26*, 235–252.

Cazden, C. B. (1998). *Classroom discourse: The language of teaching and learning.* Portsmouth, NH: Heinemann Educational Books. (ERIC Document Reproduction Service No. ED 288 206)

Clark, C. M., & Lampert, M. (1986). The study of teachers' thinking: Implications for teacher education. *Journal of Teacher Education, 37*(5), 27–31.

Clark, C. M., & Peterson, P. L. (1986). Teacher's thought process. In M. Wittrock (Ed.), *Handbook of research on teaching* (3rd ed., pp. 255–296). New York: Macmillan.

Commeyras, M., & Sumner, G. (1996). Literature discussions based on student-posed questions. *Reading Teacher, 50*(3), 262–265.

Commeyras, M., & Sumner, G. (1998). Literature questions children want to discuss: What teachers and students learned in a second-grade classroom. *The Elementary School Journal, 99*(2), 129–152.

Conrad, D., & Hedin, D. (1991). School-based community service: What we know from research and theory. *Phi Delta Kappan 72*(10), 754–575.

Cooper, P. J., & Simonds, C. (1999). *Communication for the classroom teacher* (6th ed.). Needham Heights, MA: Allyn & Bacon.

Corno, L. (1987). Teaching and self-regulated learning. In D. C. Berliner & B. V. Rosenshine (Eds.), *Talks to teachers* (pp. 249–266). New York: Random House.

Corno, L., & Mandinach, E. B. (1983). The role of cognitive engagement in classroom learning and motivation. *Educational Psychologist, 18*, 88–108.

Corno, L., & Rohrkemper, M. M. (1988). The intrinsic motivation to learn in classrooms. In C. Ames & R. Ames (Eds.), *Research on motivation in education: The classroom milieu* (pp. 53–90). Orlando, FL: Academic Press.

Costa, A., & Kallick, B. (1993). Through the lens: A critical friend. *Educational Leadership, 51*, 49–51.

Costantino, P. M., & DeLorenzo, M. N. (2002). *Developing a professional teaching portfolio: A guide for success.* Boston, MA: Allyn & Bacon.

Countryman, L. L., & Schroeder, M. (1996). When students lead parent-teacher conferences. *Educational Leadership, 53*(7), 64–68.

Cusick, P. A., Martin, W., & Palonsky, S. (1976). Organizational structure and student behavior in secondary school. *Journal of Curriculum Studies, 8*(1), 3–14.

Dagley, P. L. (1988). *The utility of cognitive self-instruction in altering teacher expectations and locus of control orientations.* Unpublished doctoral dissertation, The University of Georgia, Athens.

Daloz, L. (1986). *Effective teaching and mentoring.* San Francisco: Jossey-Bass.

Danielson, C. (1996). *Enhancing professional practice: A framework for teaching.* Alexandria, VA: ASCD.

Davies, A. (1997). Celebrating student learning with student-involved conferences. *Mindshift Connection.* Tucson, AZ: Zephyr Press.

Davies, A., Cameron, C., Politano, C., & Gregory, K. (1992). *Together is better: Collaborative assessment, evaluation, and reporting.* Winnipeg, Manitoba: Peguis.

Davis, S., & Campbell, N. (1999). *QAR Presentation.* Athens, GA: University of Georgia.

Davydov, V. (1995). The influence of L. S. Vygotsky on educational theory, research, and practice. *Educational Researcher, 24*(3), 12–21.

Dayton, J. (2002). Special education discipline law. *Education Law Reporter, 16*(3), 1–17.

Dewey, J. (1938). *Experience and education.* New York: Collier Books.

DeVries, R., & Zan, B. (1995). Creating a constructivist classroom atmosphere. *Young Children, 50*(3), 4–13.

Dillon, J. T. (1990). *The practice of questioning.* London: Routledge.

Dinkmeyer, D., & Dreikurs, R. (1963). *Encouraging children to learn: the encouragement process.* Englewood Cliffs, NJ: Prentice Hall.

Dinkmeyer, D., & McKay, G. D. (1976). *Systematic training for effective parenting (STEP).* Circle Pines, MN: American Guidance Service.

Dinwiddie, S. A. (1994). The Saga of Sally Sammy and the red pen: Facilitating children's social problem solving. *Young Children,* 13–19.

Dobbs, S. M. (1992). *The DBAE handbook: An overview of discipline-based art education.* Santa Monica, CA: Getty Center for Education in the Arts.

Dreikurs, R. (1964). *Children: The challenge.* New York: E.P. Dutton.

Dreikurs, R. (1968). *Logical consequences.* New York: Meredith Press.

Dreikurs, R. (1972). *Discipline without tears: What to do with children who misbehave.* New York: Hawthorn Books.

Duffy, G., Lanier, J. E., & Roehler, L. R. (1980). *On the need to consider instructional practice when looking for instructional implications*. Paper presented at the Conference on Reading Expository Materials, Wisconsin Research and Development Center, University of Wisconsin-Madison.

Duffy, G., Roehler, L., & Mason, J. (1984). *Comprehension instruction: Perspective and suggestions*. New York: Longman.

Eby, J. W., & Kujawa, E. (1994). *Reflective planning, teaching, and evaluation: K–12*. New York: Macmillan.

Eby, J., & Martin, D. B. (2001). *Reflective planning, teaching, and evaluation for the elementary school: A relational approach* (3rd ed.). Upper Saddle, NJ: Prentice Hall.

Ellis, A. (1977). *How to live with—and without—anger*. New York: Reader's Digest Press.

Ernst, K. (1973). *Games students play, and what to do about them*. Mellbrae, CA: Celestial Arts.

Evertson, C. M., Emmer, E. T., Clements, B. S., & Worsham, M. E. (1994). *Classroom management for elementary teachers* (3rd ed.). Needham Heights, MA: Allyn & Bacon.

Evertson, C., Emmer, E. T., & Worsham, M. E. (2000). *Classroom management for elementary teachers* (5th ed.). Boston: Allyn & Bacon.

Fennell, F., & Ammon, R. (1985). Writing techniques for problem solving. *Arithmetic Teacher, 33*, 24–25.

Forrest-Pressley, D. L., & Waller, T. G. (1984). *Cognition, metacognition, and reading*. New York: Springer-Verlag.

Freed, A. M. (1971). *TA for kids and grown ups, too. Transactional analysis for everyone series*. Sacramento, CA: Jalmar Press.

Freed, A. M. (1973). *TA for tots and other important people*. Sacramento, CA: Jalmar Press.

Friday, N. (1977). *My mother, myself*. New York: Delacorte Press.

Gallimore, R., Dalton, S., & Tharpe, R. G. (1986). Self-regulation and interactive teaching: The effects of teaching conditions on teachers' cognitive activity. *The Elementary School Journal, 86*(5), 613–631.

Georgi, D., & Crowe, J. (1998). Digital portfolios: A confluence of portfolio assessment and technology. *Teacher Education Quarterly, 25*(1), 73–84.

Georgiady, N., Sinclair, R., & Sinclair, C. (1991). What is the most effective discipline? *Principal, 71*(1), 49–50.

Giles, D. E., & Eyler, J. (1994). The theoretical roots of service-learning in John Dewey: Toward a theory of service-learning. *Michigan Journal of Community Service Learning, 1*, 77–85.

Glasser, W. (1969). *Schools without failure*. New York: Harper & Row.

Glasser, W. (1975). *Reality therapy: A new approach to psychiatry*. New York: Harper & Row.

Glasser, W. (1986). *Control theory in the classroom*. New York: Harper & Row.

Glasser, W. (1992). *The quality school: Managing students without coercion* (2nd ed.). New York: Harper & Row.

Glasser, W. (1990). *The quality school: Managing students without coercion*. New York: Harper & Row.

Gomby, S. S., Larson, S. L., Lewit, E. M., & Berham, R. E. (1993). Home visiting: Analysis and recommendations. *The Future of Children, 3*(3), 6–22.

Gonzalez, L. E., & Carter, K. (1996). Correspondence in cooperating teachers' and student teachers' interpretations of classroom events. *Teaching and Teacher Education, 12*(1), 39–47.

Good, T. L., & Brophy, J. R. (1984). *Looking in classrooms*. New York: Harper & Row.

Goodlad, J. I. (1990). *Teachers for our nation's schools*. San Francisco: Jossey-Bass Publishers.

Gorden, W., & Nevins, R. (1993). *We mean business: Building communication competence in business and professions*. New York: Harper Collins.

Gordon, T. (1974). *T.E.T.—Teacher effectiveness training*. New York: Peter H. Wyden.

Greco, N. (1992). Critical literacy and community service: Reading and writing the world. *English Journal 81*(5), 83–86.

Grosser, S. (1992). Managing the early childhood classroom. *Young Children, 47*(2), 186–191.

Guskey, T. R. (1994). *High stakes performance assessment*. Thousand Oaks, CA: Corwin Press.

Guyton, J. M., & Fielstein, L. L. (1989). Student-led conferences: A model for teaching responsibility. *Elementary School Guidance & Counseling, 24*(2), 169–172.

Hall, M. (1963) *Gilberto and the wind*. New York: Puffin Books.

Hallahan, D., Lloyd, J. W., & Stoller, L. (1982). *Improving attention with self-monitoring: A manual for teachers*. Unpublished manuscript, University of Virginia Learning Disabilities Research Institute.

Harris, K. R. (1990). Developing self-regulated learners: The role of private speech and self-instruction. *Educational Psychologist, 25*, 35–49.

Harris, T. A. (1969). *I'm OK—you're OK: A practical guide to transactional analysis*. New York: Harper & Row.

Harrison, C. (1986). *Student service: The new Carnegie unit*. Princeton, NJ: Princeton University Press.

Heaton, S., & O'Shea, D. (1995). Using mnemonics to make mnemonics. *Teaching Exceptional Children 28*(1), 34–36.

Heinich, R., Molenda, M., Russell, J. D., & Smaldino, S. E. (1999). *Instructional media and technologies for learning* (6th ed.). Upper Saddle River, NJ: Prentice-Hall.

Helmstetter, S. (1986). *What to say when you talk to yourself*. New York: Simon and Schuster.

Helmstetter, S. (1987). *The self-talk solution*. New York: William Morrow and Company.

Henderson, A. T., Marburger, C. L., & Ooms, T. (1986). *Beyond the bake sale*. Columbia, MD: National Committee for Citizens in Education.

Henkes, K. (1996). *Chrysanthemum*. New York: Mulberry Books.

Henkin, R. (1998). *Who's invited to share?: Using literacy to teach equity and social justice*. Portsmouth, NH: Heinemann.

Jackson, P. W. (1968). *Life in classrooms*. New York: Holt, Rinehart, and Winston.

Jacobs, H. H. (1997). *Mapping the big picture: Integrating curriculum and assessment, K–12*. Alexandria, VA: ASCD.

James, M., & Jongeward, D. (1971). *Born to win: Transactional analysis with gestalt experiments*. Boston: Addison-Wesley.

Jarolimek, J., Foster, C. D., & Kellough, R. D. (2001). *Teaching and learning in the elementary school* (7th ed.). Upper Saddle River, NJ: Merrill/Prentice Hall.

Jones, B. L., Maloy, R. W., & Steen, C. M. (1996). Learning through community service is political. *Equity & Excellence in Education, 29*(2), 37–45.

Kellough, R. D., & Kellough, N. G. (1999). *Middle school teaching: A guide to methods and resources* (3rd ed.). Upper Saddle River, NJ: Merrill.

Kiersey, D., & Bates, M. (1984). *Please understand me* (5th ed.). Del Mar, CA: Prometheus Books.

Kostelnik, M., Stein, L., & Whiren, A. (1988). Children's self-esteem: The verbal environment. *Childhood Education, 65*(1), 29–32.

Kottler, J. A., & Zehm, S. J. (2000). *On being a teacher* (2nd ed.). Thousand Oaks, CA: Corwin Press.

Kounin, J. S. (1970). *Discipline and group management in classrooms*. New York: Holt, Rinehart, and Winston.

Lasley, T. J. (1994). Teacher technicians: A new metaphor for new teachers. *Action in Teacher Education, 16*(1), 29–40.

Leal, L., & Rafoth, M. A. (1991). Memory strategy development: What teachers do makes a difference. *Intervention in School and Clinic, 26*(4), 234–237.

Lemlech, J. K. (1998). *Curriculum and instructional methods for the elementary and middle school* (4th ed.). Columbus, OH: Merrill.

Lena, H. F. (1995, Winter). How can sociology contribute to integrating service learning into academic curricula? *The American Sociologist, 26,* 107–117.

Leutzinger, L. (1985). Problem solving tips for teachers: Spotlight on techniques+The four step method of problem solving. *Arithmetic Teacher, 33,* 38–39.

Madaus, G. F., & Kellaghan, T. (1992). Curriculum evaluation and assessment. In P. W. Jackson (Ed.), *Handbook of research on curriculum* (pp. 119–154). New York: Macmillan.

Maltz, M. (1960). *Psycho-cybernetics*. New York: Simon and Schuster.

Manning, B. H. (1984a). A self-communication structure for learning mathematics. *School Science and Mathematics, 84*(1), 43–51.

Manning, B. H. (1984b). Problem-solving instruction and oral comprehension aid for reading disabled third graders. *Journal of Learning Disabilities, 17,* 457–461.

Manning, B. H. (1988). Application of cognitive behavior modification: First and third graders' self-management of classroom behaviors. *American Educational Research Journal, 25*(2), 193–212.

Manning, B. H. (1990, April). Self-talk and learning. *Teaching K–8,* 56–58.

Manning, B. H. (1990a). A categorical analysis of children's self-talk during independent school assignments. *Journal of Instructional Psychology, 17*(4), 208–217.

Manning, B. H. (1990b). Cognitive self-instruction for an off-task fourth grader during independent academic tasks: A case study. *Contemporary Educational Psychology, 15,* 36–46.

Manning, B. H. (1991). *Cognitive self-instruction for classroom processes*. Albany: State University of New York Press.

Manning, B. H., Glasner, S. E., & Smith, E. R. (1996). Metacognition as an aspect of self-regulated learning strategies: A component of gifted education. *Roeper Review, 18*(3), 217–223.

Manning, B. H., & Payne, B. D. (1989a). A cognitive self-direction model for teacher education. *Journal of Teacher Education, 40*(3), 27–32.

Manning, B. H., & Payne, B. D. (1996a). *Self-talk for teachers and students: Metacognitive strategies for personal and classroom use*. Needham Heights, MA: Allyn & Bacon.

Manning, B. H., & Payne, B. D. (1996b). Mental deliberations during teaching episodes: Novice teacher versus expert teacher. *Teacher Education Quarterly, 23*(1), 57–68.

Manning, B. H., White, C. S., & Daugherty, M. (1994). Young children's private speech as a precursor to metacognitive strategy use for task execution. *Discourse Processes: A Multidisciplinary Journal, 17*(2), 191–211.

Manz, C. C. (1992). *Mastering self-leadership*. Englewood Cliffs, NJ: Prentice-Hall.

Markman, E. M. (1977). Realizing that you don't understand: A preliminary investigation. *Child Development, 46,* 986–992.

Markman, E. M. (1978, October). *Comprehension monitoring.* Paper presented at the meeting of the Conference on Children's Oral Communication Skills, University of Wisconsin.

Markman, E. M. (1979). Realizing that you don't understand: Elementary school children's awareness of inconsistencies. *Child Development, 50,* 643–655.

Markman, E. M. (1981). Comprehension monitoring. In W. P. Dickson (Ed.), *Children's oral communication skills* (pp. 61–84). New York: Academic Press.

Martin, N. K. (1997). Connecting instruction and management in a student-centered classroom. *Middle School Journal, 12*(1), 177–183.

Matazano, J. (1996). Discussion: Assessing what was said and what was done. In L. Gambrell & J. Almasi (Eds.), *Lively discussions* (pp. 250–264). Newark, DE: International Reading Association.

Matthews, J. M. (1978, March). *The teacher teaches thinking skills: Dx and Rx for students' self-talk.* Paper presented at the annual meeting of the Western College Reading Association, Long Beach, CA.

Matz, K., & Leier, C. (1992). Word problems and the language connection. *Arithmetic Teacher, 39* (8)14–17.

McCall, A. L. (1989). Care and nurturance in teaching: A case study. *Journal of Teacher Education, 40*(1), 39–44.

McCall, J. (1976). Communication and negotiated identity. *Communication, 2,* 182.

McDonald, J. (1992). Dilemmas of planning backwards: Rescuing a good idea. *Teachers College Record* 94(10), 152–169.

McKay, M., Davis, M., & Fanning, P. (1983). *Messages: The communication skill book.* Oakland, CA: New Harbringer.

McRae, A. (1999). *Cognitive strategy instruction.* Unpublished class paper. Athens, GA: University of Georgia.

Meichenbaum, D. (1977). *Cognitive behavior modification: An integrative approach.* New York: Plenum Press.

Meichenbaum, D., & Goodman, J. (1971). Training impulsive children to talk to themselves: A means of developing self-control. *Journal of Abnormal Psychology, 77,* 115–126.

Milone, M. (1989). Classroom or lab: How to decide which is best. *Classroom Computer Learning, 10*(1), 34–43.

Moely, B., Hart, L., Santulli, K. R., Johnson, T. & Hamilton, L. B. (1992). *The teacher's role in facilitating memory and study strategy development in the elementary school classroom: Final report.* (ERIC Document Reproduction No. EJ 447 644)

Moore, D. W., Moore, S. A., Cunningham, P. M., & Cunningham, J. W. (1998). *Developing readers and writers in the content areas K–12* (3rd ed.). New York: Longman.

Nech, C. P., & Barnard, A.W. H. (1996, March). Managing your mind: What are you telling yourself? *Educational Leadership,* 24–27.

Nech, C. P., & Manz, C. C. (1992). Through self-leadership: The influence of self-talk and mental imagery on performance. *Journal of Organizational Behavior, 13*(7), 681–699.

Neill, S. (1991). *Classroom nonverbal communication.* New York: Routledge.

Nesin, G. (2000). *Young adolescent achievement and attitudes in various curriculum designs.* Unpublished doctoral dissertation, University of Georgia, Athens.

Nesin, G., & Lounsbury, J. (1999). *Curriculum integration: Twenty questions—with answers.* Atlanta, GA: Georgia Middle School Association.

Novaco, R. (1975). *Anger control: The development and evaluation of an experimental treatment.* Lexington, MA: Heath and Company.

O'Flahavan, J. F., & Stein, C. (1992). In search of the teacher's role in peer discussions about literature. *Reading in Virginia, 12,* 34–42.

O'Flahavan, J. F., Stein, C., Wiencek, J., & Marks, T. (1992). *Intellectual development in peer discussions about literature: An exploration of the teacher's role* (Final Report). Urbana, IL: National Council of Teachers of English.

O'Hair, M. J., & Ropo, E. (1994). Unspoken messages: Understanding diversity in education requires emphasis on nonverbal communication. *Teacher Education Quarterly, 21*(3), 91–112.

Orlando, C. A. (1993). *Using music to reinforce basic money skills taught in the TMH classroom.* (ERIC Document Reproduction Service No. ED 366 144)

Paley, V. G. (1992). *You can't say you can't play.* Cambridge, MA: Harvard University Press.

Palincsar, A. S., & Brown, A. L. (1984). Reciprocal teaching of comprehension fostering and comprehension monitoring activities. *Cognition and Instruction, 1,* 117–175.

Palkes, H., Stewart, M., & Kahana, B. (1968). Porteus maze performance after training in self-directed verbal commands. *Child Development, 39,* 817–826.

Parks, B. (1996). *Mick Harte was here.* New York: Random House.

Pate, P. E., Homestead, E. R., & McGinnis, K. L. (1997). *Making integrated curriculum work: Teachers, students, and the quest for coherent curriculum.* New York: Teachers College Press.

Pearson, J. W., & Santa, C. (1995). Students as researchers of their own learning. *Journal of Reading, 38,* 462–469.

Pintrich, P. R. (1995). Understanding self-regulated learning. *New Directions for Teaching and Learning, 63,* 3–12.

Popham, W. J. (1999). *Classroom assessment: What teachers need to know* (2nd ed.). Needham Heights, MA: Allyn & Bacon.

Pressley, M. (1995). More about the development of self-regulation: Complex, long-term, and thoroughly social. *Educational Psychologist, 30,* 207–212.

Pressley, M., & Woloshyn, V. (1995). *Cognitive strategy instruction that really improves children's academic performance* (2nd ed.). Cambridge, MA: Brookline Books.

Powell, J. (1999). *Working toward success in mathematics.* Class presentation. Athens, GA: University of Georgia.

Raphael, T. E. (1982). Teaching children question-answering strategies. *The Reading Teacher, 36,* 186–191.

Raphael, T. E. (1986). *Students' metacognitive knowledge about writing.* (ERIC Document Reproduction Service No. ED 274 999)

Raphael, T. E., & Pearson, P. D. (1985). Increasing students' awareness of sources of information for answering questions. *American Educational Research Journal, 22,* 217–236.

Raphael, T. E., & Wonnacott, C. A. (1985). Metacognitive training in question-answering strategies: Implementation in a fourth-grade developmental reading program. *Reading Research Quarterly, 20*, 282–296.

Render, G. F., Padilla, J. M., & Krank, H. M. (1989). What research really shows about assertive discipline. *Educational Leadership, 46*(6), 72–75.

Richardson, J. S., & Morgan, R. F. (1990). *Reading to learn in the content areas.* Belmont, CA: Wadsworth.

Richardson, V., & Fallona, C. (2001). Classroom management as method and manner. *Journal of Curriculum Studies, 33*(6), 705–728.

Riel, M. (1994). Educational change in technology-rich environment. *Journal of Research on Computing in Education, 26*, 452–474.

Riner, P. S. (2000). *Successful teaching in the elementary classroom.* Upper Saddle River, NJ: Merrill.

Roblyer, M. D., & Edwards, J. (2000). *Integrating educational technology into teaching* (2nd ed.). Upper Saddle River, NJ: Merrill.

Rogers, C. (1994). *On becoming a person.* Boston, MA: Houghton Mifflin.

Rogers, C. (1995). *Freedom to learn.* Upper Saddle River, NJ: Prentice Hall.

Rohrkemper, M., & Corno, L. (1988). Success and failure on classroom tasks: Adaptive learning and classroom teaching. *The Elementary School Journal, 88*, 296–312.

Rosenshine, B., & Meister, C. (1994). Reciprocal teaching: A review of the research. *Review of Educational Researcher, 64*, 479–530.

Ross, D. D., & Bondy, E. (1993). Classroom management for responsible citizenship: Practical strategies for teachers. *Social Education, 57*(6), 326–328.

Ross, E. P. (1998). *Pathways to thinking: Strategies for developing independent learners K–8.* Norwood, MA: Christopher-Gordon Publishes, Inc.

Rothenberg, D. (1997). Student involvement in the assessment of learning. *Middle School Journal, 28*(4), 54–57.

Ryan, R. M., Connell, J. P., & Deci, E. L. (1985). A motivational analysis of self-determination and self-regulation in education. In C. Ames & R. Ames (Eds.), *Research on motivation in education, Vol 2: The classroom milieu* (pp. 12–51). Orlando, FL: Academic Press.

Sachar, L. (1987). *There's a boy in the girls' bathroom.* New York: Alfred A. Knopf.

Sanders, T. (2000, June 26). Service learning unites classroom, community. *USA Today,* p. A25.

Sattler, J. (1992). *Assessment of children* (3rd ed.). San Diego, CA: Jerome M. Sattler.

Schirrmacher, R. (1998). *Art and creative development for young children* (3rd ed.). Albany, NY: Delmar.

Schukar, R. (1997). Enhancing the middle school curriculum through service learning. *Theory into Practice, 36*(3), 176–183.

Seligman, M. (1991). *Learned optimism.* New York: Alfred A. Knopf.

Sells, L., Polster, H., McEvoy, G., & Toney, B. (2000). Barnett Shoals Elementary School Teachers In-Tech Poster Presentation.

Shannon, K. C. (1997). Student-led conferences: A twist on tradition. *Schools in the Middle, 6*(3), 47–49.

Shepard, L. A., & Smith, M. L. (1989). Academic and emotional effects of kindergarten retention. In L. Shepard & M. Smith (Eds.), *Flunking grades: Research and policies on retention* (pp. 79–107). Philadelphia: Falmer Press.

Shin, I. (1997). The DLPT as a learning objective. *Dialog on Language Instruction, 12*(½), 29–30.

Short, R. J., & Short, P. M. (1989). Teacher beliefs, perceptions, of behavior problems, and intervention preferences. *Journal of Social Studies Research, 13*(2), 28–31.

Shreve, S. R. (1984). *The flunking of Joshua T. Bates.* New York: Random House.

Siegel, B. S. (1986). *Love, medicine, and miracles.* New York: Harper & Row.

Smith, F. (1988). Joining the literacy club. *The Reading Teacher, 42,* 170

Smith, M. L., & Rottenburg, C. (1991). Unintended consequences of external testing in elementary schools. *Educational Measurement: Issues and Practice, 10*(4), 7–11.

Smith, S. J. (1975). *When I say no, I feel guilty.* New York: Harper & Row.

Stanulis, R. N. (1995). Action research as a way of learning about teaching in a mentor/student teacher relationship. *Action in Teacher Education, 16*(4), 14–24.

Stanulis, R. N. (1999). Adolescent literature as virtual experience for training middle school teachers. *Middle School Journal, 31*(1), 36–40.

Steil, L. (1980). *Your personal listening profile.* Minneapolis, MN: Sperry Corporation.

Stewart, J., & D'Angelo, G. (1993). *Together: Communicating interpersonally* (4th ed.). New York: McGraw-Hill.

Tancock, S. M., & Ford, K. L. (1996). Facilitating reflective thinking: Technology-based portfolios in teacher education. *Journal of Technology and Teacher Education, 4*(3/4), 281–295.

Taylor, M. D. (1976). *Roll of thunder, hear my cry.* New York: Dial Press.

Torrance, E. P., & Myers, R. E. (1978). *Creative learning and teaching.* New York: Harper and Row.

Vygotsky, L. S. (1978). *Mind in society: The development of higher psychological processes.* Cambridge, MA: Harvard University Press.

Wade, R. C. (1993). Social action: Expanding the role of citizenship in the social studies curriculum. *Inquiry in Social Studies: Curriculum, Research, and Instruction, 29*(1), 2–18.

Wade, R. C. (1995, May/June). Developing active citizens: Community service learning in social studies teacher education. *The Social Studies Journal, 86* (3), 122–128.

Walker, B. J. (1996). *Diagnostic teaching of reading: Techniques for instruction and assessment.* Englewood Cliffs, NJ: Prentice Hall.

Weinstein, C. S. (1998). "I want to be nice, but I have to be mean": Exploring prospective teachers' conceptions of caring and order. *Teaching and Teacher Education, 14*(2), 153–163.

Weinsten, C. E., & Mayer, R. E. (1986). The teacher of learning strategies. In M. Wittrock (Ed.), *The Handbook of Research on Teaching* (3rd ed., pp. 315–327). New York: Macmillan.

Weinstein, C. S., & Mignano, A. J. (1997). *Elementary classroom management* (2nd ed.). New York: McGraw-Hill.

Weinstein, C. S., Woolfolk, A. E., Dittmeier, L., & Shanker, U. (1994). Protector or prison guard? Using metaphor and media to explore student teachers' thinking about classroom management. *Action in Teacher Education, 14*(1), 41–54.

Weiss, H. B. (1993). Home visits: Necessary but not sufficient. *The Future of Children, 3*(3), 113–128.

Wertsch, J. V. (1978). From socialization to higher psychological processes: A clarification of and application of Vygotsky's theory. *Human Development, 22,* 1–22.

White, C. S., & Manning, B. H. (1994). The effects of verbal scaffolding instruction on young children's private speech and problem-solving capabilities. *Instructional Science: An International Journal of Learning and Cognition, 22,* 39–59.

Whitford, B. L., & Jones, K. (2000). *Accountability, assessment, and teacher commitment: Lessons from Kentucky's reform efforts.* New York: SUNY Press.

Whitford, B. L., Ruscoe, G., & Fickel, L. (2000). Knitting it all together: Collaborative teacher education in Southern Maine. In L. Darling-Hammond, (Ed.), *Studies of excellence in teacher education: Preparation at the graduate level* (pp. 173–257). Washington, DC: AACTE Publications.

Whitmore, K. F., & Goodman, Y. M. (1996). *Whole language voices in teacher education.* Portland, ME: Stenhouse Publishers.

Wiggins, G. (1992). Creating tests worth taking. *Educational Leadership, 49*(8), 26–33.

Wiencek, J. (1996). Planning, initiating and sustaining literature discussion groups: The teacher's role. In L.Gambrell & J. Almasi (Eds.), *Lively discussions* (pp. 208–223). Newark, DE: International Reading Association.

Wiencek, J., & O'Flahavan, J. F. (1994). From teacher-led to peer discussions about literature: Suggestions for making the shift. *Language Arts, 71,* 488–498.

Williams, L. (1999). *The key to a positive me.* Class presentation. Athens, GA: The University of Georgia.

Williams, L., Lowe, C., Stanulis, R. N., & Manning, B. H. (1999). *Cognitive self-instruction: The key to a more positive me.* Unpublished manuscript.

Wolfe, K. & Deitz, M. E. (1998). Teaching portfolios: Purposes and possibilities. *Teacher Education Quarterly, 25*(1), 9–22.

Wolfgang, C. H. (1995). *Solving discipline problems: Methods and models for today's teachers* (3rd ed.). Needham Heights, MA: Allyn & Bacon.

Wolfgang, C. H., Bennett, B. J., & Irvin, J. L. (1999a). *Strategies for teaching self-discipline in the middle grades.* Boston: Allyn & Bacon.

Woloshyn, V. E., Paivio, A., & Pressley, M. (1994). Use of elaborative interrogation to help students acquire information consistent with prior knowledge and information inconsistent with prior knowledge. *Journal of Educational Psychology, 86,* 79–89.

Wolvin, A., & Coakley, C. (1991). A survey of the status of listening training in some Fortune 500 corporations. *Communication Education, 40,* 152–164.

Wood, K. (1997). *Interdisciplinary instruction: A practical guide for elementary and middle school teachers.* Columbus, OH: Merrill.

Woolfolk, A. E. (1995). *Educational psychology* (6th ed.). Needham Heights, MA: Allyn & Bacon.

Zemelman, S., Hyde, A., & Daniels, H. (1998). *Best practice: New standards for teaching and learning in America's schools* (2nd ed.). Reed Elsevier, Incorporated.

Zentall, S. S., & Kruczek, T. (1988). The attraction of color for active attention problem children. *Exceptional Children, 12*(4), 193–212.

Zimmerman, B. J. (2000). Attaining self-regulation: A social cognitive perspective. In M. Boekaerts, P. Pintrich, & M. Zeidner (Eds.), *Handbook of self-regulation* (pp. 13–39). San Diego, CA: Academic Press.

Zimmerman, B. J., & Schunk, D. H. (1989). *Self-regulated learning and academic achievement: Theory, research, and practice*. New York: Springer-Verlag.

Index

Entries in **Bold** indicate figure or table reference